Supreme Court Policy Making

Supreme Court Policy Making
Explanation and Prediction

HAROLD J. SPAETH

MICHIGAN STATE UNIVERSITY

W. H. FREEMAN AND COMPANY
San Francisco

Sponsoring Editor: Richard J. Lamb; *Project Editor:* Pearl C. Vapnek;
Manuscript Editor: Jeanne Singeisen Duncan; *Designer:* Marie Carluccio;
Production Coordinator: Linda Jupiter; *Compositor:* Graphic Typesetting Service;
Printer and Binder: The Maple-Vail Book Manufacturing Group.

Library of Congress Cataloging in Publication Data

Spaeth, Harold J
    Supreme Court policy making.

    Includes index.
    1. United States. Supreme Court. I. Title.
KF8742.S6   347'.73'26   78-14493
ISBN 0-7167-1013-7
ISBN 0-7167-1012-9 pbk.

Printed in the United States of America

9 8 7 6 5 4 3 2 1

In memory
of my father and
to my son

Contents

Preface

This book attempts to provide a nontechnical explanation of the activities of the United States Supreme Court: what the Court does; how it does what it does; why it decides a case in favor of one party rather than the other; and what effects the Court's activities have had on American society. Throughout the book, the Court is viewed as a policy-making body—a group of persons who authoritatively resolve the basic issues confronting American society. Why does the Court participate in the resolution of these issues? In our representative system of government, would they not be better left to the other branches of government—to Congress or the President, assisted by the administrative agencies and departments of the federal government—and to the "autonomous" state governments? Furthermore, given that the Court does authoritatively make policy, why are we so perversely reluctant to recognize the Justices as policy makers? Why do we persist in perceiving them as objective? Is it because the Court's decisions comport with our idealized vision of justice as a blindfolded woman holding the scales of justice evenly balanced in her hand?

In considering these and other matters, I openly admit to two "biases." First, I consider the Court's policy-making activity desirable and appropriate. Second, though I have often disagreed with specific rulings of the Court, I nonetheless believe that, on the whole, the policy made by the Court has been qualitatively superior to that of either legislators or executive officials. If this stance signifies lack of devotion to majority rule or participatory democracy, I stand convicted. The Framers of the Constitution did not intend the constitutional system to be one that readily implements a majority's druthers, as is pointed out in Chapter 1. And, quite frankly, I have more confidence in the Framers than I have in the membership of a past or present Congress, an occupant of the White House (past or present), or any batch of badgered and beleaguered bureaucrats.

I do not plead guilty, however, to the charge that I prefer the Justices, when they make policy, to support what are considered liberal rather than conservative policies—or conservative rather than liberal policies. I do not march to the beat of any ideological drum, and though my occasional comments about the worth of certain judge-made policies may sometimes appear caustic, I believe my evaluations will bring a relatively equal measure of comfort (or discomfort, as the case may be) to partisans on both sides of the aisle. That, at least, was the reaction of two of the persons who read the manuscript of this book. One detected a decidedly liberal slant to my personal policy preferences; the other accused me of staging a "conservative cop-out."

The book begins with a discussion of the beliefs Americans have about their judges and the reasons why we are reluctant to view our judges as policy makers. The first chapter concludes with a rendering of the reasons why—notwithstanding our belief system—American judges perforce make policy. Chapter 2 describes the mechanics of the Court's decision-making process; how litigants secure access to the Court; and the Court's jurisdiction. Judges are expected to adhere to legal norms— to abide by precedent and to employ legal reasoning. The extent to which precedent and the various modes of legal reasoning inhibit the Justices in their making of policy is the subject of Chapter 3. Although the Justices serve for life—until they resign, retire, or die—they must be nominated by the President and confirmed by the Senate. Are they representative of anybody or anything? Inasmuch as most Presidential nominees are confirmed, whom should Presidents appoint? What characteristics do they look for? These matters are considered in Chapter 4. Chapter 5 focuses on the nature of Supreme Court decision making and why the Justices vote as they do. Given the explanation provided in Chapter 5, to what extent can the votes and decisions of the Justices be predicted? What is the significance of the fact that the Justices sometimes render unpredictable decisions? Should the Justices perhaps be replaced by computers? These are the subjects of Chapter 6. Does Supreme Court decision making approximate the idealized perception of justice as being blind to the characteristics of the litigants and focusing only on the circumstances that led to the litigation? This question is addressed in Chapter 7. The book concludes with a discussion of whether the policies enunciated by the Court are always complied with and, if they are, whether they have had a meaningful impact on the course and character of American society.

Throughout the book, description of the Court's activities is illustrated by reference to pertinent Court decisions. This is as it should be; in the last analysis, the proof of the pie is in the eating.

November 1978   *Harold J. Spaeth*

Acknowledgments

Kristine J. Guthrie has worked most closely with me in the preparation of this book. Without her encouragement and assistance on matters of substance, interpretation, and style, it would not have been written. The idea for the book was first suggested by Frederic W. Hills, editor-in-chief at McGraw-Hill. My editor, Richard J. Lamb of W. H. Freeman and Company, skillfully supervised the revision of the manuscript into a textbook. Professors Lawrence Baum, Bradley C. Canon, and Sheldon Goldman, of Ohio State University, the University of Kentucky, and the University of Massachusetts, respectively, read the entire manuscript and enabled me to avoid numerous errors of fact and interpretation. Reviewers of their competence should really have their names included on the title page. So also with respect to my good friend and former colleague, David B. Meltz, now a practicing attorney in Atlanta, who gave generously of his time and expertise in the fields of law, political science, and economics. My former student assistant, Karen S. Brintnall, utilized her mastery of grammar and syntax to enhance appreciably the readability of the manuscript. Jeanne Singeisen Duncan functioned admirably as manuscript editor, as she did on my two earlier projects for W. H. Freeman and Company. Pearl C. Vapnek, project editor at W. H. Freeman and Company, effectively supplemented the work of Ms. Duncan. The organizational ability and administrative skill and efficiency of Professor Charles F. Cnudde, chairperson of Michigan State University's Political Science Department, enable his faculty to work with a minimum of demands on their time. This book is but one of many evidences of his unobtrusive leadership. Last but not least, the typing of this manuscript through all of its revisions was the work of the secretaries in the Department of Political Science: Iris Richardson, Karen Albrecht, Karen Underwood, and Linda Salemka. Without them, we would have floundered.

Supreme Court Policy Making

Judicial Policy Making: Myth and Reality

Policy making may be defined as choosing among alternative courses of action, where the chosen action affects the behavior and well-being of others who are subject to the policy maker's authority. Put another way, policy making is the authoritative allocation of resources. No one disputes that legislators, executive officials, and bureaucrats make policy. By reason of their position they exercise discretion, and in doing so they choose among alternatives with the knowledge that their choices affect those subject to their authority.

Americans, however, have resisted the idea that judges are also governmental policy makers. Such resistance is supported by a web of beliefs about the nature of law, justice, and the judicial mind. This chapter begins with a general discussion of these beliefs and some possible reasons for them. It concludes with a specification of those characteristics of the American constitutional system that allow judges to function not merely as policy makers who are adjuncts to legislators, executives, and administrators, but as the most authoritative of our society's allocators of resources.

THE MYTHOLOGY OF JUDGING

No aspect of American government is more suffused with myth than judicial decision making. Judges are viewed as bloodless incarnations of human rectitude. From their lips flows a steady stream of sapience. From their pens flows not ink but rather moral concrete into which their judgments are set. Americans believe (or at least hope) that judicial decisions are value-free, essentially nondiscretionary, and objective. Subsequent chapters assess the extent to which this belief is grounded in reality. The extent to which decisions are value-free—that is, do not impose values on society—is discussed in Chapter 5. The question of whether the law is sufficiently settled (nondiscretionary) so that there are solid and persuasive legal grounds (precedents and principles) for judges to find and use to resolve conflicting claims is the subject of Chapter 3. The question of neutrality (that is, whether justice is impartial as to the litigants themselves) is considered in Chapter 7. The matter of objectivity—whether decisions are principled and whether the rules are fairly applied—is a recurrent theme throughout the book, especially Chapters 3 and 7.

The subject of this book, as the title indicates, is Supreme Court policy making. What is said about the Supreme Court does not necessarily apply to other courts—state or federal. Lower courts, trial as well as appellate, certainly do not have the discretion that the Supreme Court has. Not only are they not free to disregard the precedents established by higher courts, but the cases and controversies that come to them are also much more "open and shut" than the unsettled issues—the unresolved questions—that distinguish the Supreme Court's docket. The cases are open and shut in the sense that they turn on questions of fact that apply to commonplace legal issues; they are not the "big" cases with wide-ranging impact (see Chapter 8) that the Supreme Court decides. And even at the High Court level, although the Justices choose which principle to apply in a given case, and although that choice is governed by the Justices' attitudes and values (as explained in Chapter 5), the resulting decision is "objective," in the sense that it is assumed to be based on a relevant principle that is evenhandedly applied.

But to the true believer, any suggestion that judges are influenced by their personal preferences—their attitudes and values—and that they consequently exercise discretion is blasphemous. True believers perceive judges as Delphic oracles; they believe that when judicial policy is made, it is not really fallible human beings who speak, but rather the Constitution and laws that speaketh through them. If a description of the deistic attributes of judges fails to convince us of judicial objectivity, the true believer supplies a second tenet: a judge's task is, after all, only a simple, mechanical one. Does the law say this or does it say that? Is the action in question constitutional or not? According to the true believer, personal beliefs, attitudes, and values do not enter in to confuse the equation. And deciding right from wrong really cannot be that difficult anyway, can it? Judging is supposedly as automatic as distinguishing between black and white, or red and green, and although occasional fuliginous shades of gray may confuse the picture, judges are deemed experienced professionals, whose perspicuity enables them to strike the balance on the scales of justice with unfailing accuracy.

Thus, according to the faithful, the judge's task is a passive one. He is not to make or change the law. His only duty is to maintain it, to apply it. No matter that the law be wise or foolish—that is no concern of his. He does not create or invent law any more than Sigmund Freud, Alfred

Kinsey, or Hugh Hefner invented sex. According to this point of view, the overruling of an earlier decision does not belie judicial objectivity. Either the earlier decision established an erroneous rule (erroneous in the sense that pre-Columbian maps of the world were inaccurate), or the judges' collective eyesight was deficient so that the correct rule was not found.

The belief that judges merely "find" or "discover" what the law is and that they never, ever make law is a refrain that has been echoed by American judges, high and low, state and federal, at least since the time of Chief Justice John Marshall. In his words:

> Judicial power, as contradistinguished from the power of the laws, has no existence. Courts are the mere instruments of the law, and can will nothing. When they are said to exercise a discretion, it is a mere legal discretion, a discretion to be exercised in discerning the course prescribed by law; and, when that is discerned, it is the duty of the court to follow it. Judicial power is never exercised for the purpose of giving effect to the will of the judge; always for the purpose of giving effect to the will of the legislature; or, in other words, to the will of the law.[1]

The classic statement of this position came from the pen of Justice Owen Roberts in *United States* v. *Butler,* a famous Depression-era decision:

> It is sometimes said that the court assumes a power to overrule or control the action of the people's representatives. This is a misconception.... When an act of Congress is appropriately challenged in the courts as not conforming to the constitutional mandate the judicial branch of the Government has only one duty,—to lay the article of the Constitution which is invoked beside the statute which is challenged and to decide whether the latter squares with the former.[2]

Reasons for Refusal to Recognize Judges as Policy Makers

The belief that judges surely reap what they sow is commonly known as the declaratory theory, frequently referred to less reverently as the phonographic theory. Americans idealize judges as learned and impartial and as the embodiment of integrity. These characteristics are supposedly the hallmarks (or more appropriately perhaps, the bench marks) of those ensconced in the temples of justice. But learning, impartiality, and integrity are not readily definable attributes. Thus, what one person considers learning, another may view as sophistry. What a minion of Madison Avenue perceives as impartiality and integrity, consumers may see as bias and duplicity. But such variance in human perception is, it has been learned, controllable. Eons ago humankind discovered and developed devices that inculcated reverence and respect. The utility of such devices was that they effected acceptance and belief with a minimum of inquiry and examination, thereby elevating the credibility of the user through what might be called theatrical illusion.* Judges today employ such ruses. They alone among governmental personnel (except for the police and the military and some postal workers) are distinctively garbed—in black robes at that, the most mysterious and solemn costume found in the wardrobe of any actor. Enter the typical courtroom (not that of a justice of the peace or a police court where minor misdemeanors and traffic offenses are processed in assembly-line fashion) and note its similarity to a church or temple. Instead of an altar, the room is dominated by the judge's bench, which is elevated so that lawyers, witnesses, spectators, and other participants look *up* at the judge. Note that the room itself has an aura of ornate dignity. Observe the ritualized proceedings, surrounded by the trappings of pomp and circumstance. Listen to the exchange between judge and attorneys, conducted in a language largely unintelligible to the layperson.

It may be parenthetically noted that the distinctive attire of police and military personnel has changed over the years in accordance with the vagaries of fashion, comfort, and convenience. But can one imagine a judge cloaked in a viridian or chartreuse robe? It would be grounds for impeachment, or at least for a long rest in a quiet sanitarium. William Howard Taft, the only person in history to be both President and Chief Justice, forthrightly expressed the utility of the judicial robe:

> It is well that judges should be clothed in robes, not only, that those who witness the administration of justice should be properly advised that the function performed is one different from, and higher than, that which a man discharges as a citizen in the ordinary walks of life; but also, in order to impress the judge himself with the constant consciousness that he is a high priest of the temple of justice and is surrounded with obligations of a sacred character that he cannot escape. . . .[3]

Again note the religious imagery: "high priest," "temple," "sacred." The coincidence is not merely fortuitous.

---

*See Milner S. Ball, "The Play's the Thing: An Unscientific Reflection on Courts under the Rubric of Theater," *Stanford Law Review* 28 (1975): 81; reprinted in Thomas C. Fischer and Richard F. Zehnle, *Introduction to Law and Legal Reasoning* (St. Paul, Minn.: West, 1977), pp. 433–444.

Individuals do not invariably need external persuasion to become true believers. They are perfectly capable of making the transformation on their own. Witness the following excerpt from a letter to the editors of the Lansing (Michigan) *State Journal* for July 15, 1977:

> . . . How on earth do these so-called "gays" expect this world to exist if many more people decide to live as they do? Who would fight our wars? We will always have those until the end of time. And with abortion as prevalent as it now is (and this too is a terrible scourge in our day), who will propagate the world as God commanded us to do?

Off the bench, a judge is expected to be a faceless member of the community. Extracurricular activities in public places are taboo: no stepping out with the boys for an evening to hoist a few at the neighborhood bar, no prancing around the dance floor at the local country club, and no hot-rodding down the main drag. When court adjourns, the velvet curtains enfold the judge until the court is next in session.

Probably the most basic reason for the refusal of most people to accept the fact of judicial policy making is that judges make decisions that profoundly affect people's lives. For reasons to be explained at the end of this chapter, judges play God with regard to the life, liberty, and property of the persons who appear before them. Judges determine the guilt or innocence of individuals accused of crime (aided and abetted by a jury in many serious criminal cases—rarely is a jury empaneled if the offense is "petty" or a misdemeanor). Judges also resolve private, noncriminal disputes between persons. And in the United States, unlike almost anywhere else in the world, it is the judges who authoritatively resolve the public policy questions of the day. The people's elected representatives—congresspersons, state legislators, members of a city council—do not authoritatively resolve such issues as abortion reform, capital punishment, sex discrimination, financial aid to nonpublic schools, electronic eavesdropping, obscenity, cross-district busing, unfair trade practices, labor relations, or environmental protection. No matter what the issue, the last word, the authoritative response, will in all likelihood be that of a judge. Indeed such decision making hardly seems a proper task for a *mere* mortal. And so mythology is born.

This is why significant precedents often seem to spring incarnate from disputes that appear to be—and sometimes are—trifling. Judges seem to allow themselves much creative liberty in labeling sow's ears as silk purses. For example, when Oklahoma prohibited the sale of "nonintoxicating" 3.2 percent beer to males under the age of 21 and to females under the age of 18, a student at Oklahoma State University and a storekeeper whose store was located near the campus brought suit in the federal district court challenging the statute as unconstitutionally violating the right of males to the equal protection of the laws. They lost and appealed to the United States Supreme Court which, by a vote of 7 to 2, ruled that Oklahoma's gender-based age differential constitutes an invidious discrimination against males, even though a survey showed that young men were more inclined to drive after having drunk beer than were young women.[4] A second example concerns two junior high-school students in Miami, Florida, who were paddled severely by their teachers because of disciplinary infractions. The students and their parents took the case all the way to the United States Supreme Court, which ruled, by a 5 to 4 vote, that such discipline does not constitute cruel and unusual punishment in violation of the Eighth Amendment to the Constitution. The power that causes college students and "nonintoxicating" beer to become the ideological components of the concept of equal protection of the laws is magic that the most powerful of black-robed sorcerers might envy.

Though judicial decisions are authoritative, they may nonetheless be overturned by constitutional amendments, as when ratification of the Sixteenth Amendment reversed the Supreme Court's decision in *Pollock* v. *Farmers' Loan and Trust Co.*, 157 U.S. 429 (1895), which had held Congress without power to levy an income tax; and when ratification of the Twenty-sixth Amendment gave 18-year-olds the right to vote in state elections, thus contravening the Court's decision in *Oregon* v. *Mitchell*, 400 U.S. 112 (1970). But unlike judicial decisions, constitutional amendments are not exactly everyday occurrences. Witness the bitter struggle to enact the Equal Rights Amendment, which would do nothing more than establish as a legal fact of life that neither women nor men may be discriminated against on the basis of their gender. Ratified amendments, moreover, are subject to judicial scrutiny and interpretation that is no different from that given any other governmental action.†

The Income Tax Amendment is an apt illustration. In 1895, by a 5 to 4 vote, the Supreme Court declared the existing income tax law unconstitutional. Eighteen years later, in 1913, the Sixteenth Amendment was ratified. In pertinent part, it authorizes Congress to levy a tax on income "from whatever source derived." This phrase, linguistically, is unequivocal. Yet for the next 26 years the Supreme Court held that "from whatever source derived" *excluded* the salaries of federal judges. The basis for this judgment was the constitutional guarantee that federal judges' salaries "shall not be diminished during their continuance in office." Since the salaries of federal judges were fixed by law, any taxation of judges' income would obviously diminish them.[5]

Accordingly, whether judges are construing and applying legal rules and principles, legislative enactments, executive orders, administrative rules and regulations, or constitutional amendments, they are authoritatively allocating society's resources. They are, in short, making policy. Such policy making is most obvious at the top of the judicial hierarchy— in state and federal supreme courts—because this is where the "big," newsworthy cases end up. But the local police court judge and justice of the peace are not without policy-making clout also. That such policy may be mundane and commonplace gainsays nothing. The local judge who invariably sends drunken drivers to jail, the judge in the next county who throws the book only at youthful drug offenders, and the judge who

---

† The United States Constitution permits ratification of amendments by a vote of three-fourths of the state legislatures. This procedure has been employed for every amendment except the Twenty-first, which repealed prohibition and which was ratified by specifically called state conventions.

sits in the courthouse making life miserable for errant spouses who have fallen behind in their child support and alimony payments—all are making policy.

Nor is judicial policy making novel. Since the Supreme Court was established, its decisions have shaped as well as reflected our political life, social structure, economic system, cultural heritage, and religious traditions. Indeed, one can make a strong case that courts in general, and the Supreme Court in particular, have shaped and directed the course of American society to a far greater extent than either Congress or the Presidency. There are those who argue (albeit with tongue in cheek) that Congress reached its legislative peak in 1789 when it enacted the two Judiciary Acts of that year, and that its legislative capability has declined steadily ever since. These laws—the twentieth and twenty-first that it passed—established and staffed the federal judiciary and regulated the federal courts' processes.[6] As for Presidents, except during periods of national emergency when they become, willy-nilly, *de facto* dictators, they do little more, Arthur L. Lippmann once said, than

> . . . issue postage stamps or face the microphones
> Or osculate with infants, or preside at corner-stones.[7]

This is a cynical statement, but it is perhaps not totally inaccurate.

Government affairs, then, are largely judicial affairs. Throughout the nation's history the courts have made basic decisions in the areas of agriculture, banking, commerce, communications, criminal justice, education, fiscal policy, industry, labor, manufacturing, mining, national defense, natural resources, public health, social welfare, taxation, and transportation. Indeed, the only area of governmental policy making that is not grist for the judicial mill is foreign affairs. But even here, noninvolvement in the past has been a sometime thing. Prior to the Civil War, the federal courts were much concerned with admiralty and maritime matters. At the turn of the century, the Supreme Court quickly followed the flag as America belatedly entered the race for colonial possessions and empire by deciding such questions as the extent to which constitutional guarantees apply to the residents of America's territorial possessions, the scope of the treaty-making power, the respective roles of the President and Congress in conducting foreign affairs, and the control over the issuance of passports.[8] The Court's current hands-off policy is one of its own choosing, which can be cast aside or retained as a majority of the Justices choose. The Court, for example, did not lack the opportunity to resolve the question of the constitutionality of the Vietnam War. For reasons that it did not articulate, the Court chose to let that cup pass. But even when it refuses to decide, the Court has an impact. Like Pontius Pilate, the Court may wash its hands of an issue, but that does not mean that the matter rests in limbo. By the Court's leave, authoritative resolution necessarily devolves upon the lower federal courts, Congress, the federal bureaucracy, the President, or the states.

Probably the most convincing explanation of why most people prefer not to accept the fact of judicial policy making is that their belief in value-free, nondiscretionary, and objective decisions reflects ideals of justice and fairness. But though individuals strive mightily, the human condition remains such that ideals often escape realization. Two more simplistic, more mundane explanations for the refusal to accept the fact of judicial policy making may also be suggested: first, the childish desire of humankind to have a fixed, unalterable legal world where judges, as surrogate father figures, protect us from harm and direct us along the path of righteousness; second, plain, old-fashioned wish fulfillment. We believe what is psychologically comforting and disregard those aspects of reality that we find painful. In other words, we assume the ostrich posture—do not confuse us with the facts.

REASONS FOR
JUDICIAL POLICY MAKING

The desire for stability and wish fulfillment continues to be widespread, even though creative and innovative decisions since the mid-1950's in such areas as race relations, criminal procedure, legislative reapportionment, abortion, and sex discrimination have made it difficult for even the most fervent true believers to keep their heads in the sand.[9] Be that as it may, explanations that focus only on why many Americans refuse to recognize the fact of judicial policy making tell only one side of the story. Equally important is an understanding of the reasons *why* American judges have virtually untrammeled policy-making authority, which allows them authoritatively to resolve public issues with less interference from other governmental officials than do judges in any other country. Five factors, directly related to the American experience, provide an answer.

Fundamental Law

A major contribution that the English colonists, especially those who settled in New England, made to American life was the concept of fundamental law,[10] which postulated that all governmental action was to be compatible with the word of God and/or the dictates of nature as these were discerned by the leadership of the particular colony. The overtly religious motivation that led to the founding of many of the colonies and the establishment of new settlements emphasized the fundamental law, which was reflected in the colonial charters and constitutions.

Belief in a fundamental law continued to be widespread long after theocratic parochialism vanished. From colonial times to the present day, Americans have lived in, and for the most part recognized the existence of, an extremely volatile environment. The lure of the frontier and the westward movement produced profound social and economic turbulence. The industrial and technological revolutions transformed what had been a scattering of yeoman farmers into a nation of urbanized employees. Mass immigration diversified the nation culturally and provided a steady supply of cheap labor to man America's farms and factories. These and other forces have produced drastic changes in the life style and status of millions of Americans, past and present. Americans have traditionally recognized change as a fact of life and have considered it synonymous with progress and freedom. The net result has been that the establishment of a fixed and stable social, economic, cultural, and religious system has been precluded.

One may label those who long for a simple, uncomplicated life as childish or primitive. But the fact remains that individuals cannot function in an overly dynamic environment. Man, after all, is a creature of habit. A shortage of life's necessities, undesired and unexpected alterations in one's relationships with others, and the demolition of cherished beliefs, all produce stress. Life becomes a frightening prospect when it is recognized that the forces of change are beyond human control and direction; individuals become only so many corks pitched endlessly about in a storm-tossed sea.

The solution, whether arrived at consciously or unconsciously, was subjection of the political sphere to control and direction. The other spheres of human activity—social, economic, cultural, and religious—were intractable. In the summer of 1787, 55 men addressed themselves to the task of replacing the hitherto parochial and essentially religious notion of fundamental law. The result was a written Constitution that, upon its ratification by the several states, was promptly enshrined as American society's secular substitute for the Holy Writ.

The Constitution of the United States has endured longer than that of any other nation, and thus another peculiarity has been added to the American way of life: political stability. Other societies secure the necessary measure of stability by means of a fixed and structured social system—a hereditary aristocracy or gentry, for example. Alternatively, the economic system may provide stability, as in nonindustrialized parts of the world where subsistence farming provides a livelihood for all but a privileged handful. Or an established state church may exist, to which all citizens pay at least *pro forma* obeisance. Or national boundaries may coincide with ethnic or tribal lines, thereby producing cultural homogeneity. In such environments, the political sphere becomes the realm of change. Changes in regime are radical; revolution—bloody or otherwise—becomes commonplace. No so in the United States.

One may argue that straws currently in the wind belie the accuracy of this analysis for the future. Political reform remains a *cause célèbre*, though it is not accompanied by the rioting and protest demonstrations of the late 1960's. But talk about political reform can be compared with talk about the weather. The assumption is that nothing ever comes of it. We are a rather homogenized middle-class society. Thanks to the public schools and the "boob tube," most Americans have been socialized and acculturated in a fairly standardized fashion; virtually everybody speaks English nowadays, albeit some speak it more correctly than others. On the other hand, change and fluidity continue to characterize the social, economic, cultural, and religious spheres. Alternative life styles and countercultures abound. Minorities have become not only visible but vocal as well. Women's Lib appears to be a fact of life, not to mention Gay Lib. Sexual behavior is somewhat looser, and sex is openly flaunted by the media. Ecumenism, Pentecostalism, and Eastern mysticism have had an impact on organized religion. Economic conditions are less than stable. If instability continues to persist in these other areas of life, then the political sphere will likely *remain* America's link with the invariant.

Distrust of Governmental Power

Americans have traditionally tended to distrust governmental power, especially that exercised from Washington. The genesis of this distrust predates the Revolutionary War. The colonists considered British policies following the French and Indian War, which ended in 1763, inimical to their rights and liberties. Opposition to these policies occasioned the Revolution, which coincided with an internal struggle for control of the newly formed state governments. This internal struggle more or less pitted the socioeconomic elite against the yeoman farmers and the urban artisans. It had by no means been resolved when the Framers convened in Philadelphia in the summer of 1787.

The socioeconomic elite sought to retain its vested economic rights. In those states where the less-privileged sector gained a measure of dominance, the burden of taxation was shifted toward the rich and wellborn. Legislative bodies were reapportioned to allow greater representation for rural and frontier regions. The passage of stay laws, which lengthened the time for the payment of debts, and the issuance of cheap paper money as legal tender were other major objectives.

The solution devised by the Framers was a governmental system that neither the "haves" nor the "have nots" were able to control. This meant a system in which the federal level would do little governing. The federal government was restricted to raising an army and maintaining a navy, coining money, operating a postal system, regulating interstate commerce, and—needless to say—levying taxes. Both "factions" accepted this arrangement. The lower strata stood to benefit because they lacked experience in managing the affairs of state. Their lack of experience except at the local and state levels left them somewhat disadvantaged in the political maneuvering. Their fundamental interest in states' rights and local self-government heightened their suspicion of a strong and efficient central government. Government, at least in their ancestors' experience, had been a vehicle of tyranny and oppression. They evidenced their distrust by insisting that a Bill of Rights be added to the Constitution as the price of their support. Finally, many of those who constituted the lower strata lived along the frontier—those parts of the country that were beyond the pale of effective governmental authority. For the next hundred years, the utility of the federal government for people on the frontier was largely limited to supplying a band of cavalry when needed to pacify unruly natives.

No less were the elite in favor of a government that was invulnerable to any group's effective control. As the privileged sector, they were paramountly concerned lest they lose their position on the top of the heap. They were also concerned that governmental power not be used *against* them. They logically assumed that they could perpetuate their position in society, given their possession and control of economic power and the social status that accompanied it. Consequently, the notion that that government is best which governs least quickly became an article of faith for everybody, for their own partisan reasons.

The means employed by the Framers to institutionalize the view that that government is best which governs least supported judicial policy making. The means were basically two in number: federalism and separation of powers. Federalism is the geographical division of power between the federal government and the states; separation of powers is the functional division of power among the three branches of government—legislative, executive, and judicial.

Note that the Framers did two things with respect to the powers of government. First, rather than simply dividing the totality of governmental power among the states and the various branches of the federal government, they severely limited the scope of the government's power. Indeed, a most striking feature of the Constitution is the plethora of negatives ("no," "not," "neither," "nor"). These negatives are far more numerous than the powers that government may exercise. Consider the equally profuse number of "thou shalt not's" in Sections 9 and 10 of Article I, which enumerate only some of the things that Congress and the states may *not* do:

SECTION 9 . . .
. . . the writ of habeas corpus shall not be suspended, . . .
No bill of attainder or ex post facto law shall be passed.
No capitation, or other direct, tax shall be laid, unless in proportion

to the census or enumeration. . . .

No tax or duty shall be laid on articles exported from any state. No preference shall be given by any regulation of commerce or revenue to the ports of one state over those of another: nor shall vessels bound to, or from, one state, be obliged to enter, clear, or pay duties in another.

No money shall be drawn from the treasury, but in consequence of appropriations made by law; . . .

No title of nobility shall be granted by the United States:—And no person holding any office of profit or trust under them, shall, without the consent of the Congress, accept of any present, emolument, office, or title, of any kind whatever, from any king, prince, or foreign state.

SECTION 10. No state shall enter into any treaty, alliance, or confederation; . . . coin money; emit bills of credit; make any thing but gold and silver coin a tender in payment of debts; pass any . . . law impairing the obligation of contracts, . . .

No state shall, without the consent of the Congress, lay any imposts or duties on imports or exports, . . . No state shall, without the consent of Congress, lay any duty of tonnage, keep troops, or ships of war in time of peace, enter into any agreement or compact with another state, or with a foreign power, or engage in war, unless actually invaded, or in such imminent danger as will not admit of delay.

Second, the Framers specified rather frequently the manner in which a given power may be exercised. For example, Article III stipulates trial by jury of all federal crimes except impeachment, and Section 7 of Article I details the procedure whereby a bill becomes a law.

Federalism

The federal government and the states were not given carte blanche to exercise these limited powers as they saw fit. Some powers, such as the power to tax, are shared. But for the most part, only the federal government can exercise certain powers; others are exercised by the states alone.

In drafting these provisions, the Framers used imprecise language. Resulting squabbles over who could do what have landed on the Supreme Court's doorstep. This steady stream of litigation has enabled the Court, since the earliest days of the nation's existence, authoritatively to determine the relative power of the federal government vis-à-vis the states and the resultant degree of centralization (which gives the federal sphere more control) or decentralization (which gives the states greater power). The decisions of the Court cause the relative balance to vary at any given point in time.[11] Thus, the Court made smooth the path of unfettered business enterprise and industrial development in the late nineteenth and early twentieth centuries by limiting the scope of Congress's power to regulate interstate commerce, while at the same time declaring that the states could not regulate such activities because their regulation of these activities would violate due process of law.[12] But in the late 1930's, the Court turned the tide toward centralization. The high-water mark of centralization may have occurred in 1942 when the Court held that a farmer who grew 23 acres of wheat for consumption within the confines of his own farm was subject to the federal marketing quotas of the Agricultural Adjustment Act of 1938.[13]

Separation of Powers

Separation of powers compartmentalizes governmental activity into three separate chambers. Each has its own personnel (who serve a term of office durationally different from that of the others—two years for representatives, four years for Presidents, six years for senators, and a lifetime for judges), and each exercises power granted to it alone. But the Framers went a step further and gave to each branch of government some power that typologically belongs to one of the others, thereby creating a system of checks and balances. Thus, the President may veto congressional legislation, and Congress curbs executive activity as a result of the constitutional requirement that all major Presidential appointees must receive senatorial confirmation.

The effect of separation of powers is to institutionalize conflict among the three branches of government, most especially between Congress and President.[14] To ensure that this condition prevails, the Framers divided the legislative branch into two separate houses, the Senate and the House of Representatives. For a bill to become a law, the measure must pass both houses, word for word, comma for comma. As a consequence, Congress must labor mightily to bring forth a mouse. But the Framers were not as jaundiced about legislators as many of the states have been. Congress may remain in session year-round if it so desires. But state legislatures commonly operate under time constraints, the rationale being that sessions of prespecified duration limit opportunities for mischief making. (Texas is a somewhat extreme example. Its legislature convenes for a 20-week session every other year.)

The Framers did not consider the federal judiciary a threat to the negative, do-nothing system that they so carefully crafted, so they put the fewest restraints upon it. They were concerned that judges might fall into the clutches of either Congress or the President. Therefore, to ensure the judiciary's independence, they provided federal judges with lifetime appointments. Neither Congress nor the President can control the selection process. Persons nominated by the President must be confirmed by the Senate. The number of federal judges, the jurisdiction of their courts, and the cases that may be appealed to the Supreme Court are legislative subjects upon which both houses of Congress must agree and which require Presidential approval. (But a Presidential veto can be overriden by a two-thirds vote of each house.)

The Framers' insistence upon a judiciary that is independent of both Congress and the President has abetted the autonomous policy-making capability of federal judges in general, and that of the Supreme Court in particular. If federal judges were not independent of Congress and the President, their ability to present themselves as impartial decision makers would be diminished. And if the federal judiciary were not independent, the public would likely assume that judges are also politicians, engaged in a dirty business that attracts only persons of minimal competence and questionable virtue. American parents, when asked what occupations they most prefer for their offspring, invariably rank "judge" at the top of the list. "Politician," by contrast, ties with peddler and is only a notch above used-car salesman.[15] Because judges are autonomous (the most striking manifestation of their autonomy being their authority to determine, by exercising their power of judicial review, the constitutionality—that is, the legality—of the actions of other public officials), they have the opportunity, litanized in their opinions, to assert that they pay obeisance to naught save the Constitution.[16]

Judicial Review

Judicial review—the power of judges to decide the constitutionality of the actions of the other branches of government—was not of the Framers' doing; but it is perhaps the most vital aspect of courts' powerful policy-making ability. The doctrine of judicial review was formally enunciated in 1803 by Chief Justice John Marshall and a unanimous Court in *Marbury* v. *Madison.*[17] The case, aptly described by historian John A. Garraty as a "trivial squabble over a few petty political plums,"[18] should never have been decided by the Supreme Court. Because Marshall himself was a principal to the action that occasioned the litigation, good legal form dictated that he disqualify himself. But Marshall, recognizing a golden opportunity to expand the power of his Court, was not one to let legalistic niceties deprive him of an opportunity that would not likely knock again.

William Marbury had been appointed a justice of the peace for the District of Columbia. His appointment was part of the strategy of the Federalist Party after their overwhelming defeat by the Jeffersonians in the election of 1800. Deprived of the Presidency and of control of Congress, the Federalists decided to fill an expanded federal judiciary and to bide their time for another foray against the now ascendant Jeffersonian faction. This was a feasible strategy because the Constitution conveniently provided that the second session of each Congress "shall assemble . . . on the first Monday in December." Congress, however, had prescribed November as the month for federal elections. Consequently, the second session of each Congress was a lame-duck session that included members who had been defeated in the previous month's election—-in this case the embittered Federalists. The lame-duck session that convened in December 1800 passed the necessary legislation creating new judicial positions, and Federalist President John Adams quickly filled them with good and faithful Federalists.

As the date for the inauguration of Jefferson (March 4, 1801) approached, John Marshall was serving in two capacities—as Adams's Secretary of State and as Chief Justice of the United States. Marshall had become Chief Justice only because of the lame-duck arrangement, having been appointed and confirmed in January 1801. (The vacancy existed because his predecessor, Oliver Ellsworth, had resigned the preceding September, and John Jay, who was nominated and confirmed in Ellsworth's stead in December 1800, declined the office.)

We may speculate whether the United States would be as we know it if Marshall had not been appointed Chief Justice. He dominated the Court as no one else had before or has since. Indeed, if one were to single out the individual most responsible for the course and direction of American government and society, that person may well be John Marshall. On such accidents of history does the fate of nations truly rest.

But it was Marshall's role as Secretary of State that gave rise to the case of *Marbury* v. *Madison*. In this capacity, he was responsible for delivering Marbury's commission as justice of the peace. Through oversight or forgetfulness, he failed to do so before Jefferson's administration took office. Madison, Jefferson's Secretary of State, refused delivery. Marbury thereupon brought suit in the Supreme Court under a provision of the Judiciary Act of 1789 that authorized such actions by "persons holding office under the authority of the United States." Marshall, in a quintessential political maneuver that would have warmed the cockles of even a Machiavelli or a Richelieu, said that Marbury had a right to his commission, but that the Supreme Court had no power to order Madison to deliver it. The reason: the original jurisdiction of the Supreme Court, unlike its appellate jurisdiction, is specified in the Constitution. By interpreting the Constitution strictly, Marshall maintained that Congress could not pass a law that was contrary to constitutional provisions even though it might enhance the Court's power. The portion of the Judiciary Act that conflicted with the Constitution was therefore null and void.

On the face of it, Marshall had ruled *against* his party's interests, not only from the point of view of Marbury and the others whose commissions were not delivered, but also from the standpoint of Federalist strategy, which was to make the judiciary a stronghold from which to blunt and counter the impact of the Jeffersonians. But by deliberately losing the battle of *Marbury* v. *Madison,* he won the war. He set a precedent that the Supreme Court, *not* Congress and *not* the President, has the authority to say what is and what is not governmentally permissible. His rationale was that each branch of the federal government, being coequal with the others, is competent to determine the constitutionality of its actions within the sphere designated by the Constitution. Inasmuch as the Constitution is the nation's fundamental law, and since the special competency of the judiciary—for which it is uniquely equipped—is to determine and apply the law, the Court has no choice but to abide by the dictates of the Constitution and to construe and apply its provisions. An awesome power was created. And the victory was complete, even though the Court did not again declare an act of Congress unconstitutional until 1857.[19] Since 1803, judicial review has been as much a part of the fabric of American government as clout, patronage, and taxes.

Though the written Constitution is without so much as an implicit reference to judicial review, the courts' arrogation of the power comports fully with the motivations and concerns that led to the drafting and ratification of the document.

First, if the Constitution is to be the fundamental law because of the need felt by Americans for a measure of stability in an otherwise fluid and dynamic environment, then some decision-making body must authoritatively interpret the provisions of this fundamental law. Congress and/or the President might be capable of doing so; they, like the judges, swear to preserve, protect, and defend the Constitution of the United States. And it would be arrogantly presumptuous to assume that they honor their oath of office less conscientiously than judges do. However, Presidents and congresspersons are subject to electoral pressures—to factious popular passions. Judges are not. So why not accept judicial interpretation as authoritative?

Second, since centralized government is to be distrusted, and since a federal system is to be established, an "umpire" is needed to resolve conflicts between the federal and state governments—especially since the constitutional provisions governing the geographical division of power are so vague. The resolution of such conflicts cannot be left to Congress, or the President, or the states. So why not leave it to the judges? Moreover, if separation of powers means that conflict prevails between the President and Congress, does it not make sense to allow the judiciary to constitute the balance of power between them?

Hence the ascendency of the judiciary. Aided and abetted by the elevating and insulating characteristics of mythology, judges remain above the hue and cry. As enigmatic technicians, as so many Delphic oracles, they dispense revealed wisdom objectively and dispassionately. Another refrain from Arthur Lippmann's "Song of the Supreme Court" summarizes the Justices' position:

Like oysters in our cloisters, we avoid the storm and strife.
Some President appoints us, and we're put away for life.
When Congress passes laws that lack historical foundation,
We hasten from a huddle and reverse the legislation.
The sainted Constitution, that great document for students,
Provides an airtight alibi for all our jurisprudence.
So don't blame us if now and then we seem to act like bounders;
Blame Hamilton and Franklin and the patriotic founders.[20]

NOTES

1. *Osborn* v. *Bank of the United States*, 9 Wheat. 738, at 866 (1824).

2. 297 U.S. 1, at 62 (1936).

3. *Present Day Problems* (New York: Dodd, Mead, 1908), pp. 63–64. Judge Jerome Frank aptly labeled and incisively criticized the symbolism surrounding judges' garb as "the cult of the robe." *Courts on Trial* (New York: Atheneum, 1963), pp. 254–261.

4. *Craig* v. *Boren*, 429 U.S. 190 (1976).

5. See *Evans* v. *Gore*, 253 U.S. 245 (1920); and *Miles* v. *Graham*, 268 U.S. 501 (1925). In 1939, the Court overruled these decisions in *O'Malley* v. *Woodrough*, 307 U.S. 277, stating that the subjection of federal judges "to a general tax . . . merely [recognizes] . . . that judges are also citizens, and that their particular function in government does not generate an immunity from sharing with their fellow citizens the material burden of the government whose Constitution and laws they are charged with administering."

6. 1 U.S. Statutes at Large, 73, 93.

7. "Song of the Supreme Court," *Life Magazine*, August 1935, p. 7.

8. See C. Herman Pritchett, *The American Constitution*, 2d ed. (New York: McGraw-Hill, 1968), pp. 93–95, 353–371.

9. See, for example, *Brown* v. *Board of Education*, 347 U.S. 484 (1954) and 349 U.S. 294 (1955); and *Mapp* v. *Ohio*, 367 U.S. 643 (1961). See also *Gideon* v. *Wainwright*, 372 U.S. 335 (1963); *Reynolds* v. *Sims*, 377 U.S. 533 (1964); *Malloy* v. *Hogan*, 378 U.S. 1 (1964); *Miranda* v. *Arizona*, 384 U.S. 436 (1966); *Katz* v. *United States*, 389 U.S. 347 (1967); *Argersinger* v. *Hamlin*, 407 U.S. 25 (1972); *Roe* v. *Wade*, 410 U.S. 113, and *Doe* v. *Bolton*, 410 U.S. 179 (1973); *Frontiero* v. *Richardson*, 411 U.S. 677 (1973); *Beal* v. *Doe*, 432 U.S. 438, *Maher* v. *Roe*, 432 U.S. 464, and *Poelker* v. *Doe*, 432 U.S. 519 (1977)—numbers 20, 21, 22, 24, 25, 29, 30, 37, 42, 44, and 54 in Harold J. Spaeth, *Classic and Current Decisions of the United States Supreme Court* (San Francisco: W. H. Freeman and Company, 1977, 1978).

10. See Edward A. Corwin, *The "Higher Law" Background of American Constitutional Law* (Ithaca, N.Y.: Cornell University Press, 1955).

11. See, for example, *Fletcher* v. *Peck*, 6 Cranch 87 (1810); *Martin* v. *Hunter's Lessee*, 1 Wheaton 305 (1816); *M'Culloch* v. *Maryland*, 4 Wheaton 316 (1819); *Dartmouth College* v. *Woodward*, 4 Wheaton 518 (1819); *Cooley* v. *Board of Wardens*, 12 Howard 299 (1852); *Younger* v. *Harris*, 401 U.S. 37 (1971); and *Stone* v. *Powell*, 428 U.S. 465 (1976)—numbers 3, 4, 5, 6, 8, 34, and 53 in *Classic and Current Decisions.*

12. See *West Coast Hotel Co.* v. *Parrish*, 300 U.S. 379; and *National Labor Relations Board* v. *Jones & Laughlin Steel Corp.*, 301 U.S. 1 (1937)—numbers 14 and 15 in *Classic and Current Decisions.*

13. *Wickard* v. *Filburn*, 317 U.S. 111.

14. See, for example, *Youngstown Sheet and Tube Co.* v. *Sawyer*, 343 U.S. 579 (1953), number 19 in *Classic and Current Decisions.*

15. According to a Chilton Research Services Survey published July 9, 1975.

16. See, for example, *Ex parte Milligan*, 4 Wallace 2 (1866); *Reynolds* v. *Sims*, 377 U.S. 533 (1964); *Powell* v. *McCormack*, 395 U.S. 486 (1969); *New York Times* v. *United States*, 403 U.S. 713 (1971); *United States* v. *U.S. District Court*, 407 U.S. 297 (1972); and *United States* v. *Nixon*, 418 U.S. 683 (1974)—numbers 10, 24, 32, 36, 40, and 47 in *Classic and Current Decisions.*

17. 1 Cranch 137 (1803), number 2 in *Classic and Current Decisions.*

18. John A. Garraty, *Quarrels That Have Shaped the Constitution* (New York: Harper & Row, 1962), p. 13.

19. In *Scott* v. *Sandford*, 19 Howard 393, number 9 in *Classic and Current Decisions.*

20. *Op. cit.*, note 7 *supra.*

The Mechanics of Supreme Court Policy Making: Process, Access, and Jurisdiction

How does the Court operate? This is the subject of the first part of this chapter. At the heart of the Court's operations are its conferences—those highly secret proceedings in which the Justices decide which cases they will hear and who will write the opinions in those cases in which they have heard argument. Why are these conferences conducted in utmost secrecy? What procedures govern the Justices in these deliberations? What is the role of the law clerks who assist the Justices? Where do the Court's cases come from and how do the Justices act upon them? How are the opinions written?

Not everyone who so desires will have his or her case reviewed by the Supreme Court. To gain access to the High Bench—or any other court—the plaintiff must have "standing to sue." In addition, the court to which the litigant brings his or her case must have jurisdiction to decide the controversy. The various requirements of standing to sue that plaintiffs must meet to gain access, and the determination of which court has jurisdiction are the subject of the last part of this chapter. What types of cases may the federal courts—including the Supreme Court—hear? In describing the jurisdiction of the federal courts, reference is made to one of the most basic aspects of the American judicial system: the adversary process. What is it, why do we use it, and how well does it work?

Even though a litigant has standing to sue and the Supreme Court has jurisdiction to decide the case, the Justices may nonetheless refuse to hear the matter. How is this possible? What criteria does the Court use to determine which cases within its jurisdiction it will decide? The chapter concludes with a discussion of three cases that illustrate that both common, everyday occurrences and momentous issues receive the Court's attention.

INSIDE THE MARBLE PALACE

On Capitol Hill, at One First Street NE, sits a bone-white temple— longer than a football field—that since 1935 has housed the United States Supreme Court.* Inside the main entrance is an imposing hall, beyond which lies the courtroom. Outside the main hall and the court- room are four courtyards—two on each side. Separating the courtyards are conference and reception rooms, a lawyers' lounge, and the mar- shall's office. Around the periphery of the building are the chambers and offices of the Justices and their staffs. Behind the red velvet curtains in back of the bench at which the Justices sit when the Court is in session is the conference room. The Justices gather here to vote on the cases on which they have previously heard argument and to decide which of the cases they have been requested to review will receive the benefit of a formal decision. The upper and lower floors of the 250-room building contain the Court's library, a reading room, a cafeteria, an infirmary, and the offices and work areas of the 250 persons who assist the Justices in their labors, such as police officers, cooks, laundry workers, a seamstress, a nurse, carpenters, electricians, librarians, printers, pages, messengers, and clerks.†

---

*As evidence that governmental programs and projects do not invariably result in cost overruns, note may be made that the building cost approximately $94,000 less than the $9,740,000 appropriated for it. *Equal Justice Under Law* (Washington, D.C.: Foundation of the Federal Bar Association), 1965, p. 121.

†Although the Court's employees are extraordinarily loyal (many of them devote their entire lives to service on the Court), they are not one big, happy family. The Court's employees are not part of the federal civil service. Salaries, hours and conditions of work, pensions, and fringe benefits are governed by the Court's own rules. In 1973, the Court's fifty-member police force organized a union because of what they regarded as low pay, long hours, and unfair promotion policies. All but two of the officers signed cards authoriz- ing the union to represent them. The Court, however, has refused to recognize the union, notwithstanding that the Court has been ordering other employers to bargain with unions for decades. To be sure, the Court is a small agency by federal standards, and this fact, plus the Court's independence from the civil service, has resulted in its administering itself in a highly personalized fashion—the Chief Justice makes most appointments with the con- currence of the other Justices. The basis for the Court's refusal to recognize the police officers' union was a 1962 Presidential order that, while encouraging union activity among federal employees, exempted the FBI and the CIA from unionization, as well as any other governmental body that is "primarily performing intelligence, investigative, or security functions if the head of the agency determines that the provisions of this order cannot be applied in a manner consistent with national security requirements and considerations." Whether President Kennedy, who issued the order, meant it to be applicable to the Su- preme Court is an interesting, if unanswerable, speculation. See Linda Mathews, "Supreme Court—a Miniature World Governed by Tradition," *Los Angeles Times,* February 2, 1974; and Warren Weaver, Jr., "High Court Bars Union for Own Police," *New York Times,* April 20, 1974.

But not all the Court's employees are unhappy. According to Jack Anderson, writing in his syndicated column of June 10, 1977, the Court's carpenters have been willing not only to repair and maintain the furniture and woodwork within the Supreme Court building, but also to build coffee tables, bookcases, and picture frames to adorn the homes of several of the Justices.

The Law Clerks

Working most closely with the Justices are their law clerks.‡ Each Justice is entitled to three; the Chief Justice is entitled to four. They are recent law school graduates who usually work a year for the Justice who selects them. (Chief Justice Burger, however, has begun a practice of hiring clerks who are permanently assigned to his office.) The duties to which their Justice assigns them are varied. Their most intensive duty is the research that precedes the writing of an opinion by the Justice: checking the relevance of previously decided cases and checking historical data, statutory and administrative provisions, and congressional records. They also write footnotes, draft opinions, and advise their Justice which of the cases in which the losing party seeks review are worthy of the Court's consideration. They ease the Justices' tasks, but they do not function as members of the Court. Their title—clerk—aptly describes the extent of their responsibilities. They are not powers behind the throne; nor are they drones.

The Term of the Court

For over a century, it has been the Court's practice to sit for nine months a year—currently from the first Monday in October until the end of June. Occasionally an issue requiring immediate resolution surfaces that requires the Court to convene in a special summer session. This happened in 1972 when the Court met early in July to hear and resolve a dispute challenging the composition of the delegates to the Democratic National Convention, which was scheduled to convene on July 10.[1] But do not assume that the Justices are idle the rest of the year. During the summer, though they may not be in Washington, the Justices read the lower-court opinions and the briefs submitted by attorneys in those cases that the Court has agreed to review but has not yet decided.

During the months that the Court is in session, most of the activity occurs within each Justice's suite of offices. The courtroom is utilized only for the purpose of hearing oral argument in the cases the Court has agreed to decide and to announce the decision in the cases that have been decided. The Court normally hears oral arguments on Monday through Thursday two weeks during each month while in session. On these days, decisions are also announced, as they become ready, when the Court is called to order at 10 A.M. The Court sits until noon and also from 1 to 3 P.M.[2] The time allotted attorneys to argue their cases is

---

‡Most of the law clerks have been males. The first female clerk was appointed by Justice Douglas in 1944. Henry J. Abraham, *The Judicial Process,* 3rd ed. (New York: Oxford University Press, 1975), p. 239. The first female page was not appointed until 1972. "Notes on People: High Court Hires Girl," *New York Times,* September 20, 1972.

rigorously limited: either one hour or one-half hour for each side per case. Reading from a prepared text is frowned upon and the attorneys may expect frequent interruptions from the Justices, who pepper them with questions at will.

The Conference

On Fridays, at 9:30 A.M., the Justices gather in their conference room. They spend the entire day there discussing and voting how to decide the cases on which they have heard oral argument. These regular Friday conferences are supplemented by additional conferences on Wednesday afternoons during the week in which they have heard oral argument. Thus, the Justices must be prepared to decide (tentatively, at least) each and every case 24 to 96 hours after they have heard oral argument. Theoretically, any Justice may change his initial vote at any time before the Court publicly announces its decision (which it usually does 1 to 6 or 8 months after oral argument is heard), and occasionally one or more Justices do so. However, a lot of vote switching would disrupt the Court's decisional process, because the task of writing the Court's opinion is assigned on the basis of the initial vote. If more than one or two Justices change their minds, the Court, if narrowly divided, may find itself without a majority opinion coalition. A majority of the participating Justices must join in a single opinion. Failure to obtain a majority results in a "judgment" rather than an "opinion" of the Court. The judgment merely stipulates which party to the case has won and which has lost, whereas the opinion of the Court is of paramount importance to the Court as a policy-making body. The Court's opinions exert a policy impact far beyond the immediate interests of the parties to the case. Through them, the constitutional and legal principles governing the Court's decision are communicated; they create precedents that presumably bind the lower courts in their consideration of related cases that will subsequently arise; and affected persons and governmental agencies are expected to make their activities conform with the guidelines provided in the Court's opinions. For example, a judgment that a person is entitled to a new trial because he or she was deprived of counsel is quite distinct from an opinion that holds that *no* person convicted of a crime may be sentenced unless represented by an attorney.[3] Similarly, a judgment that a given business may not refuse service to blacks differs from an opinion that opens virtually all places of public accommodation on a color-blind basis.[4] And a decision that orders the payment of welfare benefits is distinct from an opinion that declares such benefits to be a matter of right rather than a privilege.[5]

Washington's best-kept secret is what transpires in the Justices' weekly conferences. No one but the Justices themselves participates in these sessions, at which they discuss the cases on which they have heard oral argument, assign opinions, and decide which cases they will hear in the future. Until 1910, two pages attended the Justices' conferences. But in that year an attorney who had argued a case before the Court sold his stock in the corporation whose case he had argued a few hours before the Court announced its decision. Although the lawyer denied having had any advance knowledge, maintaining instead that he had made an educated guess about the outcome of the case, the Justices did not believe him. Convinced that one or the other of the pages was responsible, they banished them forever from the conference room.[6]

Ousted along with the pages was a porter who served drinks. Chief Justice Marshall had begun this tradition a century earlier, insisting that the Justices begin their conferences with a drink if it was raining anywhere within the Court's jurisdiction.[7] Inasmuch as the Court's jurisdiction encompassed virtually all the land east of the Rocky Mountains subsequent to the purchase of the Louisiana Territory in 1803, the porter's presence could be expected as regularly as that of Marshall himself.

The most serious leak occurred in connection with the infamous Dred Scott case.[8] President-elect Buchanan was informed how the Justices had voted by one of the proslavery Justices (presumably John Catron) a month before he took office. At the same time various Northern newspapers received copies of the dissenting opinion of antislavery Justice Curtis. In his inaugural address, Buchanan stated that the much disputed questions of whether blacks were citizens and whether any provisions in the Constitution protected them would soon be settled. Two days later the Court announced its proslavery decision, which, as subsequent events proved, did anything but calm the waters.

Although the other branches of government have opened their proceedings somewhat to public scrutiny—either voluntarily, as a result of so-called sunshine laws, or because of the Freedom of Information Act§—the Court has not followed this trend. But unlike Congress and the executive branch, the Court has provided the public with all relevant materials pertaining to its decisions: briefs, transcripts of oral argument, lower-court decisions, and of course the opinions of the Justices. The Justices base their opposition to opening their conferences to the public on the ground that to do so would seriously undermine the Court's effectiveness as an authoritative policy-making body. In a recent speech at the Washburn University School of Law in Topeka, Kansas, Justice Rehnquist gave what apparently was the first full-blown defense of the

---

§ The Freedom of Information Act, enacted in 1966 as an amendment to the Administrative Procedure Act, does not open proceedings of federal decision makers to the public. Rather, it requires disclosure of government records to "any person" except as "specifically stated" in its provisions. See Kenneth Culp Davis, *Administrative Law Text*, 3rd ed. (St. Paul, Minn.: West, 1972), pp. 68–87.

secrecy of the Court's deliberative processes.[9] "From public sessions of oral argument and published opinions and orders, we already know precisely what business the Supreme Court transacts, and we know a fair amount about how it transacts that business," Rehnquist said. "The deliberations of the Court's conference are not public, and should not be made public, because the added information about the workings of the Court would be more than offset by the probability that the usefulness of the conference as a deliberative institution would be seriously impaired." Rehnquist gave four reasons to justify the Court's secrecy: (1) "A re-remarkably candid exchange of views" occurs. "No one feels at all inhibited" that he might be quoted or that "half-formed or ill-conceived ideas" might later be "held up to public ridicule." (2) With no one else in attendance, each Justice, unlike a member of the President's Cabinet who is "generally flanked by aides," is forced to personally "prepare himself for the conference deliberation." (3) Public scrutiny or press coverage could generate "lobbying pressures" intended to affect decisions before they become final. (4) Conferences are marked by "occasionally short-tempered remarks or bits of rancorous rhetoric," which are transcended by a cordiality among the Justices that might not survive if they were displayed in a public record.[10]

The procedure in the conference with regard to the cases that have been orally argued allows the Chief Justice to state his views first; then the Associate Justices speak their minds in order of their length of service on the Court. When discussion is finished, the Justices vote in reverse order of seniority—the junior member first and the Chief Justice last. These votes are tentative, subject to change after opinions have been drafted and circulated among the Justices. The Chief Justice keeps notes, and each of the other Justices has his own docket book in which all votes are recorded. The newest member of the Court answers the door to take and deliver messages.

In addition to discussing orally argued cases, the Justices in their conference also determine which of the many cases in which the losing party requests review of a lower-court's ruling warrant their consideration. The Chief Justice prepares a list of the cases that he and his staff deem worthy of Court review and submits a copy to each Justice two weeks in advance of the conference at which they will be considered. Annually, the Court receives approximately 4,000 to 5,000 requests to review lower-court decisions, but the vast majority of them do not receive conference attention. On the average Friday there may be 10 to 40 cases on the Chief Justice's list, and if the number is especially large, the Justices may require about three hours to select those that they will hear.[11] Over the course of a term, the Justices agree to hear oral argument and decide only about 150 of the several thousand cases filed with the Court.

Bringing Cases to the Court

Most of the Supreme Court's cases come from the federal district courts, the federal courts of appeals, and the state courts of last resort (usually a state's supreme court, but occasionally a lower state court if that state's supreme court has no jurisdiction to hear the case). A small handful of cases also comes from such federal courts of specialized jurisdiction as the Court of Claims and the Court of Customs and Patent Appeals. Depending on the issues involved, a petition for Supreme Court review must be filed with the Clerk of the Supreme Court 30 to 90 days after the lower court has made its decision.[12] The Court's Rules (15 and 23) specify the format that requests for review shall take and the information that is to be included. Notice is given the other party to the litigation that review is being sought and that, in accordance with Rules 16 and 24, a statement may be submitted by that party giving reasons why the Court ought not consider the case.

When a losing party petitions the Court for review of a lower court's decision and after the winning party has submitted a statement giving reasons why the Court should disregard that petition, the documents are reviewed by the Clerk of the Supreme Court (who is a permanent employee of the Court, unlike the clerks selected by the Justices each year). If the Clerk of the Court believes the petition is "frivolous"—that is, undeserving of review—he so indicates to the Chief Justice who, in turn, has his staff prepare a brief digest of the case. These digests are distributed to the Justices, who also have access to the original petition and supporting documents. If the Chief Justice's clerks consider a petition frivolous and if the Chief Justice agrees, the case is "dead listed." Meanwhile, the other Justices also review the case, assisted by their clerks. If all the Associate Justices concur that a case ought to be dead listed, that case has reached the end of the line. It will not be discussed in conference and the request for Supreme Court review will be automatically denied. This fate befalls the vast majority of the petitions—somewhere between 50 and 75 percent of the total.[13] But if either the Chief Justice or any one of the Associate Justices requests that a petition be discussed in conference, the case will be placed on the "discuss list." If, following discussion, any 4 of the 9 Justices vote to hear the case, oral argument is scheduled, and the case will be among the 150 or so that, in the average term, the Court formally decides. If fewer than 8 of the Justices participate in the consideration of a petition, only 3 votes are needed for formal consideration.[14]

In addition to denying or granting petitions to review lower-court judgments, the Justices have two other options. One is a summary decision that either affirms, reverses, or remands the case back to the lower court for further proceedings. This option falls between the extremes of refusal and acceptance; outright dismissal is not warranted, but neither is oral argument followed by a formal decision. Perhaps 200 to 300 of the approximately 5,000 requests for review that the Court receives per year are disposed of in this fashion.[15] The Court writes no opinion; it only specifies that the lower court's decision is "affirmed," "reversed," or returned to the lower court "for further proceedings." Occasionally, the Court will append the title and citation of one of its previously decided cases as authority for affirming, reversing, or remanding. The other option is a *per curiam* ("for the Court") decision, which is similar to a summary decision in that no oral argument is scheduled, but differs from the summary decision in that a formal opinion accompanies the Court's decision. The *per curiam* option is commonly utilized in cases engendering slight disagreement and in which little legal reasoning is required to justify the result. These opinions are unsigned and rather brief. Of 22 such opinions in the 1974 term, 14 (64 percent) were unanimous. In 2, 3 Justices dissented; in 1, 4 Justices dissented. The remaining 5 were decided by an 8 to 1 vote, Douglas alone dissenting. The Court produced 37 *per curiam* opinions during the 1975 term, 22 (59 percent) of which were unanimous. In 7, only 1 Justice dissented; in 6, 2 Justices dissented; in 1 case each, 3 and 4 Justices disagreed with the result.

Once the Court accepts a case for review, the lawyers for both parties to the litigation submit briefs stating the legal arguments and precedents for the position they plan to argue. Each party is also permitted to file a reply brief countering the arguments and contentions of the other party.[16] Responsibility for enforcing the Rules governing briefs rests with the Clerk of the Court. Perhaps a dozen times per year he rejects briefs that, in format or length, fail to comport with the Rules. In 1974, in an apparently unprecedented action, the Justices themselves refused to accept a brief in a case involving the closing of a theater that featured obscene movies because the brief failed to comply with paragraph 5 of Rule 40: "Briefs must be compact, logically arranged with proper headings, concise and free from burdensome, irrelevant, immaterial, and scandalous matter." The lawyer in question, who was the prosecuting attorney of an Ohio county, filed a 100-page brief that was supplemented by a 500-page appendix of sexually oriented photographs. The Court, over the dissent of Justice Douglas, flatly stated that "oral argument will be allowed only by counsel who have filed briefs that conform to the Rules," and gave the lawyer 20 days to submit a conforming brief.[17] Twice during the 1976 term, individual Justices castigated attorneys for submitting lengthy briefs. When an attorney, during oral argument, sought permission to file a supplemental brief, Justice Blackmun curtly noted that the attorney had already filed two briefs totaling 250 pages. "Do you expect," he asked, that "we can absorb that with the energy you would like?" Another Justice, when a reporter asked him his reaction to Blackmun's remarks, stated that he doubted that any of his colleagues had read the briefs to their end. In a subsequent case, Chief Justice Burger, at the close of oral argument, echoed Justice Blackmun's complaint. Addressing the offending lawyer, he said: "I am making an observation to the bar in general as well as to you. You have filed a 216-page brief when 75 pages easily would have done it."[18] Both those attorneys, incidentally, lost their cases.[19]

The Writing of Opinions

One to four days after oral argument has been heard, the Justices, in conference, discuss the case and then vote on how it should be decided. Once a majority has agreed on the outcome, one of the Justices voting with the majority will be assigned the task of writing the opinion of the Court.‖ If the Chief Justice is in the majority, he assigns the opinion, either to himself or to one of the other Justices who voted with him. If the Chief Justice is not in the majority, the senior Associate Justice among those constituting the majority assigns the opinion.[20] Virtually never do the Chief Justice and the two senior Associate Justices find themselves simultaneously in the minority. Accordingly, opinion assignment is monopolized by these three Justices—effectively by only the Chief Justice and one senior Associate.

The Justice who is assigned an opinion of the Court begins by writing a draft that is circulated among the other Justices, who may either agree with its contents, suggest changes as the price of their support, or disagree altogether. Opinion writing is the most time-consuming task for the Justices, especially where opinions of the Court are concerned. The writer must satisfy not only himself, but also at least four of his col-

---

‖ On rare occasions, the Court will decide an orally argued case via a *per curiam* opinion. The two most recent notable examples concerned issues that the Court was under great pressure to decide with dispatch: the Pentagon Papers controversy in 1971 (*New York Times* v. *United States,* 403 U.S. 713, number 36 in *Classic and Current Decisions*) and the constitutionality of the Federal Election Campaign Act and a related amendment to the Internal Revenue Code providing for public financing of Presidential nominating conventions and general election and primary campaigns in 1976 (*Buckley* v. *Valeo,* 44 LW 4127). All 9 Justices wrote a separate opinion in the former case; in the latter, 5 of the 8 who participated wrote separate opinions. The *per curiam* opinion in the Pentagon Papers case ran three paragraphs; that in *Buckley* v. *Valeo,* with its appendix, ran in excess of 100 pages.

The information that the Justices avail themselves of in resolving major public issues has been the subject of a couple of intriguing studies: Arthur S. Miller and Jerome A. Barron, "The Supreme Court, the Adversary System, and the Flow of Information to the Justices," *Virginia Law Review* 61 (1975): 1187–1245; and Charles M. Lamb, "Judicial Policy Making and Information Flow to the Supreme Court," *Vanderbilt Law Review* 29 (1976): 45–124.

leagues. Absent such accommodation, there is no opinion of the Court. All that results is a decision that upholds, qualifies, or reverses the action of the lower court.# Justice Powell, in a recent statement, describes the writing of the Court's opinion as "a process, not an event. The process is similar to the writing of a major appellate brief by a top-flight law firm: There may be a dozen drafts within the chambers before an opinion is deemed suitable for circulation to other justices. Even then, the process of editing and revision continues—spurred by criticisms and suggestions from other chambers."[21] An outside observer describes the procedure as follows:

> Once Powell is assigned an opinion, either he or his clerk roughs out a draft opinion. Who does the first draft depends on what the workload is in the office at the time. The opinion then goes back and forth between the Justice and his clerk like a shuttlecock, being worked and reworked, drafted and redrafted, until both are satisfied. Then the opinion is given to a second clerk, who goes over it like an editor, looking for mistakes, poor reasoning, unclear writing. Then the opinion is sent to the print shop the Court maintains inside the building. Then the third Powell clerk reads the opinion, acting as an editor-proofreader.
>
> Once the opinion is written so that a Justice is satisfied with it, it is circulated to the other Justices. "You wait for the join memos from the people who voted with you and pray," one Justice says. And then the memos begin to fly.
>
> "It can be very difficult to get one Court opinion, even if people agree with the judgment," explains one Justice. "To write a Court opinion you have to sew a big enough umbrella for five guys to get under, and that can require some pretty fancy sewing."[22]

Justices who do not agree with the majority's decision indicate their disagreement by a dissenting vote that is usually—but not always—coupled with a dissenting opinion. The dissenters usually await completion of the opinion of the Court before writing their opinions. This

---

In the 1974 term, a majority assented to an opinion in every formally decided case, but in the 1975 term, no majority assented to an opinion in 10 cases, 5 of which concerned the constitutionality of the death penalty. See, especially, *Gregg* v. *Georgia,* 44 LW 5229 (1976); and *Woodson* v. *North Carolina,* 44 LW 5267 (1976)—number 52 in *Classic and Current Decisions.* In the 1976 term, no majority was formed in 8 cases. When no majority opinion results, the prevailing opinion is labeled the "Judgment of the Court." As a policy-making vehicle, a judgment of the Court provides little guidance and has little precedential value. Thus, the 1976 death penalty cases merely held that capital punishment is not inherently cruel and unusual under the Eighth Amendment, but that a mandatory death sentence upon conviction for specified crimes is. Hence, for a death sentence to be constitutional, a required—but not necessarily sufficient—condition is that the pertinent statute specify the mitigating and aggravating circumstances that the trial court judge and/or jury must consider before passing sentence.

provides them an opportunity for more effective rebuttal. Not infrequently, a dissenting opinion may be signed by more than one Justice. The dissenting Justices (or Justice) obviously have much greater freedom to give free rein to their personal views about how a case ought to be decided. Unlike the author of the Court's opinion, they need satisfy nobody but themselves. A Justice may also write a concurring opinion. These are of two types. They are similar in that both agree with the result—the decision—of the majority, but different in that one type, the special concurrence, does not agree with the reasoning whereby the majority justified its policy views. Occasionally a Justice will concur in the result without stating his reasons for disagreeing with the reasoning behind the majority's opinion. The regular type agrees completely with the contents of the opinion of the Court. A Justice will write this type of concurring opinion either to add additional bases for the majority's opinion, to identify his particularized understanding of the policy made in the Court's opinion, or to rebut the arguments contained in a dissenting opinion.**

Although the Court's decisions and the vast majority of their opinions are a group product, the Court remains, in the words of Justice Powell, "one of the last citadels of jealously preserved individualism. To be sure, we sit together for the arguments and during the long Friday conferences when votes are taken. But for the most part, perhaps as much as 90 percent of our total time, we function as nine small, independent law firms." Most of the Justices' contacts with one another occur "by correspondence or memoranda." As a matter of fact, "a Justice may go through

---

** Although they may not be representative, data from the 1975 term reveal that the Justices cast 174 concurring votes, 96 of which were regular (55.2 percent) and 78 of which were special. These votes generated 126 opinions, 67 of which were regular (53.2 percent) and 59 of which were special. Powell and Burger cast the most concurring votes, 31 and 23 respectively. Powell alone accounted for more than a quarter of the regular concurrences: 25 of 96. Powell, White, and Stewart were the most prolific writers of concurring opinions: 26, 18, and 17 respectively. Stevens's 17 concurring votes were each coupled with an opinion, as were 18 of White's 19 concurring votes. Apart from Douglas, who resigned shortly after the term began, Rehnquist concurred the least: 6 votes and 2 opinions, one of which was written jointly with Burger.

Excluded from these totals are a series of opinions in *Buckley* v. *Valeo*, 424 U.S. 1, in which 5 Justices wrote opinions "concurring in part and dissenting in part."

In the 1976 term, the Justices cast 204 concurring votes (an increase of 30 over the preceding term)—69 of which were regular, 135 of which were special. These votes generated 151 opinions (an increase of 25)—56 of which were regular, 95 of which were special. Burger and Blackmun cast the most concurring votes, 43 and 29 respectively. Blackmun and Stewart were the most prolific opinion writers, with 23 opinions each. White and Stevens concurred the least—14 votes each—and all but one of their votes were accompanied by an opinion, as were all 20 of Brennan's concurrences. Rehnquist again wrote the fewest opinions—a total of 9.

An instructive effort to explain why the Justices write separate opinions has been made by Gregory J. Rathjen, "An Analysis of Separate Opinion Writing Behavior as Dissonance Reduction," *American Politics Quarterly* 2 (1974): 393–411.

an entire term without being once in the chambers of all of the other Justices."[23]

ACCESS

"I'll fight this all the way to the Supreme Court." This is the typical refrain of a person (or that person's attorney) who has just lost his or her case and who believes that an injustice has been done. As a statement of dogged determination it expresses a noble sentiment, evocative of John Paul Jones's "I have just begun to fight" or David Farragut's "Damn the torpedoes. Full steam ahead." But is it realistic? Or is it merely the frenzy of a drowning person clutching at a straw?

More often than not, such a statement will at least buy the loser some time before he pays his debt to society or whomever he has injured. The sentence or judgment of a court will usually be stayed pending the outcome of an appeal. But the time, energy, and costs of an appeal may not be worth the candle. Lawyers do not come cheaply. Without support from a public-interest law firm, a public defender, or a legal aid society, the private citizen will shell out bucks that can easily run into five figures. Organizations working on behalf of the average citizen choose their cases carefully, whereas public defenders and legal aid societies service only those who are indigent or virtually so. But if the losing litigant deems the stakes high enough, courts do provide a means whereby the system may be bucked. The odds against success may be long, but avenues of appeal do exist. They exist not by reason of any language in the Constitution—the Court has said on numerous occasions that only a fair *trial* is guaranteed—but because of provisions in statutes and state constitutions.[24]

The hurdles to be surmounted are imposing. Initially, for a court to decide a matter two conditions must be met: the person who institutes the litigation must have "standing to sue," and the case must be one over which the court has jurisdiction.

Standing to Sue

Standing to sue is a technical term that means that a court considers a dispute to be worthy of judicial resolution—that the person instituting the suit is a proper plaintiff. Standing pertains to whether the disputants are properly before the court, whereas jurisdiction refers to whether the dispute is one that the court has the authority to resolve. Although the Supreme Court, in a leading decision, accurately observed that "generalizations about standing to sue are largely worthless as such,"[25] the various aspects of standing lend themselves to some degree of specification. First, a bona fide "case" or "controversy"—that is, a real dispute between two or more persons whose interests conflict—must exist.[26] The issue cannot be moot; it must be a live controversy. For example, the case of a state prisoner who claimed that his constitutional rights were violated because he was not provided notice of the issues that would be considered at his parole hearing or the opportunity to present arguments in support of his release was declared moot when the prisoner was granted parole.[27] The Court similarly refused to decide the constitutionality of quota systems—reverse discrimination—when the issue first reached the High Bench. The reason? The student who challenged the practice had been admitted to law school and was in the final semester of his senior year and would "receive his diploma regardless of any decision this Court might reach on the merits of this case."[28] But what about short-lived controversies, such as a pregnant woman desirous of an abortion or an allegedly illegal strike? These cases, in the words of the Court, are "capable of repetition, yet evading review," so that petitioners are adversely affected "without a chance of redress."[29] In such situations, the Court tends to treat mootness less formalistically. Through such devices as class action suits and declaratory judgments, the requirement that the dispute be a "real" one is made less stringent. Class action suits allow an individual to sue on his own behalf and, as well, on behalf of all other similarly situated persons. The utility of the class action suit is that the case will not be mooted if the circumstances of the individual who initiated the litigation or on whose behalf the litigation is instituted change. Class action suits are common in the field of civil rights. Thus, if a parent files a class action suit on behalf of his minor child seeking desegregation of the local school system, the suit continues even if the child graduates or the family moves to another town. Declaratory judgments obviate the need for a person to break the law in question before a judicial determination of his rights and duties can be secured. The 1973 abortion decisions were decided by means of a declaratory judgment, thereby enabling pregnant women and their physicians to challenge state antiabortion statutes without subjecting themselves to criminal penalties in the event the laws were held to be constitutional.[30]

Second, judges do not render advisory opinions on hypothetical issues. (There are some isolated exceptions in the state court systems.) For example, a federal court will not decide the legality and constitutionality of such questions as: What if the President did y? What if Congress enacted a law that decreed z? Similarly, judges will not decide "friendly" or feigned disputes for the simple reason that the interests of the affected persons do not conflict. Not so simple is the Court's task in ascertaining whether the suit is actually feigned. This is especially difficult to judge when a stockholder sues his corporation to prevent it from complying with a statute or regulation that adversely affects his—as well as the corporation's—pocketbook. Some authorities suspect the litigation in which the federal income tax was declared unconstitutional, thereby necessitating the Sixteenth Amendment, to have arisen from a feigned dispute.[31]

Third, a mere conflict of interest does not suffice to assure a party of standing to sue. The conflict must concern a "legal injury"—a statutory or constitutional right or some personal or property interest. Historically, such conflicts as businesses adversely affected by competition, persons convicted of a crime of which they were subsequently found innocent, and a decline in property values because of changes made in local zoning ordinances have not been considered to affect "recognized legal interests." But in a pair of 1970 decisions, the Court knocked the props out from under the legal injury standard and replaced it with two new tests. The first, based on Article III of the Constitution, specified the necessity of an "injury in fact, economic or otherwise." The "otherwise" has been interpreted to include "aesthetic, conservational, and recreational" values. The second test, the zone of interest test, was concerned with "whether the interest sought to be protected by the complainant is arguably within the zone of interests to be regulated or protected by the statute or constitutional guarantee in question."[32] The injury in fact test has had salutary effects in that it tends to give effect to the simple and natural proposition that one who is hurt in fact should have standing to sue.[33] But the zone of interest test has proved to be deficient because statutes frequently make no reference to what interests are "to be regulated or protected," and even when they do, the reference is often unclear. Consequently, courts have tended to ignore the zone of interest test, focusing instead on injury in fact.[34]

Fourth, the injury suffered must be "direct." A person lacks standing to sue if he himself has not been directly injured. One may not bring legal action solely on behalf of a friend or relative except in the case of a legal guardian or next of kin where the injured person is a minor or otherwise legally incompetent. Lack of direct injury is classically illustrated by the efforts that have been made to challenge the constitutionality of Connecticut's anticontraception law. A physician, Dr. Wilder Tileston, argued that the law, if applied to him, would prevent his giving advice to several of his female patients whose lives would be endangered by bearing children. The Supreme Court unanimously dismissed his suit because the physician's patients were not parties to the litigation. Consequently, Tileston himself had no standing to secure adjudication of their rights.[35] Those who were opposed to Connecticut's law persisted, however. The next challenge was brought by patients as well as a physician. But again the Court refused to decide, holding that the plaintiffs had suffered no injury because none of them had been subject to prosecution.[36] But when a physician was convicted late in 1961, the Court agreed that a direct injury had occurred and, by a 7 to 2 vote, declared that Connecticut's law unconstitutionally invaded the privacy of married persons.[37]

Fifth, standing to sue does not exist if a court deems the controversy "nonjusticiable"—if, in other words, the matter is one the court considers more appropriate for resolution by legislators or executive officials. Such cases are termed "political questions." Examples include: whether a constitutional amendment was properly ratified; the length of time the United States may rightfully occupy conquered territory; and the deportation of an enemy alien whom the Attorney General considered dangerous to the public peace and safety.[38] Until 1962, how equitably state legislative and congressional districts were apportioned was considered a political question. But in that year, the Court ruled that this was a justiciable question and that private citizens have standing to sue.[39] What constitutes a political question is best—although inadequately—defined as whatever a court says it is.[40] The irony is that the label "political question" is itself a misnomer. All judicial decisions and all issues that come before the Court are political, for they deal with allocation of society's resources, which is what politics is all about. Nonetheless, the label has utility. The designation of certain matters as political questions helps judges recognize the limitations on their policy-making capacity.

Sixth, courts will not decide a controversy if their decision is not final and binding on the litigants. The fact that a higher court may reverse the decision of a lower one does not negate this element of standing; nor does the possibility that the legislature in the future may change the law; nor does the possibility that a constitutional amendment may overturn a court's decision. All that is required is that, at the time of decision, the court's judgment be binding on the parties. The rationale for this aspect of standing is that the judiciary would lose its autonomy if legislators and bureaucrats could override court decisions in specific cases. The eligibility of veterans for pension benefits exemplifies this aspect of standing. An early statute authorized the Secretary of War to authoritatively determine eligibility; today the authority is lodged in the Veterans' Administration.[41]

Finally, a person who otherwise has standing will be "estopped," or precluded from suing, if he or she has previously alleged or denied facts or engaged in activity that is inconsistent with what is now being alleged or challenged. Estoppel, then, is merely one of the many more or less self-evident principles that have been given the force of law. The applicable axiom here is that one may not have his cake and eat it also. Hence, if a person has benefited from the provisions of a law, he or she may not subsequently challenge its constitutionality. Similarly, a person who has received compensation from the government for property taken for public use forfeits his or her right to challenge the taking of that property. Estoppel, however, does not apply if no benefits were received or if they were obtained under duress. A recent decision of the Virginia Supreme Court is a good example of the application of the principle of estoppel. The question to be decided was whether a man who knew that his wife was pregnant by another man at the time he married her was obligated to support that child following their divorce. The evidence showed that prior to the marriage the woman had planned to move to another state, have her baby, and put the child up for adoption. Having full knowledge of her pregnancy, the husband-to-be promised the woman that if she would become his wife, he would care for the child after its birth "as if it were his own." The authorities at the hospital where the child was born gave the child the surname of the husband-to-be with his approval, and he himself listed the child as a tax exemption and secured an increased Navy dependency allowance. The Virginia court found these facts sufficient to establish an oral contract. But that state's statute of frauds provides that no action shall be brought to enforce an agreement in consideration of marriage. Nonetheless, the court held that the mother's reconsideration of her plans to place the baby for adoption "resulted in critical changes in the lives of both mother and child." The court therefore ruled that "the husband's promises to the wife, in reliance upon which she changed her position, acted to her detriment, and substantially performed her obligations until her husband made further performance impossible, have estopped him from pleading the statute of frauds. Accordingly, we hold that the wife has established an enforceable express oral contract by the husband to continue to support the child as if he were the natural father of the child."††

---

††*T.* v. *T.*, 44 LW 1179, 2523–2524 (1976). Although the concept of estoppel binds private parties, the government is somewhat excluded. So-called equitable estoppel, which precludes a person from denying the truth of statements made to another when that other has reasonably relied upon the statement to his detriment, and precludes him from a financial gain because he subsequently takes a position that is inconsistent with his original statement, has not been consistently applied to governmental actions. See Kenneth Culp Davis, *Administrative Law Text,* 3rd ed. (St. Paul, Minn.: West, 1972), pp. 343–352. By contrast, the Supreme Court has held that "collateral estoppel" does estop the government because it is an essential component of the Fifth Amendment's guarantee against double jeopardy. Thus, "when an issue of ultimate fact has once been determined by a valid and final judgment, that issue cannot again be litigated between the same parties in any future lawsuit." *Ashe* v. *Swenson*, 397 U.S. 436 (1970), at 443. Consequently, in criminal proceedings in which the accused has allegedly committed a crime simultaneously against several persons, if he is acquitted of the crime against one member of the group, the government cannot subsequently try him for that same crime against a second member.

In summary, these elements of standing effectively limit the types of controversies that courts will hear in order that judges may avoid hypothetical and officious questions and unnecessary conflicts with other policy makers. The rules governing standing also provide judges with a tactical flexibility that enables them to maneuver around issues they prefer not to resolve and to cite good legal form as their rationale.

Jurisdiction

The other condition that must be met before a court will decide a controversy is proper jurisdiction. Jurisdiction is simply the authority by which judges take cognizance of and decide matters brought to their attention. A court's jurisdiction is determined by legislative enactment or constitutional provision. Because courts cannot determine their own jurisdiction, they are wholly at the mercy of their environments, in the sense that, with the exception of the Supreme Court (as we shall see) and about half of the state supreme courts, they have no way to limit the number of cases they must decide. The result, especially for trial courts in urban areas, is dockets crowded with cases that are delayed for months and even years before they are decided. If justice delayed is truly justice denied, then American trial courts have reached a point of crisis. Unfortunately, no court can increase the number of its judges—the simplest solution to the problem. Responsibility for that rests, rather, with Congress and the state legislatures. But for them nothing is simple. Indecision is their stock in trade. And so Nero fiddles while Rome burns.

There are three types of jurisdiction: subject matter, geographical, and hierarchical. A court may hear only those cases that deal with the types of controversies that fall within its subject matter competency. A court whose jurisdiction is exclusively criminal may not hear civil cases, or vice versa. In addition, a court may decide only those cases within its subject matter jurisdiction when one or the other of the parties to the litigation, or the thing being litigated, resides in or is located in the geographical area over which the court has jurisdiction—a city, county, or state. Hierarchical jurisdiction distinguishes trial from appellate courts. The former are courts of first instance in that they hear cases that have not been heard before; decisions of trial courts can be appealed to appellate courts.

The fact that a trial court has heard and decided a case normally means that the matters of standing and jurisdiction have been resolved and that the losing party may appeal the merits of the controversy to a higher court. But it is possible that the trial court's decision may not have reached the merits but turned instead on an aspect of standing or a question of jurisdiction, or some procedural consideration—a defective indictment or an improperly empaneled jury, for example. The losing litigant may appeal such decisions just as readily as if the case had been decided on the merits, but with one difference: if the appellate court upholds the contention of the trial court loser on any of these bases, the participants return to ground zero—to a consideration of the merits of the controversy.

Federal questions.   The vast majority of trial court litigation is decided on the merits, however. The losing litigant (or attorney) then utters his or her vow to fight the matter all the way to the Supreme Court. Standing and jurisdictional hurdles have been surmounted—but not completely. The jurisdiction of the federal courts does not even begin to cover the waterfront of litigable issues. Only a small handful of cases originate in the federal courts. If a person has been injured by someone who resides in another state, and if the amount of damages sought is $10,000 or more, he may bring his case to a federal court for trial.[42] Many such cases end up in state courts, however. What usually falls within federal court jurisdiction is a "federal question": an issue that pertains to an act of Congress, a treaty of the United States, or a provision of the Constitution. Examples of such questions are: whether the Social Security Act entitles one to certain benefits; whether the Interstate Commerce Commission exceeded its authority by imposing certain freight rates; whether a foreign business was authorized to engage in certain domestic activities; whether a person was deprived of due process of law or whether a person's First Amendment freedoms were abridged.

Many state courts derive their subject matter jurisdiction from the state constitution. However, the United States Constitution makes no reference to any federal court except the Supreme Court and specifies only its original jurisdiction (see the footnote on pages 40–41). The lower federal courts—the district courts and the courts of appeals— were created by Congress and are staffed by Congress. Their authority to hear federal questions and "diversity of citizenship" cases is also established by Congress, as is the entirety of the Supreme Court's appellate jurisdiction, on which it depends for its policy-making capabilities.

Obviously, if a case is heard and decided by a federal trial court, federal jurisdiction exists, especially if the case has been decided on the merits. There is thus no need to establish the existence of a federal question. But if the case was originally heard in a state court, it is absolutely essential to show that a federally protected right was abridged. This, however, is not especially difficult, particularly if a person has been accused of committing a crime. The Fourth, Fifth, Sixth, and Eighth Amendments of the Bill of Rights, along with the due process clause of the Fourteenth Amendment, provide fairly specific guidelines that the states must follow with respect to criminal proceedings.[43] These guidelines apply not only to the conduct of the trial, but also to events antecedent to what happens in the courtroom: arrest, detention, indictment, and the gathering of evidence. The major substantive rights (freedom of speech, press, religion, assembly, and association) are also within the realm of federal jurisdiction, as are those of a political and civil nature: voting and racial and sex discrimination. Judicial proceedings in which a person claims violation of these types of rights need not allege criminal activity. Whether the activity is criminal or not, a federal question exists. The same is true of some of the procedural guarantees contained in the Bill of Rights and the Fourteenth Amendment. Due process, for example, requires that affected persons be given notice and hearing regardless of whether the judicial proceedings are civil or criminal.[44]

Nor is it uncommon for federal legislation to concern matters that are also subject to state regulation. In such areas as labor-management relations, regulation of business, civil rights, poverty law, and consumer and environmental protection, both the states and the federal government may act. When state and federal laws conflict, the supremacy clause of the Constitution gives precedence to federal regulation.[45] Accordingly, if a person has been sanctioned under state law, he or she may be able to establish an incompatibility with the overriding federal law and thereby invoke federal jurisdiction over the case.

The adversary process.   Although the existence of a federal question is not especially difficult to establish, the process of raising it in a proper legal fashion is not so simple. Adherence to proper procedure is part of that wondrous legacy bequeathed to America via the customs and traditions of medieval England: the adversary process. In a trial, litigants, through their respective attorneys, engage in a battle of wits, the outcome of which determines who wins and who loses. The origins of this system can be traced to trial by combat, in which the litigants did physical battle. God presumably protected the innocent party. If a person did not want to confront his accuser, professional champions were available for a fee. Lesser folk could settle for a trial by ordeal. A litigant was made to grasp a red-hot iron and if, after three days, no infection had set in, he was deemed innocent. Alternatively, he could be tossed into the village pond. If he floated, he was guilty; if he sank, he was innocent. It is noteworthy that in these ordeals, as in their variations, the improbable outcome proved the accused's innocence, and thus was evidence of the judgment of God.

By the end of the thirteenth century, trial by jury had replaced these earlier methods of determining guilt and innocence. This was a major humanitarian advance, most assuredly, but not one that removed the element of chance. The process remained a contest—a battle of intellect, guile, and will, rather than one of physical prowess. As a method of determining truth, of ascertaining precisely what the facts of the matter are, it does not always work very well. Ascertaining truth becomes a game in which witnesses and evidence are used to score points, to out-maneuver the opponent. And so the attorneys carefully calculate the most propitious time to play their trump cards, the probability of drawing to an inside straight, the possibility of establishing a marked finesse. A trial is entertaining and frequently engenders considerable public interest—the same type of interest that attends the "big game" or the championship match. Speculation over the outcome dominates conversation, and the media cover the event—before, during, and after—down to the smallest detail.[46]

The underlying assumption is that two persons arguing, as partisanly as possible, will produce the fairest decision. And so witnesses are cajoled and intimidated, evidence is suppressed or exaggerated, false impressions are created, irrelevancies are emphasized—as theatrically as the judge will allow. It is more than passing strange that in no other crucial area of human activity where knowledge and information are vital to decision making are such theatrics built into the fact-discovery system. Businessmen do not make decisions under such circumstances, nor do scientists or military officers, or even public officials, including bureaucrats (other than trial court judges, of course). It should be emphasized that these theatrics are not part of the decision-making process of appellate courts, including the Supreme Court.

However, our adversary system does work. Miscarriage of justice occurs, perhaps too often. But no system could be flawless. Of all American institutions and processes, probably none is more deeply ingrained or highly cherished. Such deficiencies or excesses as exist are considered the fault of the players, not the system—they are attributable to an overly zealous prosecutor, a deceitful witness, or an unduly flamboyant defense attorney. Any effort at significant reform would be an exercise in futility. I do not mean to suggest that the system has been set into concrete and made impervious to change. So-called discovery procedures require that the litigants disclose evidence to each other in advance of trial. Judges may take a hand in the examination and summoning of witnesses. And the use of plea bargaining and out-of-court settlements has produced a marked decline in the proportion of cases that go to trial. The great majority of criminal cases, for example, are settled by a guilty plea in which the accused admits guilt to a lesser charge and/or a reduced sentence.[47] Notwithstanding such alterations, a reincarnated court watcher of 700 years ago would readily recognize today's trial procedures.

Review of state court decisions. In such a setting, a litigant must be prepared for an eventual appeal. Assuming that the case originates in a state court, it is absolutely essential that the existence of a federal question be established at the beginning of the trial, and not as an afterthought. As one authority has noted, "unless you build the record in your state litigation so that you *do* make a federal case out of it, you not only do not have a rosy chance of review, you don't have any chance at all."[48] The federal question must be more than a formal one. It must not be so devoid of merit as to be frivolous. Nor can it be so explicitly foreclosed by prior Supreme Court decisions as to leave no room for real controversy. On the other hand, no particular formula need be followed in raising a federal question. The federal claim and the basis of it need only be stated with as much precision and detail as possible. It is necessary, however, that the litigant adhere to state procedures and requirements in raising, presenting, and documenting his or her federal question.

Failure to do so has cost at least one plaintiff his life. In 1955, in *Williams* v. *Georgia,* the Court reversed a conviction for murder and remanded the case to the state courts for further proceedings because the jury had been selected in a manner incompatible with the equal protection clause of the Fourteenth Amendment. (The names of prospective white jurors had been placed on white cards; those of blacks had been placed on yellow cards. The accused was black.) The state supreme court, however, refused to order a new trial, observing that *under state law* a defendant must challenge a jury when it is "put on" him, not after the trial is over. This requirement did not affect the United States Constitution or federal law. Consequently, when the convict's attorneys again petitioned the Supreme Court for review, the Justices denied the request. Two and one-half months later, he was electrocuted.[49]

As the foregoing example illustrates, a litigant's success in properly prosecuting a federal question depends directly upon his or her attorney's skill and competence. Although opposing attorneys and the states cannot prevent a litigant from raising a federal question, state procedural requirements do nothing to facilitate the raising of such issues—as the *Williams* case indicates.[50] State judges do not welcome the intrusion of federal questions. They are obviously much more comfortable and familiar with their state's laws and regulations than with those of the federal government. Nor do state judges idolize their federal counterparts. Although both share the mystique of "the cult of the robe," they nonetheless compete for control and dominance within the judicial arena. No judge likes to be overruled by a higher court. The best way to minimize this possibility is to keep litigation simple. The infusion of issues that bear upon federal rights is thus a threat to the state judge's autonomy.

Finality of action.   Assuming that the losing litigant has successfully injected a federal question into his case, by no means is it now ripe for review by the federal judiciary. One additional element of standing to sue must be satisfied: finality of action. The litigant must exhaust any additional remedies provided by state law before seeking access to the federal courts. So if, as is probably the situation, the case falls within the jurisdiction of the state court of appeals and/or the state supreme court, the litigant must seek redress there before the federal judiciary will entertain his or her plea. The same is true if administrative remedies are available. A person who challenges the amount of income tax owed must exhaust the remedies provided by the Internal Revenue Service before a court will agree to hear his or her case. There are, however, some situations when state or administrative remedies need not be pursued to the bitter end: when an agency is acting *ultra vires* (beyond the scope of its authority); when an agency or state court is being deliberately dilatory; when irreparable harm or injury may result; or when pursuit of these remedies is obviously futile. Examples are the bureaucrat who orders the taking of a person's property without compensation; the clerk of a county or township who refuses to register voters during a certain period because other duties have precluded attention to the task of voter registration; local officials who threaten and harass an unpopular organization in its exercise of such constitutionally protected rights as speech, press, and association; and the state court that adamantly refuses to accept the unconstitutionality of deliberately racially segregated schools. Such situations are very much the exception, and a correspondingly heavy burden of proof falls on those who seek to bypass finality of action.[51]

If the losing litigant has established the existence of a federal question and if all the requirements of standing to sue have been met, the case may be carried to the federal judiciary. If the case originated in the state courts, the request for federal review is addressed directly to the Supreme Court, which forms the major link between the state and federal judicial systems because only the Supreme Court has geographical jurisdiction over the entire United States.[52] To ensure that the Constitution, acts of Congress, and United States treaties receive uniform interpretation throughout the country, Congress, in the Judiciary Act of 1789, authorized the Supreme Court to review state court decisions that concern a federal question.‡‡ On the other hand, if the losing litigant's case originated within the federal system, Supreme Court review becomes available only after remedies in the lower federal courts have been exhausted.

---

‡‡ See *Martin* v. *Hunter's Lessee,* 1 Wheaton 305 (1816), number 4 in *Classic and Current Decisions.*

Selection of cases for review. Does the Court automatically review all cases properly brought to its attention? By no means. Contrary to popular belief, the Court does not exist to right each and every legal wrong that an individual believes he or she has suffered. Since 1925, the Court has had complete and total discretion to decide for itself which cases it will hear and decide. In this regard, the Court is unique. No other court, state or federal, has such absolute discretion over its caseload. The means used to determine which cases it will accept is the so-called rule of four—the votes of four of the nine Justices that a case warrants their attention.

The losing litigant petitions the Court for either a writ of appeal or a writ of certiorari. Although writs of appeals theoretically entitle a petitioner to Supreme Court review, whereas writs of certiorari are issued at the Court's discretion, the "rule of four" applies equally to both. Petitioners utilize a writ of appeal when a lower court has declared a federal law or treaty unconstitutional; when a federal court of appeals

---

In addition to its appellate jurisdiction to review cases from the lower federal courts and the state courts, the Supreme Court also possesses a modicum of original jurisdiction—it hears cases that have not previously been heard by any other court. Henry J. Abraham, *The Judicial Process*, 3rd ed. (New York: Oxford University Press, 1975), pp. 170–171, reports that between 1789 and October 1974 the Court formally exercised original jurisdiction in only 155 instances. Article III of the Constitution authorizes the Court to exercise such jurisdiction in controversies between the United States and one of the fifty states; controversies between two or more states; controversies involving foreign diplomatic personnel; and controversies commenced by a state against residents of other states, citizens of foreign countries, or foreign countries themselves. The Eleventh Amendment, however, bars citizens, aliens, and foreign countries from the Court's original jurisdiction. They must commence their cases in the appropriate state's court. Rarely does the Court's exercise of its original jurisdiction result in significant policy making. Most such cases concern the demarcation of the boundary between two states, an issue that commonly arises when a river changes course, leaving a few acres on the other side of its new channel. If the states' border is the channel, the benefiting state arguably has expanded its domain a notch. For an example, see *Mississippi* v. *Arkansas,* 415 U.S. 289 (1974). In preference to taking testimony—*à la* a trial court—the Court appoints a "special master," who is usually a retired judge, to hear arguments, receive evidence, make findings, and write a report that is usually accepted without much ado by the Justices, who enter a decree containing the essence of the special master's report (for example, *Mississippi* v. *Arkansas,* 415 U.S. 289, at 302). The only recent decision in which original jurisdiction had a major policy impact upheld the constitutionality of the Voting Rights Act of 1965. As a result of that decision, the historic barriers preventing Southern blacks and certain Northern minorities from voting with the ease accorded white were lifted. See *South Carolina* v. *Katzenbach,* 383 U.S. 301 (1966), number 27 in *Classic and Current Decisions.*

Interestingly, although the Court's original jurisdiction is specified in the Constitution, the Court receives its appellate jurisdiction—the heart of its policy-making capability—from Congress. And what Congress has given, Congress may take away. See *Ex parte McCardle,* 7 Wallace 506 (1869). But though Congress has had opportunities to curb the Court when it disagreed with the Court's policy making—particularly in such areas as school desegregation and the Red scare of the 1950's—it has not effectively done so. See Walter F. Murphy and C. Herman Pritchett, *Courts, Judges, and Politics,* 2d ed. (New York: Random House, 1974), pp. 311–312; David W. Rohde and Harold J. Spaeth, *Supreme Court Decision Making* (San Francisco: W. H. Freeman and Company, 1976), pp. 195–196.

has declared a state law or constitutional provision unconstitutional; when a state court upholds its own law or constitutional provision against a challenge that it violates federal law or the Constitution; when the United States is party to a civil suit in a federal district court under the federal antitrust, interstate commerce, or communications laws; and when a three-judge federal district court has granted or denied an injunction. Actions other than these can only be reviewed by means of a writ of certiorari.

A rather nebulous set of criteria governs whether review will be granted. The case must concern a "substantial" federal question, which may be one not previously decided by the Supreme Court, or one decided by a state court "in a way probably not in accord with applicable decisions" of the Supreme Court. Or the decision of one federal court of appeals conflicts with the decision of another federal court of appeals. (This is by far the most specific of the criteria.) Or the question for review is one that "should be" settled by the Supreme Court, or is one that is "in conflict with applicable decisions" of the Supreme Court.[53] In short, so long as the case concerns a federal question (which is not always a matter of crystal clarity), the vote to review is a matter of the individual Justice's discretion. The Court never reports how the Justices vote when a case is granted review. But when review is denied, any Justice who voted to accept the case may note his disagreement with the majority and write an opinion stating his reasons.

What proportion of cases passes through the screen imposed by the "rule of four"? Of the cases on the Court's main docket, about 15 percent or a little less are accepted: an average of 1 of every 7 or 8 cases. If, however, a lower court has declared a federal law unconstitutional, review is virtually a certainty. If the federal government is the losing litigant, the proportion accepted is approximately 50 percent.[54] If these types of cases are excluded, the proportion of the remaining petitions that are accepted is somewhat less than 1 in 10. Greater precision is not possible short of access to the several thousand petitions for review that are received annually. The Court usually does not specify the reason for refusing to review a case, and even when it does, only the most cryptic explanation is offered: "for want of a substantial federal question" and "for want of jurisdiction" are the most common. Nor does the Court ever provide a statement of the issues raised by cases that are denied review.

Of the cases on the Court's other docket, no more than 1 in 20 or 30 is accepted. This docket contains the requests of persons proceeding *in forma pauperis*—mostly convicts, unrepresented by counsel, who cannot afford the financial costs of having their petitions placed on the other docket. This distinction may smack of rank discrimination against indigents, but it ain't necessarily so. By any standard, most of these petitions are frivolous—motivated by a spirit of nothing ventured, nothing gained. Actually, the Court bends over backward to accommodate those seeking review by this means. Only one copy of the petition need be filed instead of the usual 40. Technical requirements of form and style are waived, and the petition need not even be typed. Even more importantly, the procedure whereby the Court evaluates the merits of these requests does not differ from that whereby it evaluates others.

In view of the hurdles that must be surmounted in perfecting an appeal so that it is ripe for review by the Supreme Court and the limited access to the Court that the typical litigant has, is an appeal worth the time, expense, and trouble? If the answer has been "yes" all through the lower courts, a litigant finds that the additional investment required to carry the case to the Court does not significantly increase the costs previously incurred. Merely because the Court agrees to hear the plea does not guarantee a favorable verdict. Even if the verdict is not favorable, the petitioner will be no worse off than he or she is now—a loser. Common, everyday occurrences are just as likely to precipitate a Supreme Court decision as are those of a novel sort. Consider the following.

Sam Thompson, an elderly black handyman, was arrested in a bar in Louisville, Kentucky, in January 1959 for loitering and disorderly conduct. He was fined $10 for each offense. This was not Thompson's first brush with the law. He had been arrested dozens of times before. But unlike most persons picked up for loitering and vagrancy, Thompson had gotten himself a lawyer to contest an earlier charge. This apparently annoyed the police, who, he claimed, were now arresting him on sight. Kentucky law made no provision for an appeal of a fine of less than $20. Accordingly, the highest state court that had jurisdiction over his case was the lowest. Thompson's attorney, believing that he had been denied due process of law, appealed directly to the United States Supreme Court, alleging that there was no evidence to support the state court convictions. The Court accepted the case for review.

In the oral argument, Louisville's attorney said that Thompson was charged with loitering because he was in a bar shuffling his feet to the music from a jukebox while waiting for a bus. In response to the Justices' questions, the city attorney admitted that the bar owner did not object to Thompson's presence. But, he said, Thompson was doing a "shuffle dance," which, although it was not illegal per se, occurred on premises that had no dancing license. If the bar had no such license, said Justice Frankfurter, the city should have charged the bar owner, not Thompson.

Chief Justice Warren picked up the point that loitering occurred because Thompson had not bought anything in the bar. If a woman were in a department store for half an hour and did not buy anything, would that constitute loitering? The city attorney said that in some circumstances it could. Then, said Warren, "there would be a lot of women in jail."

With regard to the disorderly conduct charge, the arresting officers' testimony merely indicated that Thompson "was very argumentative." No abusive language was used and no physical resistance occurred. Chief Justice Warren asked: "Do you really put a man in jail for arguing with a police officer?" The city attorney replied: "That's what happened in this case." Justice Brennan inquired when an argument becomes disorderly conduct. "Any argument tends to lead to disorder," replied the city attorney—"You are making an argument now, aren't you?" Brennan responded, "Do you see any signs of disorder?"

When the Court handed down its decision two months later, the Justices were unanimously in agreement: Conviction without evidence of guilt violates due process of law. This was a landmark decision. The routine use by police of loitering and vagrancy statutes as a basis for hassling those whom they considered undesirable would no longer be permissible.[55]

Consider another example. In 1963, the Supreme Court ruled that in all state criminal prosecutions the defendant, if accused of a felony, had an absolute right to be provided the services of an attorney. This also was a landmark decision. It overruled the precedent that a state was required to furnish the accused with counsel only if the crime was a capital offense or if other special circumstances existed with regard to the age and literacy of the defendant, or the complexity of the litigation.

The case was brought by Clarence Earl Gideon, a ne'er-do-well, a drifter who had spent most of his life in and out of prison. He was not a professional criminal or a man of violence. Rather, he was one of life's outcasts, who made his way by gambling and occasional theft. In 1961, he was convicted of breaking into and entering a poolroom in Panama City, Florida. He had requested the assistance of counsel and been denied by both the trial court and the state supreme court. But Gideon did not give up. On five sheets of lined paper, he penciled a petition to the Supreme Court. Five months later, after having received a response to Gideon's petition from the attorney general of Florida and a four-page reply from Gideon, the Court agreed to hear his case.

Gideon's claim that he had been unconstitutionally deprived of his right to be represented by counsel was not one he would have to argue for himself. It is the Court's unvarying practice to appoint counsel for any indigent whose petition has been granted. And as evidence perhaps that the rich do not always have an advantage over those less well off, the caliber of the person appointed to represent an indigent petitioner is markedly superior to that of petitioners who hire their own. The attorney whom the Justices appointed to represent Gideon became one of their own number three years later: Abe Fortas.[56]

The common, everyday occurrences that comprise so large a piece of the Supreme Court's action are not necessarily those which produce potentially momentous decisions. Sometimes their impact does not extend beyond the parties themselves. As an illustration, consider a 1957 decision, *Ringhiser* v. *Chesapeake and Ohio Railway Co.*[57]

A railroad employee's leg was crushed while he was working and he sued to recover for the injury sustained. A jury verdict in favor of the employee was set aside by the trial judge on the basis that the railroad was not negligent. The Court, by a 5 to 4 vote, reinstated the jury's verdict, holding that the railroad "was or should have been aware of conditions which created a likelihood that the petitioner would suffer just such an injury as he did." Just what were these "conditions"? As summarized by the trial judge, they were the following:

> On October 7 . . . the plaintiff . . . arose in the afternoon, made preparation to report for duty at 4:45 p.m., had a bowel movement, made a mental calculation, and thereby set in motion a chain of events which created a result both unusual and tragic.
>
> The sequence of these events is as follows: The plaintiff's bowel movement was unsatisfactory: "This won't do," said he to himself . . . he took a dose of salts and washed it down with sweet cider; he got in his car and drove to Parson's Yard, the switching yard of the defendant, and had a bowel movement at the roundhouse. He then got on his engine and maneuvered it to track twelve, where it was coupled on to a train scheduled for Walbridge Yard at Toledo. While sitting in his engine waiting for his air brake test, he had an urgent call of nature and "had to go quick." He dismounted from his locomotive cab to go to a toilet a short distance west. A long train of empties passed between him and the object of his immediate attention. He could not wait for this train to pass and went to No. 8 switch track and climbed into a low-sided gondola to answer his call of nature. While thus engaged, a yard crew switched two cars into No. 8 switch track. These cars came in contact with the car ahead of plaintiff's car and it likewise came in contact with plaintiff's car. The gondola car in which plaintiff had taken his position was loaded with steel plates and when the cars made contact the plates shifted, caught plaintiff's right leg and crushed it so that a few days later, it had to be amputated.[58]

There is no argument that this was an exceptional chain of circumstances. But there was nothing exceptional about the status of the petitioner. In a more systematic vein, the identification of the litigants in the cases whose decisions were announced on June 9 and June 16, 1975, should prove persuasive. I make no claim that these cases are representative in any statistical sense. Indeed, the fact that decisions were announced within three weeks of the Court's adjournment indicates the cases were among the more important of those decided during the 1974–1975 term. (Most of the so-called big cases are commonly saved for last.) I chose these decisions simply because as I was writing this, volume 421 of the *U.S. Reports* was at hand, and I leafed through the last 200 pages to identify the litigants whose cases' decisions were announced on June 9 and June 16. They were: a criminal defendant convicted of murder; unemployed parents; a retail drug company; a woman who challenged as sexually discriminating Louisiana's procedures for selecting jurors; a married couple; Jack Murphy, better known as "Murph the Surf," who was seeking a new trial on robbery charges; the editor of an underground newspaper; tenants of a nonprofit housing co-operative; a construction worker; and the president of a national supermarket chain.[59]

With the exception of the drug company and the supermarket chain president, these litigants were rather average Americans. For what it may be worth, six of them won their cases; the drug company and the supermarket chain president both lost. The former lacked standing to sue a trading stamp company for questionable financial statements, and the latter was held personally responsible for unsanitary conditions in a company warehouse.

Much more than is commonly realized, it is the little person's case that affects the course of justice. Upon reflection, one sees that it could hardly be otherwise. Those who buck the system are in large part those whom society has disadvantaged or sanctioned. The rights accorded persons accused of crime are the legacy of those who themselves have stood in the dock. So also with regard to the First Amendment freedoms, civil rights, and the welfare benefits that have been written into poverty law. Whatever the issue, in a society in which the decisions of judges reign supreme, it is the plea of the losing litigant that determines the course of justice.

In an epitaph to Clarence Earl Gideon, Anthony Lewis, a columnist for the *New York Times,* wrote:

> His case shows that, in the United States, the least influential of men can persuade those in charge to re-examine the premises of justice in society. That is no small thing when so many people feel defeated by the political system.
>
> In a huge country with overwhelming problems it is easy for the individual to feel helpless in the mass, to doubt that the system can respond to his needs. But the courts still do listen to the individual: That is what Gideon showed us.[60]

NOTES

1. *O'Brien* v. *Brown*, 409 U.S. 1 (1972).
2. Henry J. Abraham, *The Judicial Process*, 3rd ed. (New York: Oxford University Press, 1975), pp. 190–191; Anthony Lewis, "Supreme Court Ends 1873 Rule; Will Meet at 10 Instead of Noon," *New York Times*, October 3, 1961.
3. *Argersinger* v. *Hamlin*, 407 U.S. 25 (1972), number 37 in Harold J. Spaeth, *Classic and Current Decisions of the United States Supreme Court* (San Francisco: W. H. Freeman and Company, 1977).
4. *Heart of Atlanta Motel* v. *United States*, 379 U.S. 241 (1964), and *Katzenbach* v. *McClung*, 379 U.S. 294 (1964)—number 26 in *Classic and Current Decisions*.
5. *Goldberg* v. *Kelly*, 397 U.S. 254 (1970), and *Wheeler* v. *Montgomery*, 397 U.S. 280 (1970)—number 33 in *Classic and Current Decisions*.
6. Linda Mathews, "Supreme Court—a Miniature World Governed by Tradition," *Los Angeles Times*, February 2, 1974.
7. *Ibid.*
8. *Scott* v. *Sandford*, 19 Howard 393 (1857), number 9 in *Classic and Current Decisions*.
9. Mort Mintz, "Rehnquist Strongly Defends Secrecy in Supreme Court," *Washington Post*, January 28, 1977.
10. *Ibid.* Also see John P. Mackenzie, "Douglas Illness Raises Issue of High Court Secrecy," *Washington Post*, May 11, 1975.
11. Warren Weaver, Jr., "Justices Reject Most Cases Filed," *New York Times*, May 24, 1973.
12. See Rules 11 and 22 of the *Rules of the Supreme Court of the United States*, 398 U.S. 1015, at 1021, 1033–1034.
13. S. Sidney Ulmer, "The Decision to Grant Certiorari as an Indicator to Decision 'On the Merits,'" *Polity* 4 (1972): 439; Weaver, *op. cit.,* note 11 *supra.*
14. S. Sidney Ulmer, *et al.,* "The Decision to Grant or Deny Certiorari: Further Consideration of Cue Theory," *Law and Society Review* 6 (1972): 643, fn. 6; Warren Weaver, "The Supreme Court at Work: A Look at the Inner Sanctum," *New York Times*, February 6, 1975; Nina Totenberg, "Behind the marble, beneath the robes," *New York Times Magazine*, March 16, 1975, pp. 58, 60.
15. These figures have been culled from the data appearing in David W. Rohde and Harold J. Spaeth, *Supreme Court Decision Making* (San Francisco: W. H. Freeman and Company, 1976), pp. 120–121.
16. The format and the contents of the briefs and reply briefs are specified in Rules 36–41, *op. cit.,* note 12 *supra.*
17. *Huffman* v. *Pursue*, 42 L Ed 2d 136; Warren Weaver, Jr., "Supreme Court, in Rare Action, Rejects Brief as Being Lengthy," *New York Times*, October 25, 1974. The lengthy brief did not prejudice the merits of the attorney's case,

however. By a vote of 6 to 3, he won. *Huffman* v. *Pursue,* 43 L Ed 2d 482 (1975).

18. Lesley Oelsner, "Burger Warns Bar Against Long Briefs in High Court Cases," *New York Times,* November 10, 1976.

19. They were Ruth Weyand, who represented Martha Gilbert in *General Electric* v. *Gilbert,* 50 L Ed 2d 343 (1976), and Sylvester Petro, who represented D. L. Abood in *Abood* v. *Detroit Board of Education,* 45 LW 4473 (1977).

20. A perceptive analysis of the strategic considerations governing the decision to whom the opinion of the Court will be assigned is found in David W. Rohde, "Policy Goals and Opinion Coalitions in the Supreme Court," *American Journal of Political Science* 16 (1972): 208–224; and "Policy Goals, Strategic Choice, and Majority Opinion Assignments in the U.S. Supreme Court," *American Journal of Political Science* 16 (1972): 652–682. Also see Gregory J. Rathjen, "Policy Goals, Strategic Choice, and Majority Opinion Assignments in the U.S. Supreme Court: A Replication," *American Journal of Political Science* 18 (1974): 713–724; and Rohde and Spaeth, *op. cit.,* note 15 *supra,* chaps. 8–9.

    Also see the exchange of views by R. W. Hoyer, Lawrence S. Mayer, and Joseph L. Bernd, "Some Problems in Validation of Mathematical and Stochastic Models of Political Phenomena: The Case of the Supreme Court," *American Journal of Political Science* 21 (1977): 381–403; Micheal W. Giles, "Equivalent Versus Minimum Winning Coalition Size: A Test of Two Hypotheses," *ibid.,* pp. 405–408; and David W. Rohde, "Some Clarifications Regarding a Theory of Supreme Court Coalition Formation," *ibid.,* pp. 409–413.

21. Address to the Labor Law Section of the American Bar Association, Atlanta, Georgia, August 11, 1976.

22. Totenberg, *op. cit.,* note 14 *supra,* p. 66. It has been reported that after the death of Justice Brandeis the thirty-fourth draft of an opinion was found among his papers. Mathews, *op. cit.,* note 6 *supra.* That, I trust, is the all-time record.

23. *Op. cit.,* note 21 *supra.*

24. But the constitutional right of an indigent to be provided counsel in a criminal proceeding stops after the first appeal—usually to a state or federal court of appeals. See *Ross* v. *Moffitt,* 417 U.S. 600 (1974).

25. *Association of Data Processing Service Organizations* v. *Camp,* 397 U.S. 150 (1970), at 151.

26. The quoted words appear in Article III of the Constitution and limit the jurisdiction of the federal courts to cases or controversies that pertain to the subjects listed in Article III, plus those found in various federal statutes.

27. *Scott* v. *Kentucky Parole Board,* 429 U.S. 60 (1976).

28. *DeFunis* v. *Odegaard,* 416 U.S. 312 (1974), at 317.

29. *Southern Pacific Terminal Co.* v. *Interstate Commerce Commission,* 219 U.S. 498 (1911), at 515.

30. *Roe* v. *Wade,* 410 U.S. 113, and *Doe* v. *Bolton,* 410 U.S. 179—number 42 in *Classic and Current Decisions.* For an example of a declaratory judgment in the area of labor-management relations, see *Super Tire Engineering Co.* v. *McCorkle,* 416 U.S. 115 (1974). Also see Kenneth Culp Davis, *Administrative Law Text,* 3rd ed. (St. Paul, Minn.: West, 1972), pp. 444–446, 460–461.

31. *Pollock* v. *Farmers' Loan and Trust Co.*, 157 U.S. 429, 158 U.S. 601 (1895). C. H. Pritchett, *The American Constitution*, 2d ed. (New York: McGraw-Hill, 1968), p. 168.

32. *Op cit.*, note 25 *supra*, at 152, 154, 153. *Barlow* v. *Collins*, 397 U.S. 159 (1970).

33. Indeed, the Court had so held in a number of pre-1970 decisions, concerning such injuries as a fine of $5.00 and costs (*McGowan* v. *Maryland*, 366 U.S. 420 [1961]), fractional differences in the populations of legislative districts (*Baker* v. *Carr*, 369 U.S. 186 [1962]), a poll tax of $1.50 (*Harper* v. *Virginia Board of Elections*, 383 U.S. 663 [1966]), and the disadvantage to children who absented themselves from a public school classroom while a prayer was being recited (*Engel* v. *Vitale*, 370 U.S. 421 [1962]). The question that judges must answer with regard to injury in fact is how trifling or remote the injury must be in order for the plaintiff to sue. See Davis, *op. cit.*, note 30 *supra*, pp. 429–431.

34. Davis, *op. cit.*, note 30 *supra*, pp. 431–437.

35. *Tileston* v. *Ullman*, 318 U.S. 44 (1943).

36. *Poe* v. *Ullman*, 396 U.S. 497 (1961).

37. *Griswold* v. *Connecticut*, 381 U.S. 479 (1965). More recently, the Court held that a licensed vendor of alcoholic beverages had standing to contest the constitutionality of a gender-based statute that prohibited the purchase of beer by males under 21 and females under 18. The Court reasoned that the vendor suffered "injury in fact" because "she is obliged either to heed the statutory discrimination, thereby incurring a direct economic injury through the constriction of her buyers' market, or to disobey the statutory command and suffer, in the words of Oklahoma's Assistant Attorney General, 'sanctions and perhaps loss of license.' . . . Accordingly, vendors and those in like positions have been uniformly permitted to resist efforts at restricting their operations by acting as advocates for the rights of third parties who seek access to their market or function." *Craig* v. *Boren*, 45 LW 4057 (1976), at 4058.

38. *Coleman* v. *Miller*, 307 U.S. 433 (1939); *Neely* v. *Henkel*, 180 U.S. 109 (1901); *Ludecke* v. *Watkins*, 335 U.S. 160 (1948).

39. *Baker* v. *Carr*, 369 U.S. 186 (1962). Also see *Reynolds* v. *Sims*, 377 U.S. 533 (1964), number 24 in *Classic and Current Decisions*.

40. Other equally cryptic definitions may be found in Abraham, *op. cit.*, note 2 *supra*, pp. 364–365.

41. *Hayburn's Case*, 2 Dallas 409 (1792). The federal courts do, however, have finality of decision over *constitutional* questions concerning veterans' benefits. See *Johnson* v. *Robinson*, 415 U.S. 361 (1974); and *Hernandez* v. *Veterans' Administration*, 415 U.S. 391 (1974).

42. This jurisdiction is known as "diversity of citizenship." The Framers of the Constitution made provision for it because they feared that the parochialism of the state court judges would cause them to decide favorably to their residents and against residents of other states.

43. The Fourth Amendment prohibits the police from engaging in "unreasonable searches and seizures," and requires that search warrants be issued only on a showing of "probable cause." The Fifth Amendment protects against double jeopardy and self-incrimination. The Sixth Amendment states that all persons accused of crime are entitled "to a speedy and public" trial by

jury; to be informed of the charges against them; to confront their accusers; to have "compulsory process" for obtaining favorable witnesses; and to be represented by counsel. The Eighth Amendment forbids "cruel and unusual punishments." The Fourteenth Amendment prohibits state and local governments from denying persons due process of law and also prohibits them from denying "the equal protection of the laws."

44. See, for example, *Goldberg* v. *Kelly*, 397 U.S. 254 (1970), and *Wheeler* v. *Montgomery*, 397 U.S. 280 (1970); *Fuentes* v. *Shevin*, 407 U.S. 67 (1972); *Goss* v. *Lopez*, 419 U.S. 565 (1975), and *Wood* v. *Strickland*, 420 U.S. 308 (1975)—numbers 33, 38, and 49 in *Classic and Current Decisions*.

45. Article VI, paragraph 2: "This constitution, and the laws of the United States which shall be made in pursuance thereof; and all treaties made, or which shall be made, under the authority of the United States, shall be the supreme law of the land; and the judges in every state shall be bound thereby, any thing in the constitution or laws of any state to the contrary notwithstanding."

46. For examples of trials that produced so much publicity that unfairness allegedly resulted, see *Frank* v. *Magnum*, 237 U.S. 309 (1915); *Moore* v. *Dempsey*, 261 U.S. 86 (1923); *Rideau* v. *Louisiana*, 373 U.S. 723 (1963); *Estes* v. *Texas*, 381 U.S. 532 (1965); and *Sheppard* v. *Maxwell*, 384 U.S. 333 (1966). With regard to the efforts of trial judges to gag the press, see *Nebraska Press Assn.* v. *Stuart*, 427 U.S. 539 (1976).

47. Plea bargaining is not only constitutional (see *Boykin* v. *Alabama*, 395 U.S. 238 [1969]; and *Brady* v. *United States*, 397 U.S. 742 [1970]), but in *Santobello* v. *New York*, 404 U.S. 257 (1971), at 260, the Court described plea bargaining as "an essential component of the administration of justice. Properly administered, it is to be encouraged." Also see James Eisenstein, *Politics and the Legal Process* (New York: Harper & Row, 1973), pp. 98–142, 243–246; and Herbert Jacob, *Justice in America*, 3rd ed. (Boston: Little, Brown, 1978), pp. 168–193.

48. Quoted in Robert L. Stern and Eugene Gressman, *Supreme Court Practice*, 3rd ed. (Washington, D.C.: Bureau of National Affairs, 1962), fn. p. 90.

49. *Williams* v. *Georgia*, 349 U.S. 375 (1955); *Williams* v. *State*, 88 S.E. 376 (1955); *Williams* v. *Georgia*, 350 U.S. 950 (1956).

50. Stern and Gressman, *op. cit.*, note 48 *supra*, pp. 94–100.

51. The Court's policies toward finality of action are enunciated in *Younger* v. *Harris*, 401 U.S. 37 (1971), number 34 in *Classic and Current Decisions*.

52. The most important exceptions are writs of habeas corpus, which are utilized to secure review of state court convictions in the federal district courts. See *Stone* v. *Powell*, 428 U.S. 465 (1976), number 53 in *Classic and Current Decisions*. The Court's decision in this case, however, limited the availability of habeas corpus review, at least in search-and-seizure cases.

53. Rule 19 of the *Rules of the Supreme Court of the United States*, 398 U.S. 1015, at 1030–1031.

54. See Rohde and Spaeth, *op. cit.*, note 15 *supra*, pp. 124–126; Joseph Tanenhaus, *et al.*, "The Supreme Court's Certiorari Jurisdiction: Cue Theory," in Glendon Schubert, ed., *Judicial Decision-Making* (New York: Free Press, 1963), pp. 111–132; S. Sidney Ulmer, *et al.*, "The Decision to Grant or Deny Certiorari: Further Consideration of Cue Theory," *Law and Society*

Review 6 (1972): 637–643; and Lawrence Baum, "Policy Goals in Judicial Gatekeeping: A Proximity Model of Judicial Discretion," *American Journal of Political Science* 21 (1977): 13–35.

55. *Thompson* v. *Louisville,* 360 U.S. 199 (1960); Joseph P. Blank, "The High Court and Shufflin' Sam," *Reader's Digest,* November 1961, pp. 94–98.

56. Gideon won his case, *Gideon* v. *Wainwright,* 372 U.S. 335 (1963), number 22 in *Classic and Current Decisions,* and a new trial was ordered. This time he was provided an attorney, and after 65 minutes of deliberation the jury found him not guilty of breaking into and entering the poolroom.

57. 354 U.S. 901.

58. *Ibid.,* at 904–905.

59. *Mullaney* v. *Wilbur,* 421 U.S. 684; *Philbrook* v. *Glodgett,* 421 U.S. 707; *Blue Chip Stamps* v. *Manor Drug Stores,* 421 U.S. 723; *Edwards* v. *Healy,* 421 U.S. 772; *Goldfarb* v. *Virginia State Bar,* 421 U.S. 773, number 50 in *Classic and Current Decisions; Murphy* v. *Florida,* 421 U.S. 794; *Bigelow* v. *Virginia,* 421 U.S. 809; *United Housing Foundation* v. *Forman,* 421 U.S. 837; *Intercounty Construction Corp.* v. *Walter,* 422 U.S. 1; and *United States* v. *Park,* 421 U.S. 658.

60. "Gideon: An Epitaph," *New York Times,* February 12, 1972.

Legal Influences on Decision Making

In reaching their decisions and writing their opinions, judges are guided by two norms: adherence to precedent, and the use of legal reasoning. Adherence to precedent precludes judges from writing on a clean slate. The wisdom of the past, not the free choice of the present, controls their decisions. They are expected to be guided by not only their own decisions but also those of their predecessors. The specific form that a judge's reasoning takes depends upon the law that is being applied: whether it is a constitutional provision or, more frequently, a statute. A judge must ask such questions as: What did the Framers of the Constitution intend by the phrase "To regulate commerce . . . among the several states"? What was the meaning of the words "ex post facto law"? What does the record show the purpose of Congress to have been when it enacted a certain law?

It is commonly assumed that adherence to precedent and use of legal reasoning preclude judges from exercising any discretion. Is this assumption correct? In this chapter, evidence is provided that neither precedent nor legal reasoning *necessarily* restricts judicial discretion. Certainly most judges are faithful most of the time to what their predecessors have wrought. But if a judge is so minded, he or she can easily utilize precedent and legal reasoning to reach a creative, innovative decision.[1] If this is puzzling, read on.

PRECEDENT

Arguments that judicial decision making is objective are grounded on the fact that judges base their decisions on precedent. Precedent, or *stare decisis,* means quite simply to abide by or adhere to what has previously been decided. Today's decisions are thus linked with what transpired yesterday, and the law develops a quality of connectedness, an appearance of stability. A measure of certainty, of predictability, presumably results. Because judges base their decisions on precedent, their discretion would seem to be circumscribed—indeed, almost nonexistent. Consequently, the art of judging becomes an objective, dispassionate exercise.

No one seriously disputes that judges actually do base their decisions on precedents in the sense that they cite previously decided cases to justify their decision in the case at bar. A cursory reading of any opinion will show it to be larded with extensive citation of previously decided cases. And if one then reads through the cases cited as precedents, one will indeed find that those earlier decisions do relate to the case at hand. So, on the face of the matter, precedent appears to reduce, if not totally preclude, judicial discretion. However, appearances can be deceiving, and nowhere are appearances more susceptible of deception.

First, go back to that cursorily read opinion with its references to previously decided cases. If it was a decision of an appellate court, one or more of the judges may have dissented. If so, read the dissenting opinion or opinions. Note that there are many references to previously decided cases. Read through these references. Note that these cases bear as much on the issue as those cited by the majority. The conclusion is inescapable: Precedents are available to support a decision in favor of either party to the litigation. Moreover, the precedents on either side are probably equally numerous and of equal weight.

How is it possible that an approximately equal number of precedents can be found to support the contentions of either party in a lawsuit? First, if precedents did not exist on both sides of an issue, one or the other of the parties would not have much of a case. Such a situation would not preclude litigation, of course. People *are* known to bang their heads against stone walls. The stakes may be sufficiently high to cause a party to press a case even though the precedents are stacked against him or her.

This circumstance prompted the litigation that produced the school desegregation cases of 1954, *Brown* v. *Board of Education*.[2] The weight of precedent overwhelmingly supported the "separate but equal" doctrine that had been enunciated in 1896.[3] Indeed, the precedents were so one-sided that the Court was unable to cite so much as a single precedent to support its judgment that "separate educational facilities are inherently unequal." This decision outlawing racial segregation in public facilities is certainly the most notable example of a judicial decision that had not a stitch of precedent to cloak the nakedness of its decree.[4] Decisions unembarrassed by precedent are very much the exception. The only other example at the Supreme Court level that comes to mind is the school prayer case of 1962, *Engel v. Vitale*.[5] But here the failure to cite precedent was conscious and deliberate, not a result of the absence of authority. To the majority, the answer to the question that the case presented was so patently obvious that it did not warrant dignification with precedent: "the constitutional prohibition against laws respecting an establishment of religion must *at least* mean that in this country it is no part of the business of government to compose official prayers for any group of the American people to recite as a part of a religious program carried on by government." (Emphasis added.)

The second reason for the availability of precedents supporting the contrary contentions of the parties to a lawsuit is that a precedent has two components: the court's decision, and the material facts that gave rise to the decision. Quite clearly, the facts in two different cases are rarely, if ever, identical. They may be substantially the same on occasion, but then only at the most mundane level—traffic violations, for example. To find substantial similarity at an appellate court level is not exactly commonplace, if only because decisions tend to be appealed only when they pertain to heretofore unresolved or unsettled issues. The range of precedents from which appellate judges may choose is so great that they are able to justify almost any decision they desire.

A third and final reason for the multiplicity of precedents is that jurists disagree over what constitutes a precedent. One school accepts the definition just mentioned: the court's decision, plus the material facts that gave rise to the decision. Others maintain that precedent is the *ratio decidendi*—the ground of decision, the underlying principle upon which the case was decided. According to this view, the authoritative part of a decision is neither what the court decided, nor the rule on which the court based its decision, but rather some more basic principle. Just what this is supposed to mean is anybody's guess. It does appear, however, that the *ratio decidendi* is not the reasons that a judge gives for his decision; nor is it the rule of law stated in the opinion. Not even all the ascertainable facts of the case are always pertinent. Some facts may have been immaterial to the decision.[6]

All that may be said about precedent with any degree of precision is that it is a norm that governs judicial decisions. Therefore, a judge need merely make reference to previously decided cases to justify his or her decision in the case at hand. Precedent is a matter of form rather than substance. It does not require that a certain number of judges hearing a given case arrive at the same decision—only that each judge support his contrary judgment with a substantial list of previously decided cases that somehow or other bear on the controversy before him.

That, however, is by no means the full story. If a judge should find his discretion limited more than he wishes by a restrictive precedent or two, several options are available whereby he may properly (that is, in accordance with good legal form) minimize the constricting effects of such previously decided cases.

Obiter Dicta

Among the devices used to limit the scope of precedent is to distinguish obiter dicta—those parts of an opinion that are not pertinent to the reasoning by which that court arrived at its decision. Determination of which portions of an opinion constitute dicta is, of course, made by a subsequent court. Hence, if a judge wishes to confine a precedent more narrowly than on its face it appears to be, the judge simply declares the troublesome reasoning upon which the earlier decision was based to be dicta.

A classic example occurred in 1935, in the case of *Humphrey's Executor* v. *United States.*[7] Nine years previously, the Court had declared unconstitutional congressional efforts to restrict the right of the President to remove federal officials from office.[8] In the aftermath of the Civil War, Congress was battling President Andrew Johnson on a wide variety of fronts. In 1867, the Tenure of Office Act was passed, which forbade the President to remove the members of his Cabinet without Senate approval. Twenty years later Congress repealed the law, but in the meantime it enacted a law stipulating that postmasters could be removed from their four-year terms of office only "by and with the advice and consent of the Senate." (Civil service at the time was little more than a gleam in a few reformers' eyes.) In 1920, without senatorial approval, President Wilson removed the postmaster of Portland, Oregon, from office before his term expired. The postmaster sued for the balance of his salary. The case reached the Supreme Court in 1925 and, in one of the lengthiest opinions on record, Chief Justice Taft—the only person in history to occupy both the White House and a seat on the High Bench—ruled that any and all executive officials were removable at the will of the President. The early 1930's saw a sharp increase in the number of regulatory agencies that at most were only indirectly accountable to the President. An appointee to one such agency, the Federal Trade Commission, which had been established twenty years earlier, was removed by President Roosevelt on the basis that he and Roosevelt did not see eye to eye. In its 1935 decision, the Supreme Court held that much of Taft's 1926 opinion was dicta and that the President could remove at will only those officials whose responsibilities were purely executive and who were not covered by civil service regulations.

That much of an earlier opinion is dicta is especially easy for a subsequent court to establish if the earlier court buttressed its opinion with a raft of arguments, rather than reaching its decision by a single chain of reasoning. Dicta are also easy to establish if the decision was a group product, and decisions of appellate courts invariably are. Although the decision had majority support, the coalition behind it may well have been built on compromise—that is, the majority coalition agreed upon the result to be reached, but disagreed over the precise wording of their opinion. To resolve such differences, the pet reasons of the several members of the majority may have required inclusion, with the ultimate result that much of the reasoning is subsequently declared to be dicta, and the scope of the precedent is thereby narrowed.[9]

Distinguishing a Precedent

A less drastic means of limiting precedent is for a court to rule that the situation presented in the case being decided is sufficiently dissimilar from that presented in a previously decided case. This tactic is known as "distinguishing a precedent." It is less drastic than distinguishing obiter dicta because the scope of the previously decided case is not permanently narrowed. Instead, it is deemed irrelevant as a guide to reaching a decision only with respect to the case being decided. Inasmuch as the facts of two cases are never identical, precedents may be distinguished at will. All that the court need do is to detail the situational differences between the case at bar and one decided earlier. Three recent decisions, which sharply focused upon a single issue, aptly illustrate this particular device. All three cases came from Louisiana; all concerned inheritance rights—specifically, those of illegitimate children.

The first case was decided in 1968. By a 6 to 3 vote, Harlan, Black, and Stewart dissenting, the Court held that the five illegitimate children of one mother could sue for damages because of her death due to negligent medical treatment.[10] Starting from the premise, which the dissenters did not dispute, that illegitimate children "are clearly 'persons' within the meaning of the Equal Protection Clause of the Fourteenth Amendment" (this fully 100 years after the Amendment's ratification), the Court went on to declare the statute prohibiting such suits unconstitutional. "Why," asked the Court rhetorically, "should the illegitimate child be denied rights merely because of his birth out of wedlock?" After all, "the rights asserted here involve the intimate, familial relationship between a child and his own mother."

In the second case, decided three years later, the same three dissenters were joined by Nixon's first two appointees, Burger and Blackmun, in holding that Louisiana could constitutionally prohibit acknowledged illegitimate offspring from sharing their father's estate equally with his legitimate children.[11] The majority distinguished the earlier decision, *Levy* v. *Louisiana,* stating that it "did not say . . . that a State can never treat an illegitimate child differently from legitimate offspring." The statute, moreover, had a rational basis: "to establish, protect, and strengthen family life." The dissenters, on the other hand, argued that *Levy* was controlling and that the discrimination lacked a rational basis: "It is . . . like answering a complaint of Negro school children against separate lavatories for boys and girls."

The third decision, *Weber* v. *Aetna Casualty & Surety Co.*, was decided one year later, in 1972.[12] A deceased male who had been covered by Louisiana's workmen's compensation laws left a household of dependents: a woman to whom he was not married, two *unacknowledged* illegitimate children by this woman, and four minor children by his wife who, at the time of his death, was in a mental hospital. A majority of eight, the newly appointed Rehnquist alone dissenting, held that the law in question unconstitutionally discriminated against unacknowledged illegitimate children. The Court said that *Levy* v. *Louisiana,* rather than the previous year's decision, *Labine* v. *Vincent,* controlled the facts in this case. The reason: a state's legitimate interest in protecting legitimate family relationships is not promoted by distinguishing legitimate from illegitimate children in a statutory compensation scheme where dependency on the deceased is a prerequisite to anyone's recovery. Further, though society condemns "irresponsible liaisons beyond the bonds of marriage," to visit "this condemnation on the head of an infant is illogical and unjust. Moreover, imposing disabilities on the illegitimate child is contrary to the basic concept of our system that legal burdens should bear some relationship to individual responsibility or wrongdoing. Obviously, no child is responsible for his birth and penalizing the illegitimate child is an ineffectual—as well as an unjust—way of deterring the parent."

As a consequence of these three decisions, the Court has a perfectly good precedent on either side of the issue. If it subsequently wishes to rule in favor of illegitimate children, the first and third of these decisions provide justification. If it wishes to rule against them, the second decision will do quite nicely. This is a classic example, by no means atypical, of how judges manage to have their cake and eat it too.[13]

Limiting a Precedent in Principle

In addition to distinguishing dicta and precedents, judges may also limit precedents in principle. This device is considerably more drastic than distinguishing a precedent but its effect is similar to declaring part of a previous opinion to be obiter dicta. But when a court limits a precedent in principle, the precedent loses its original scope for all subsequently decided cases as well as the one to which it is being applied.

An apt example is the matter of taxpayer's suits—cases brought by a taxpayer to challenge the purpose for which government is spending money. When, for example, a state legislature or a city council embarks upon a new program that entails the expenditure of tax dollars, someone, frequently an unknown young attorney, will file suit alleging that the program in question is illegal or unconstitutional. In 1923, a unanimous Supreme Court flatly prohibited taxpayer's suits as a device for challenging the purpose for which federal funds were spent.[14] The Court reasoned that there are millions of federal taxpayers. None of them deserve judicial resolution of their claims. The decision implied that their interests are minute and indeterminable and that any injury suffered is at best indirect. More than an indirect injury must be shown before a federal court will heed a taxpayer's claim.

But in 1968, the Court limited the scope of this decision by carving out an exception: If a federal taxpayer challenges the purposes for which Congress appropriates money on the basis that the expenditures exceed some specific constitutional limitation upon Congress's power to tax and spend money—in this case, the establishment of religion clause of the First Amendment—then, said the Court, the case may be heard.[15] The federal funds in question were those disbursed by the Elementary and Secondary Education Act of 1965 to parochial schools to purchase textbooks and other instructional materials and to hire teachers and guidance counselors.

Two more recent examples concern *Miranda* v. *Arizona,* the 1966 decision in which the Court placed severe restrictions on the power of the police to interrogate suspects.[16] Although guilty pleas did not grind to a screeching halt as many persons had predicted, the Court's decision did much to cement its reputation as soft on criminals, and spurred the erection of additional "Impeach Earl Warren" billboards along America's highways and byways. The most important of the principles laid down in *Miranda* stipulated that no statement made by a person while in custody could be used as evidence against him unless he had previously been warned of his right to remain silent, and that he had a right to have a lawyer present during interrogation.

The initial limitation on the scope of the *Miranda* decision was imposed in 1971, in the case of *Harris* v. *New York.* By a 5 to 4 vote, the Court held that statements made by the accused, though inadmissible as evidence of guilt because he had not been informed of his right to counsel, could nonetheless be used to impeach his credibility on the witness stand.[17] A second limiting decision, *Michigan* v. *Tucker,* was handed down three years later. With only Justice Douglas dissenting, the majority ruled that the testimony of a witness could be used notwithstanding the fact that the witness's identity was learned during an interrogation of the suspect at which he was not advised of his right to have counsel present.[18]

Overruling Precedent

Although these devices for avoiding adherence to precedent give judges a substantial amount of discretion, judges have yet another option: the outright overruling of precedents. Because the other methods effectively achieve the same end, precedents are rarely overruled. During its history, the Supreme Court has overruled itself perhaps 100 times,[19] and frequently at an excessively high cost. The overruling of a precedent is an admission that judges are human and sometimes make mistakes. What they decided yesterday may return to haunt them tomorrow. To wit: the legalization of segregation in 1896 made the process of desegregation in the 1950's and 1960's immeasurably more difficult than it would have been if there had been no *Plessy* v. *Ferguson* to overrule.[20]

But not all overrulings jar the myth of judicial sapience. As often as not, courts are able to justify overruling a precedent on the basis that precedents other than the one being overruled support the decision arrived at. A court, in other words, may overrule a precedent on the basis of *stare decisis*. For example, in 1961 the Court held that no person could be convicted on the basis of evidence secured from an illegal search or seizure, thereby overruling a 1949 decision that allowed state officials to use such evidence. The basis for its holding was another 1961 decision that no person could be convicted by means of a coerced confession.[21]

On numerous occasions, members of the Supreme Court have rationalized the need to overrule precedent. A typical statement is that of Justice Powell, concurring in a 1974 decision, *Mitchell* v. *W. T. Grant Co.*:

> To be sure, *stare decisis* promotes the important considerations of consistency and predictability in judicial decisions and represents a wise and appropriate policy in most instances. But that doctrine has never been thought to stand as an absolute bar to reconsideration of a prior decision, especially with respect to matters of constitutional interpretation. Where the Court errs in its construction of a statute, correction may always be accomplished by legislative action. Revision of a constitutional interpretation, on the other hand, is often impossible as a practical matter, for it requires the cumbersome route of constitutional amendment. It is thus not only our prerogative but also our duty to re-examine a precedent where its reasoning or understanding of the Constitution is fairly called into question. And if the precedent or its rationale is of doubtful validity, then it should not stand. As Chief Justice Taney commented more than a century ago, a constitutional decision of this Court should be "always open to discussion when it is supposed to have been founded in error, [so] that [our] judicial authority should hereafter depend altogether on the force of the reasoning by which it is supported."[22]

The "doubtful validity" of a precedent or its rationale, to which Powell refers, is itself rationalized because of changed circumstances or conditions, or as a result of additional knowledge or experience. Both bases were utilized in *Brown* v. *Board of Education:*[23] changes in the character of public education between the 1890's and 1954, and knowledge of the adverse psychological effects that segregation has upon school children.

But at least as important as changed circumstances and additional knowledge are changes in a court's personnel. The classic example is the legal tender cases of 1870 and 1871. The three-member minority of 1870 was transformed into the five-member majority of 1871 by reason of President Grant's careful filling of the two 1870 vacancies with persons known to support the constitutionality of the Legal Tender Act.[24] Similarly, the Liberal output of the Warren Court during the 1960's was a result of Kennedy's replacement of Frankfurter with Arthur Goldberg in 1962. He provided the necessary fifth vote—along with the votes of Douglas, Black, Warren, and Brennan—in support of issues pertaining to the value of freedom. And the replacement of Tom Clark with Thurgood Marshall in 1967 provided a similar majority supportive of equality. But Liberal dominance collapsed with the resignation of Fortas (Goldberg's successor) in 1969 and the accession of Burger to the Chief Justiceship in 1969.[25]

May one conclude, then, that courts will overrule precedent because of changes in personnel or changed conditions only when the issue is a constitutional question? Not at all. Overruling precedent may require a bit of legalistic gobbledygook, but judges are not exactly unskilled in this regard. Consider the matter of the arbitration of labor-management disputes. In a 1962 decision, *Sinclair Refining Co.* v. *Atkinson,*[26] the Supreme Court ruled that federal courts have no power to halt strikes over grievances that a collective bargaining agreement requires to be arbitrated. The Court based its decision on provisions of the Norris-LaGuardia Act, which forbids federal courts to issue injunctions in labor disputes. Eight years later, in *Boys Markets* v. *Retail Clerk's Union,* the Court overruled itself.[27] Justice Brennan spoke for the Court: "At the outset, we are met with respondent's contention that *Sinclair* ought not to be disturbed because the decision turned on a question of statutory construction which Congress can alter at any time. Since Congress has not modified our conclusions in *Sinclair,* even though it has been urged to do so, respondent argues that principles of *stare decisis* should govern the present case." Brennan further stated: "We fully recognize that important policy considerations militate in favor of continuity and predictability in the law."[28] So far so good. But then there was a change in tune: "It is precisely because *Sinclair* stands as a significant departure from our otherwise consistent emphasis upon the congressional policy to promote the peaceful settlement of labor disputes through arbitration and our efforts to accommodate and harmonize this policy with those underlying the anti-injunction provisions of the Norris-LaGuardia Act that we believe *Sinclair* should be reconsidered."[29] Brennan thereupon asserted, albeit gratuitously, that in light of subsequent developments, "it has become clear" that *Sinclair* "does not further but rather frustrates realization of an important goal of our national labor policy."[30]

Then Brennan added the clincher:

> Nor can we agree that conclusive weight should be accorded to the failure of Congress to respond to *Sinclair* on the theory that congressional silence should be interpreted as acceptance of the decision. . . . Therefore, in the absence of any persuasive circumstances evidencing a clear design that congressional inaction be taken as acceptance of *Sinclair,* the mere silence of Congress is not a sufficient reason for refusing to reconsider the decision.[31]

Obviously, this is a most persuasive argument. But Justice Black, dissenting, was not convinced. What, he asked, has changed since the *Sinclair* decision? Black's answer is complete and accurate: "Nothing at all has changed, in fact, except the membership of the Court and the personal views of one justice."[32] Very true. Two members of the five-man majority in *Sinclair* had retired—Clark and Warren. The three dissenters in *Sinclair*—Douglas, Brennan, and Harlan—adhered to their position and picked up the vote of Burger, who was not a member of the Court when *Sinclair* was decided. The Justice who switched sides was Stewart. And what did he have to say for himself? Simply that he was taking "refuge" in an aphorism of former Justice Frankfurter: "Wisdom too often never comes, and so one ought not to reject it merely because it comes late."[33]

Frankfurter's comment about the belated arrival of wisdom is nicely illustrated by a 1975 decision, *United States* v. *Reliable Transfer Co.*[34] For well over a century the Court had consistently adhered to a maritime damage rule that was originally promulgated by one Eleanor of Guienne in the middle of the *twelfth century.* Eleanor governed a French duchy south of Brittany, and the rule she promulgated was part of the Laws of Oleron, an island in the Bay of Biscay. The laws governed mariners and merchants throughout Western and Northern Europe. The rule stated that ships colliding at sea must share the resulting damages equally, even if one was more responsible for the accident than the other. The reasons for the rule seem to have been (1) the difficulty of determining proportionate responsibility for a collision, and (2) the expectation that it would cause mariners to be more careful and vigilant.

By the beginning of the twentieth century dissatisfaction with the rule had become prevalent, and many of the world's maritime nations began to drop it in favor of a rule of proportionate, rather than equally divided, damages. Not so the United States. The Senate had twice refused to ratify the Brussels Collision Liability Convention of 1910, which provided for apportioning damages proportionately. The Court, however, noting that the lower federal courts were following the original rule grudgingly—terming it unfair, illogical, and archaic—and that "Congress has largely left to this Court the responsibility for fashioning the controlling rules of admiralty law," abruptly made a 180-degree turn in mid-passage, and thereby put the United States on the same course as the rest of the world's major maritime nations. Thus the demise of a rule that had been observed for 825 years. If there be a hoarier precedent extant, I, for one, am ignorant of it. So, if I have given the impression that the Court changes its tune with the frequency of a sing-along chorus, the decision in the *Reliable Transfer Co.* case should provide evidence that sometimes the Court is unwilling to yield to the winds of change until long after the rest of the world has trimmed its sails.

That the Court occasionally changes its mind and reverses itself would seem to be a predictable result of changes in the Court's membership. However, unfortunately for those desiring certainty in matters legal, precedents are sometimes uprooted or qualified absent any change in personnel whatsoever. Consider replevin laws. They affect every person who purchases goods on credit, whether bought on an installment plan or charged to a charge account via the ubiquitous credit card. Failure to meet the easy monthly payments may result in repossession of the goods in question. What rights, if any, does a purchaser have against such repossession? What recourse does the seller have? The Supreme Court has addressed these questions. The answers, however, are less than enlightening.

The first of the relevant decisions, *Fuentes* v. *Shevin,* was handed down in June of 1972.[35] By a 4 to 3 vote, Powell and Rehnquist not participating, the Court declared unconstitutional state laws that allow installment sellers to obtain court orders authorizing repossession of property from allegedly delinquent purchasers without giving prior notice and hearing to the buyer. A hearing after the fact is not sufficient. Nor, said the Court, does the language of the sales contracts constitute a waiver of the purchaser's right to a fair hearing. Powell and Rehnquist did not participate in the decision because the case was orally argued two months before they joined the Court. But when the issue was next brought before the Court, in May of 1974, participate they did. The result: a 5 to 4 vote that held that sellers need *not* provide notice or a hearing to purchasers before seizure of goods if the seller has posted bond to protect the buyer against loss if the seizure should prove to be invalid.[36] The majority stated that Louisiana's statutory scheme appropriately accommodates the conflicting interests of buyers and sellers. The due process clause does not guarantee purchasers the use and possession of merchandise until all issues have been judicially resolved. If that were the constitutional mandate, a purchaser might destroy, sell, or remove the goods from the court's jurisdiction before legal proceedings were completed.

Four members of the new majority distinguished the *Fuentes* precedent on the grounds that Louisiana's law differed from those of Pennsylvania and Florida, which were at issue in *Fuentes.* The fifth member of the majority, Lewis Powell, expressed the view that *Fuentes* had been overruled. The dissenters, speaking through Justice Stewart, agreed with Powell: "the Court today has unmistakably overruled a considered decision of this Court that is barely two years old, without pointing to any change in either societal perceptions or basic constitutional understanding that might justify this total disregard of *stare decisis.*"[37]

The Court handed down its third replevin law decision in January 1975.[38] By a 6 to 3 vote, the Court resuscitated the *Fuentes* precedent while simultaneously asserting that the Louisiana decision was still alive and well. The Court struck down a Georgia law that permitted creditors to garnish debtors' bank accounts—but not their wages—without notice or hearing. All that the statute required was that the creditor post a bond for double the amount due. The debtor, however, could dissolve the garnishment by depositing a bond to cover the alleged indebtedness. The majority found this statute deficient because property "was impounded and . . . put totally beyond use" pending litigation of the debt, "all by a writ of garnishment issued by a court clerk without notice or opportunity for an early hearing and without participation by a judicial officer."[39]

Justice Stewart, concurring, observed that "it is gratifying to note that my report of the demise of *Fuentes* v. *Shevin* . . . seems to have been greatly exaggerated."[40] The dissenters—Blackmun, Burger, and Rehnquist—were less amused: "the commercial communities in other states [are] uncertain as to whether their own established and long-accepted statutes pass constitutional muster with a wavering tribunal off in Washington, D.C. This Court surely fails in its intended purpose when confusing results of this kind are forthcoming and are imposed upon those who owe and those who lend."[41]

This was a valid complaint, to be sure. And though such tergiversation is hardly typical, one ought not expect much more when one has so gossamer a constraint as precedent.

LEGAL REASONING:
THE VENEER OF OBJECTIVITY

Legal reasoning, like precedent, is a norm that guides and controls the decisions of judges. But no more than precedent does legal reasoning inhibit the discretion that judges are able to exercise. Legal reasoning and precedent serve a common purpose: to give judicial decision making the appearance of stability, uniformity, and certainty. Both maintain public respect for the law by the specious, yet plausible, fiction that it is known and precise.

Essentially, legal reasoning is nothing more than the use of analogy and examples to reach a conclusion. When a case is brought to court for resolution, the task of the judge is to ascertain whether and to what extent the facts of the matter are congruent with those of related controversies. The weakness of such a mode of procedure is that never are the facts of two cases identical. Judges, consequently, analogize among cases that are dissimilar. This lack of factual identity among cases gives the law its flexibility, with the result that judges have discretion to base decisions on their personal policy preferences or other subjective considerations. The reason, of course, is that what one judge considers an analogous set of facts will not necessarily be so perceived by another.

The basic weakness of legal reasoning is that it is a low form of rational behavior. It certainly is the most primitive—the first to be learned and to be employed. Consider the matter of children's bedtime. When the preschooler is told that the appointed hour is fast approaching, a plaintive objection is heard: "Why do I have to go to bed now? Susie doesn't." The patient parent points out that Susie is in first grade and thus is entitled to stay up longer. The parental explanation, more often than not, is promptly rebutted: "Susie got up earlier than me"; "I took a nap"; or "I'm not sleepy."

By basing decisions upon presumably similar examples, law develops inductively—from the specific to the general. For this reason and because purely logical and empirical processes need not be employed, law is not, properly speaking, a science. Science is concerned with the formulation of interrelated constructs, concepts, and propositions that present a systematic view of phenomena by specifying relationships among variables for the purpose of predicting and explaining the phenomena being investigated. Law, by comparison, is not concerned with prediction and explanation, but rather with the specification of the rules of action prescribed by the governing power of the community. These rules regulate, limit, control, and protect the activities of the members of the community. Though one may find numerous references to law as a science, it is no more a science than are creative writing, necromancy, or finger painting. But this is not to say that reasoning by example lacks utility. It is quite suitable for poetry, where ambiguity and blurred imagery are used to produce aesthetic effects. Where precision and agreement on the appropriate examples are required, reasoning by example simply does not work very well.

Modes of Legal Reasoning: Constitutional Interpretation

Although legal reasoning enables the user to rationalize almost any conclusion desired, there does exist a limited number of specific types, or modes, of legal reasoning that judges use. Each of these modes is based on a premise from which a judge reasons to reach a conclusion. Rarely do these modes appear in their pure form; rather they appear in some combination. Four pertain to controversies in which the issue is one of constitutional interpretation. Two others pertain to cases in which the question is the meaning of the provisions of a law or government regulation. We turn first to constitutional interpretation, the heart of judicial review.

The intention of the Framers. What did the Framers have in mind when they drafted the provision that we must now interpret? It is difficult to determine just who the pertinent "they" were in both body and opinion. With regard to the original document, the Framers are defined as the 55 males who were delegates to the Constitutional Convention, held in Philadelphia in the summer of 1787. But not all were present during the entirety of the proceedings. Many came and went. At the end of their deliberations, only 39 signed the document. Were these 39 of a single mind? Certainly not. Some probably had not even read the final draft. The more casual participants may have signed at the behest of others. We do know that some of the major participants had serious reservations—not the least of whom was Alexander Hamilton.

What about those who refused to sign? And what about the delegates to the various state conventions that were called for the purpose of ratifying the Constitution, to say nothing of those who elected these delegates in the first place? Because of a paucity of historical records (none were kept at the Convention), these individuals and groups are excluded completely from consideration. History has left, however, the notes taken by James Madison, upon which the historically minded judge is largely dependent, but by Madison's own admission his notes are incomplete. Moreover, he took the liberty of editing them some twenty years after the events described therein took place.

On the other hand, we do have *The Federalist*, a collection of essays written by Hamilton, Madison, and John Jay within seven months after the Convention adjourned. The purpose of these essays, however, was not to document the Convention's proceedings for the sake of posterity but to influence New Yorkers to support ratification of the Constitution. As such, they must be classified as political propaganda—of the highest order, to be sure. Closely reasoned and brilliantly articulated, they are a model that modern candidates and advocates might usefully emulate, but they are propaganda nonetheless. The fact that judges do rely on *The Federalist* to divine the Framers' intent unequivocally demonstrates the inadequacy of the historical record.

Apart from the record, can we know with any precision what were the Framers' intentions? This mode of reasoning obviously assumes we can. It is an assumption, however, that cannot withstand scrutiny. In the first place, intentions are highly subjective and decidedly personal. As individuals, we are frequently unaware of why we say and do certain things.

Psychoanalysts do not lack for business. At the group level, ascertaining intent is an exercise in futility. The Framers undoubtedly agreed that the United States needed a governmental system that was superior to that established by the Articles of Confederation. What specifically constituted such a system was assuredly not a matter of consensus. Decisions made one day were changed or rescinded the next. The final document, equally clearly, was a bundle of compromises. Obviously, it had to be; otherwise, ratification would not have occurred. Consider the division of power between the federal government and the states. Both national supremacists and states' righters have, since 1789, seen fit to cite "the Framers' intent" as support for their nearly mutually exclusive positions. Accordingly, one may, with difficulty, make a reasonable assessment of the Framers' intentions. But such assessments can be no more precise than brain surgery performed with a meat ax.

Nor does interpretation of intent inhibit judicial discretion when the provision at issue is a constitutional amendment. Many congresspersons and senators do not participate in legislative debate of any sort. Obviously, those who do, do not speak with a single voice. The intended meaning of the phrase "due process of law" in the Fourteenth Amendment generated heated controversy even during the lifetime of the very members of Congress who proposed that Amendment. Since its adoption in 1868, the due process clause has been the most litigated of all the Constitution's provisions.

The meaning of the words. This approach is an attempt to define the meaning of the Constitution according to what the words used therein meant at the time the document or an amendment to it was written. Some authorities allege that this and the preceding mode are backward-looking; that they make American society the prisoner of its past; and that the words and phrases of the Constitution have been set in concrete—alterable only by means of constitutional amendment. Such allegations are false. Whatever problems may result from the use of these methods, legalistic inertia is not one of them. Most of the innovative and precedent-shattering decisions of the later years of the Warren Court have been made using either or both of these modes of reasoning. For example, in 1964 Justice Black used the intention of the Framers and the meaning of certain words in Article I of the Constitution as the basis of a ruling that a state's congressional districts had to contain an approximately equal number of people.[42] With this one fell swoop, rural domination of Congress was toppled and the path cleared for the Court to declare, four months later, that the one person, one vote principle applied as well to both houses of the state legislatures.[43]

Nor are these approaches to constitutional interpretation susceptible to innovative use only by a Liberal court. The Burger Court is certainly not the spitting image of its predecessor. Yet in 1972 it declared the death penalty unconstitutional.[44] Seven months later, that precedent-shattering decision was followed with one that held that all state antiabortion laws also violated the Constitution.[45]

A classic nineteenth-century example of the use to which the "meaning of the words" method can be put concerns the right of access of corporations to the federal courts. Article III of the Constitution provides that disputes between "citizens of different states" may be heard in the federal courts. The purpose of this provision was to overcome the possibility that state courts might favor their own residents in ligitation that involved those from other states. On the basis of the eighteenth-century meaning of the words, corporations could in no way be deemed "citizens." But if one were to ignore the corporation's existence and look instead at the stockholders, and if the stockholders were all residents of a single state, then diversity would be complete if the other party to the litigation resided in a state different from that of the stockholders. Such was the rationale of an opinion by John Marshall in 1810.[46] But, when business enterprise was no longer localistic, and stockholders of national corporations no longer resided in only one state, Marshall's decision became a millstone around the neck of American business. With access to the federal courts now denied stockholders, their only recourse for judicial redress of grievances was to throw themselves on the often not-so-tender mercies of their respective state courts.

In 1845, the Supreme Court rode to business's rescue.[47] Noting that Marshall himself had subsequently regretted his 1810 decision, the Court coupled the phrase "citizens of different states" with the phrase that gave Congress its power to establish the jurisdiction of the lower federal courts. Congress, said the Justices, "may give the courts jurisdiction between citizens in many other forms than that in which it has been conferred."[48] Hence, for jurisdictional purposes, a corporation was to be deemed a "citizen" of the state in which it was incorporated. In the words of John P. Frank:

> In the next two decades the Court polished the . . . theory, trimmed its appearance, and finished with the most remarkable fiction in American law. A conclusive and unrebuttable presumption was established that all stockholders of a corporation were citizens of the state in which the corporation was chartered. By operation of this fiction, every one of the shareholders of the General Motors Corporation is a citizen of Delaware despite the fact that there are more stockholders than there are Delawareans.[49]

Logical analysis. This mode is based upon the syllogism, which consists, quite simply, of a major and a minor premise and the conclusion that follows therefrom. The major premise sets forth a proposition: "A law

repugnant to the Constitution is void." The minor premise is an assertion related to the major premise: "Law X is repugnant to the Constitution." From the major and minor premises, the conclusion inescapably
follows: "Law X is unconstitutional." The foregoing example illustrates
John Marshall's reasoning in *Marbury* v. *Madison*,[50] in which the Court
enunciated the doctrine of judicial review, and which is perhaps the
classic example of the use of logical analysis in American constitutional law.

Marshall began his opinion by noting that the American governmental system is one of limited powers and that it is the Constitution that
sets these limits. He then asserted: "It is a proposition too plain to be
contested, that the Constitution controls any legislative act repugnant to
it"; otherwise, "the legislature may alter the Constitution by an ordinary
act."[51] From this Marshall concluded that "all those who have framed
written constitutions contemplate them as forming the fundamental
and paramount law of the nation, and consequently, the theory of every
such government must be, that an act of the legislature, repugnant to
the Constitution, is void."[52] This argument, which is logically unassail-
able, implies that Congress would enact a law they believed to be unconstitutional if they could get away with it. Such an assumption is obviously demeaning to Congress. Indirectly, Marshall addressed himself to
it: "It is, emphatically, the province and duty of the judicial department
to say what the law is. . . . If two laws conflict with each other, the courts
must decide. . . . So, if a law be in opposition to the Constitution . . . so
that the court must either decide that case, comfortable to the law,
disregarding the Constitution; or conformable to the Constitution, disregarding the law; the court must determine which . . . governs the
case; this is of the very essence of judicial duty."[53] The argument is again
plausible, but nonetheless specious. It omits from consideration the
possibility that Congress is at least as capable as the courts to determine
the constitutionality of its own actions. But Marshall anticipated this
objection: "Why does a judge swear to discharge his duties agreeably to
the Constitution of the United States, if that Constitution forms no rule
for his government?"[54] A note of indignation is added: "How immoral
to impose it on them [the judges], if they were to be used as the instruments, and the knowing instruments, for violating what they swear to
support!"[55] This argument, however, is sheer dissimulation. All federal
officials—elected as well as appointed—take an oath either to "preserve, protect, and defend" or to "support and defend" the "Constitution of the United States." Why assume that congresspersons are less
honorable than judges? Marshall had his reasons for making such an
assumption, but nowhere does he document this implied premise.

The point of the foregoing is that logical analysis exists independently
of fact or experience. Almost any conclusion can be given logical form.

The correlation between logic and a reasonable decision may be—and sometimes is—zero. Logical reasoning may be unjust or even absurd, but as long as the argument conforms with the requirements of proper inference, the decision may not be impugned as illogical. Thus, logical analysis, even more than the other two modes of legal reasoning, enables judges—if they are so minded—to make decisions that are compatible with their personal policy preferences, while at the same time imbuing their opinions with a semblance of order and a degree of connectedness. Oliver Wendell Holmes stated the matter well:

> The life of the law has not been logic: it has been experience. The felt necessities of the time, the prevalent moral and political theories, intuitions of public policy, avowed or unconscious, even the prejudices which judges share with their fellow-men, have had a good deal more to do than the syllogism in determining the rules by which men should be governed.[56]

The adaptive approach. The adaptive approach is based upon changing conditions and the lessons of experience. John Marshall stated the matter well in *M'Culloch* v. *Maryland* (a decision at least equal in importance to *Marbury* v. *Madison*), in which he broadly construed the powers of the federal government at the expense of the states: "we must never forget that it is a Constitution we are expounding," a Constitution that was "intended to endure for ages to come, and consequently, to be adapted to the various crises of human affairs."[57] At the heart of the adaptive mode is the recognition that though the Framers built exceedingly well, neither they nor anyone else was able to foresee the needs of a rapidly changing society very far into the future. In comparison with the other types of constitutional interpretation, use of the adaptive mode by the courts is politically risky. It does not preserve the outward appearance of stability that a fundamental law ought to have. Hence, its use stirs opposition to the Court's policy making from those supportive of the status quo and those who desire political certainty and governmental absolutes. Consequently, adaptive arguments are seldom used and, even then, only in conjunction with one or more of the other modes.

Modes of Legal Reasoning: Statutory Construction

In addition to interpreting the Constitution, courts must construe and apply statutes, the rules and regulations of regulatory agencies and commissions, and the procedural rules that govern the activities and operations of the judiciary itself. They must also rule on the actions of executive officials. Although decisions on these matters tend not to be of landmark proportions or to possess the dramatic quality that stems from the exercise of judicial review, they constitute the bulk of all courts' output. Two modes of legal reasoning apply to these types of cases: the plain-meaning rule and legislative intent.

The plain-meaning rule.   The plain-meaning rule is the equivalent of the "meaning of the words" mode of constitutional interpretation. The focus is upon the literal text of the statute, rule, or regulation and the objective is simply to construe what the provision says, but not in a "wooden or unimaginative" fashion.[58] The difficulty with the plain-meaning rule is that English is an ambiguous language. It is a rare word for which Webster gives but a single definition. Since definitions are not usually expressed in mathematical symbols, precision can at best be only approximated. When decision making is a collective enterprise, as is the situation in a legislature or bureaucracy, the probability of ambiguity increases prodigiously. Moreover, because most legislative enactments are a result of compromise, clarity and precision are further obfuscated. The result is that the words of a statute, rule, or regulation may be treated like so many empty bottles into which judges pour whatever contents they wish.

As an illustration, consider the following passage. It is the key provision of the Mann Act, enacted in 1910 for the purpose of outlawing what was then known as "white slavery." As such, the Mann Act is one of the myriad measures by which American officialdom, in the best Puritanical tradition, attempts to legislate sexual morality.

> . . . any person who shall knowingly transport or cause to be transported, or aid or assist in obtaining transportation for, or in transporting, in interstate or foreign commerce, or in any territory or in the District of Columbia, any woman or girl for the purpose of prostitution or debauchery, or for any other immoral purpose, or with the intent and purpose to induce, entice, or compel such woman or girl to become a prostitute or to give herself up to debauchery, or to engage in any other immoral practice . . . shall be deemed guilty of a felony.[59]

The language is straightforward, as much as legalese ever is, and the meaning is clear. Indeed, the passage is about as clear and unequivocal as one could find in any statute. Its constitutionality was upheld, three years after passage, as an appropriate exercise of Congress's power to regulate interstate commerce.[60] (Of that, advocates of women's rights may wish to take note.) The interesting feature of the Mann Act was not that it was found constitutional, but rather that it spawned three decisions of the Supreme Court that attempted to spell out the meaning of the previously quoted provision.

The first case concerned three men who transported their respective mistresses across a state line. Over the objections of three Justices, including both of the Roman Catholics then on the Court (Chief Justice Edward White and Joseph McKenna), the majority affirmed the convictions on the basis that the phrase "immoral purpose" in the Mann Act included persuading a woman or girl to become a "concubine and mistress," even though the venture was nonremunerative.[61] The second case involved a madam and her husband who took two of their employees on a trip to Yellowstone National Park, crossing state lines in the process. The girls did not work while on vacation but did resume their profession upon their return. By a 5 to 4 vote, the Court reversed the proprietors' convictions, ruling that the sole purpose of the trip "was to provide innocent recreation and a holiday" for their employees. Hence, there was no immoral purpose.[62]

The third case pertained to members of a Mormon sect who practiced polygamy. Each had transported his several wives across state lines for the purpose of cohabitation. The Court, speaking through Justice Douglas, affirmed the convictions. "The establishment or maintenance of polygamous households," he said, "is a notorious example of promiscuity." Of the three dissenters, Frank Murphy's remarks were most trenchant: "etymologically, the words 'polygyny' and 'polygamy' are quite distinct from 'prostitution,' 'debauchery' and words of that ilk."[63] Apparently, the crucial distinction for Justice Douglas, who has been married four times, is that four wives are permissible so long as a man has them consecutively rather than concurrently.

Legislative history. The other mode of statutory construction, legislative history, looks behind the face of the law in an effort to ascertain the spirit of the law, that is, to determine what the legislators really meant, as distinct from what the law, rule, or regulation says. This approach, then, is equivalent to the "intention of the Framers" mode of constitutional interpretation. But unlike those interpreting the Constitution, those analyzing legislative history have much more information at their disposal: debates that preceded passage of the legislation; majority and minority committee reports; the statements and views of the sponsors of the legislation; testimony and comments of individual legislators, government officials, and interested private persons given at legislative committee hearings; and previous court decisions interpreting the statute.

Though the legislative history approach may appear to be superior to the plain-meaning rule, it is not. As guides to legislative intent, both approaches allow judges virtually untrammeled discretion. Many legislative committees are notably biased and self-serving; much of the *Congres-*

sional Record was never uttered on the floor of either the House or the Senate.* Congress rarely, if ever, acts with singleness of purpose; and not uncommonly it communicates no more clearly than does a whispered phrase in the midst of the clamorous din of a rock concert. For example, in an opinion in a case concerning a section of the Social Security Act's provisions for Aid to Families with Dependent Children that required states participating in the program to redefine eligibility for public assistance and to rework the scale used in determining how much money should be given to each eligible person, the Court stated that "the background of [the pertinent section] reveals little except that we have before us a child born of the silent union of legislative compromise. Thus, Congress, as it frequently does, has voiced its wishes in muted strains and left it to the courts to discern the theme in the cacophony of political understanding." Further, "Congress, sometimes, legislates by innuendo, making declarations of policy and indicating a preference while requiring measures which, though falling short of legislating its goals, serve as a nudge in the preferred direction."[64]

---

*The significance of the fact that, according to Congressman William A. Steiger of Wisconsin, "70 percent of the Congressional Record now consists of remarks never uttered" on the floor of either the House or the Senate produces a classic *Catch-22* situation: A federal court is called upon to interpret a provision of an act of Congress; the court uses the legislative history approach and concludes that the provision means "this" rather than "that" on the basis of statements contained in the *Congressional Record.* But what if the statements were not actually part of the debates leading to the provision's enactment? The court could then have relied as validly on a Ouija board or an astrological chart as the basis for its decision.

Note ought also be made that the ramifications of the *Catch-22* situation extend beyond the decision making of the federal courts to that of federal agencies. As Congressman Steiger points out, administrative officials "look to Congressional debate for guidance in writing regulations for Congressionally mandated programs." And "in an era of increasingly complex legislation, the possibility of error in interpretation is heightened by falsification."

Occasionally the falsification is evident to the close observer. Hale Boggs of Louisiana is recorded as having addressed the House of Representatives two days after his tragic disappearance in an Alaska plane crash. And there is irony as well:

> . . . the Congressional Record's account of the debate on a new House ethics code contains unspoken speeches by 24 members. Eight of them specifically said "I rise," most in support or strong support, but one with reluctance and one with serious reservations. One mythically thanked the chairman "for the opportunity to address this body on the question of the ethic code"; another, *in absentia,* chided his colleagues that "we can talk all day and into the night about and around the issue before us."

William A. Steiger, " 'Say,' the Senator Asked, 'Read Any Fiction Lately?' 'Yes, The Congressional Record.' " *New York Times,* August 29, 1977.

In addition, words uttered on the floor of Congress are sometimes *omitted* from the *Congressional Record.* See the interesting "debate" among Congressmen Ronald Dellums of California, Robert Bauman of Maryland, and Richard Ottinger of New York, recounted by William Miller and Frances S. Leighton, *Fishbait: The Memoirs of the Congressional Doorkeeper* (Englewood Cliffs, N.J.: Prentice-Hall, 1977), p. 207.

As evidence of the Court's willingness to exploit congressional ambivalence even to the extent of rewriting the legislation in question, consider the decision in the case of *Muniz v. Hoffman*,[65] where the Court was asked whether a union and its officials had the right to a trial by jury when tried for criminal contempt of court because of their disobedience of an injunction obtained by the National Labor Relations Board. The pertinent statute provides: "In all cases of contempt arising under the laws of the United States governing the issuance of injunctions or restraining orders in any case involving or growing out of a labor dispute, the accused shall enjoy the right to a speedy and public trial by an impartial jury. . . ."[66] "All" and "any" are unequivocal words; nonetheless, the majority refused to grant the union's request for a jury trial because, quoting from an 1892 decision, it has long been a "familiar rule, that a thing may be within the letter of the statute and yet not within the statute, because not within its spirit, nor within the intention of its makers."[67] Moreover, the majority added, "we are construing a statute . . . which . . . created an exception to the historic rule that there was no right to a jury trial in contempt proceedings. To read a substantial change in accepted practice into a revision of the Criminal Code without any support in the legislative history of that revision is unsupportable." Why? Because (and here the majority quoted an 1884 decision) "it will not be inferred that the legislature, in revising and consolidating the laws, intended to change their policy, unless such an intention be clearly expressed."[68] And so, though the plain meaning of the statute might be unmistakably clear (as the four dissenters pointed out[69]), Congress may also be required—when a majority of the Court so dictates—to apply its statutory change to all related provisions and, as well, to make its purpose clear in the reports and debates that precede passage of the law.

As another example of the Court's willingness to rewrite legislation, consider the Civil Rights Act of 1964, in which Congress ended the conflict over sit-in demonstrations by prohibiting racial discrimination in places of public accommodation.[70] But what about demonstrators who had been prosecuted under state law before the Act's passage? The Court ordered these persons released and the charges against them dropped, even though—as Justice Black pointed out in a biting dissent—"Congress nearly a century ago passed a 'saving' statute . . . to keep courts from imputing to it an intent to abate cases retroactively, unless such an intent was expressly stated in the law it passed." And "unless judge-made rules of construction have some sort of superiority over congressionally enacted statutes" [which they apparently do, as the previous example, *Muniz v. Hoffman,* so neatly illustrates], the Court has no "authority for disregarding the Federal Saving Statute." The majority's declaration, Black wryly observed, "that 'there is no public interest to be served' in upholding the convictions of these trespassers" is "a conclusion of policy which I had thought was only for legislative bodies to decide."[71]

Perhaps the adequacy of legislative history as a mode of legal reasoning was best described some years ago by noted authority Glendon Schubert as "the psychoanalysis of Congress":

> The assumption that congressmen behave like judges are supposed to behave just isn't supported by the available research findings, notwithstanding the fact that the highest title that one can bestow upon a member of the national legislature is to call him—even if he was only a justice of the peace once forty years earlier—not "Senator," but "Judge." Such admiration is reciprocated by the majority of Supreme Court justices who have had no congressional experience and who exhibit the greatest confidence in their capacity for the divination of legislative intent through the study of legislative history.[72]

As a matter of fact, until 1950 only approximately 27 percent of the Justices had congressional experience. But in the quarter century between 1950 and 1976, not a single one of the fourteen Justices who took his seat was an ex-congressman. Not that their presence would have made any difference in the free play of personal policy preferences. The modes of legal reasoning effectively cloak the real bases on which judges decide their cases—their individual beliefs, attitudes, and values.

Although the mythology supporting the cult of the robe has remained fixed for the better part of two centuries, the rhetoric surrounding judicial policy making adapts to changing circumstances and conditions. Perhaps the two most frequent modifications that have been made in the relatively recent past are modifications in the doctrines of judicial restraint and of strict construction.

As the principles of laissez-faire economics widened the gap between rich and poor during the first decades of the twentieth century, and as dissenting opinions became more commonplace beginning in the 1930's, the concept of the impartial, impersonal judge strained credulity. Judges themselves became aware that they were not neutral technicians, but were as much the prisoners of their own mythology as was the public at large. Hence the need for new labels to make more palatable the sometimes bitter elixir dispensed from the judicial trough.

Two doctrines, of reasonably recent vintage, that are sometimes considered modes of legal reasoning are judicial restraint and strict construction. Because of the frequency with which both terms are bandied about, each is discussed in the remainder of this chapter. It should be emphasized that though they are frequently put to ideological uses—judicial restraint by Liberals during the 1930's and by Conservatives during the Warren Court years—neither judicial restraint nor strict construction is necessarily an ideological term, any more than are any of the modes of legal reasoning that have been previously discussed.

Judicial Restraint

Judicial restraint became the rallying cry of those who sought accommodation of judicial policy making with the social and economic reforms of the New Deal. The collapse of the stock market in 1929 sounded the death knell of the old order of unrestrained competition, monopoly capitalism, and unorganized labor. Since the 1880's, judicial policy making had forbidden governmental regulation that was hostile to business or favorable to labor. What the Supreme Court needed was a solution that would allow it to have its cake and eat it too, a rationale whereby the Justices could make policy while retaining a semblance, at least, of objectivity. To be sure, the Justices would no longer be able to justify probusiness or antilabor decisions on the basis of laissez-faire economics. The invisible hands of Adam Smith and Herbert Spencer were now dead hands and could no longer pilot the ship of state. But this was a small price to pay. There was, after all, more than one way to skin a cat. And judicial restraint was not so uniform a standard that it could not be put to conservative as well as liberal uses.

The wisdom and necessity of judicial restraint are based on the postulates that judges, especially those serving lifetime appointments, are remote from the needs and wishes of the public, and that their decision-making competency is limited. Hence, runs the argument, they should defer to those decision makers who are publicly accountable. Deference should also be accorded state governmental officials because of the federal character of the governmental system. Concession is made to the possibility that not all wisdom emanates from Washington, and that the Justices' Marble Palace may not be wisdom's only font. Furthermore, many issues, especially those of an economic nature, are exceedingly technical and complex. Such matters should be left to the experts for resolution. Accordingly, then, courts should not declare congressional or executive acts unconstitutional (except perhaps in the most wanton instances), state decision making should be upheld, and the rules and regulations of the various federal regulatory commissions should receive judicial support.

Synonymous with the concept of judicial restraint is the name of Justice Felix Frankfurter. He became identified with it long before he became a member of the Supreme Court in 1939. His teaching and writings during the 1920's and 1930's, his unofficial membership in FDR's brain trust, and his reputation as the supplier of eager and able young government attorneys (the "Happy Hot Dogs") made Frankfurter the spokesman par excellence for those disgruntled with judicial demolition of reformist and New Deal legislation. Like a broken record, he didactically iterated at every opportunity his zealous dedication to judicial restraint. Friend and foe alike accepted Frankfurter's assertions at face value. The concluding statements from a book by one of the Justice's staunchest supporters, Professor Wallace Mendelson, are by no means atypical.

The Court, Mendelson notes, must decide controversies entailing clashes of interests, each of which has some, but no clearly preponderant, legal foundation. The intrinsic problem thus becomes: for whom or in what direction shall doubt be resolved? Some Justices, indeed most of those who sat during the 1920's and the first half of the 1930's, made uncertainty the servant of selected business interests. Others have been guided "by more generous considerations." But, in the Gospel according to Frankfurter, "this 'sovereign prerogative of choice' is not for judges." He would resolve all "reasonable doubt" in favor of the integrity of sister organs of government and the people to whom they answer. He would adhere "to the deepest of all our constitutional traditions, the dispersion of power," even though the immediate result might "offend his own generous heart's desire."[73]

The test of reasonableness.   Taken at face value, the foregoing statements are enough to warm the cockles of a curmudgeon's heart. Their accuracy, however, is on a par with the pitch of a barker at a circus sideshow. Note the use of the word "generous." Did Frankfurter consider it his mission to transform the Supreme Court into an eleemosynary institution, so that the Marble Palace would become a forum for the dispensation of largesse rather than justice? A federal Department of Public Welfare? Consider the reference to "reasonable doubt." The use of the word "reasonable" and its converse, "unreasonable," is favored by judges at all levels of the judicial hierarchy. No assertion better clinches an argument than one that labels the action or practice in controversy "reasonable" or "unreasonable." As the politician cloaks his personal preferences in the name of liberty, so the judge cloaks his in the name of reason. Patriotism may be the last refuge of a scoundrel, as Samuel Johnson observed. A judge's last refuge is his solipsistic perception of reasonableness.

Justice Brennan recently remarked—quite correctly—that "reasonableness generally has signified the most relaxed regime of judicial inquiry."[74] And though this statement suggests that the criterion of reasonableness is as pliant as a piece of bubble gum, it governs not only much of our constitutional law, but most of our tort, contract, and property law as well. Paradoxically, the use of "reasonableness" and related words and phrases is an attempt to create an objective, not a subjective, standard by which to judge human actions. (Unfortunately, the alternatives are equally lacking in precision: a set of rigidly codified rules, often of questionable applicability to a given situation, or an interpersonal comparison of subjective utilities.) The law of nuisance is an example of the test of reasonableness. Consider a person who, late of an evening, turns his radio dial to the emissions of a rock station. The *reasonable person test* (the conventional label is "reasonable man") stipulates that the judge, in light of all the circumstances, must weigh the reasonableness of the defendant's action against the plea for damages as reasonable persons would estimate them. Thus, each case is decided on its own merits. The *rigid rule test,* by contrast, might prohibit radio playing above a specified decibel level after 10:00 P.M.—clearly a silly rule for a person residing on a 160-acre farm or in a college dormitory, where everyone likes the music, and peace and quiet are as welcome as cockroaches or acne. The *subjective utility test* dictates that the personal quirks of the plaintiff should determine the outcome—that a person who intensely dislikes rock music should collect more in damages than someone who does not because his *subjective* loss of utility is greater. Thus, the problem becomes an evidentiary one: Whom should the jury believe and how are utilities to be compared? Considering these alternatives, the test of reasonableness, although it does not exude objectivity, seems to be the best that can be hoped for in an imperfect world.

An empirical analysis of judicial restraint. Let us return to Frankfurter and judicial restraint. Frankfurter was reputedly "wary" of judicial attempts to "impose Justice" on the community—attempts to deprive it of "the wisdom that comes from self-inflicted wounds" and "the strength that grows with the burden of responsibility." It was "his deepest conviction" that no group of judges is "wise enough or good enough" to wield such power. In his view, "humanitarian ends are served best" when the people "by a balance of power seek their own destiny." True to the "faith upon which democracy ultimately rests," Frankfurter left to the political process "the onus of building legal standards in the vacuum of doubt"—for only that people is free "who chooses for itself when choice must be made."[75]

The logic of these statements leaves much to be desired. I doubt that "self-inflicted wounds" produce much in the way of "wisdom." They may result in suicide, or a hangover, or lung cancer. At the societal level, experimentation is a luxury that government can rarely afford. Solutions, once adopted, quickly become as set as concrete. They cannot be erased like chalk on a blackboard. Americans might do things differently if given the chance to start from scratch in such areas as public welfare, unemployment, energy and transportation policy, and the conservation of natural resources. Unfortunately, the die is cast. We can tinker with the mechanism, but Frankenstein's monsters are a fact of life. To leave to the political process "the onus of building legal standards in the vacuum of doubt" would deny judges meaningful policy-making authority. The blind would lead the blind. Ignorance, if not blissful, would assuredly chart the path to the Promised Land. The nation's future would rest in the hands of legislative and executive officials. The fact that the public has chosen to invest its judges with the authority to make policy is, according to Frankfurter, a failure to be true to "the faith upon which democracy ultimately rests." Instead, the nation's fate should be entrusted to legislative and executive officials, even though surveys consistently show that politicians are viewed by the public as only slightly more trustworthy than used-car salesmen. (Among the most recent of such studies is a July 1975 Chilton Research Services Survey.)

Whether Frankfurter actually practiced what he preached can be determined by an analysis of his votes in cases where judicial restraint was exercised. Unlike many other legal principles, judicial restraint is amenable to empirical analysis. If it truly guides judicial policy making, it ought to be employed in a relatively evenhanded fashion, across the board. To ascertain whether this hypothesis is valid, we can analyze all the nonunanimous cases that concerned state economic regulation and the activity of the various federal regulatory commissions that were decided with a formal opinion during the first seven terms of the Warren Court (1953–1959).[76] These cases were chosen because judicial restraint is most susceptible of utilization in these types of cases. The voting behavior of only six of the Justices who sat on the Court between 1953 and 1959 is analyzed: Justice Frankfurter, and the two Justices who voted most frequently with him—John Marshall Harlan and Charles Whittaker—and the three Justices who most frequently disagreed with Frankfurter and Company—Hugo Black, William Douglas, and Earl Warren.

The following table shows the votes of these Justices in the state action cases. A pro-state vote is one that supports the action in question. As

Justice	Vote		
	Pro-state	Antistate	Percent pro
Frankfurter	18	19	49
Harlan	14	8	64
Whittaker	8	12	40
Black	20	16	56
Douglas	19	19	50
Warren	19	17	53

such, it constitutes deference to the state and is thereby compatible with the principle of judicial restraint. The pattern is virtually random. Each of the Justices could have flipped a coin and approximated these results. But note what happens when these state cases are divided into labor and business subsets:

Justice	Labor Cases			Business Cases		
	Pro-state	Antistate	Percent pro	Pro-state	Antistate	Percent pro
Frankfurter	10	1	91	8	18	31
Harlan	6	1	86	8	7	53
Whittaker	6	0	100	2	14	14
Black	1	9	10	19	7	73
Douglas	1	11	8	18	8	69
Warren	1	10	9	18	7	72

The data show that Frankfurter and friends supported the states when they regulated labor, but not when they regulated business. The pattern is precisely the opposite for Black, Douglas, and Warren. Strange, is it not?

Not really. The state's regulation in all 12 of the labor cases was antiunion. Consequently, a pro-state vote in any of these 12 cases was simultaneously antiunion. A pro-state vote in the business cases was simultaneously antibusiness in 20 of the 26 cases. In the other 6, the state's regulation supported business. The conclusion is inescapable: those Justices voted the way they did because of their attitudes toward business and labor. Frankfurter and associates are simply good economic conservatives—probusiness and antilabor. Just as clearly, Black, Douglas, and Warren are economic liberals—antibusiness and prolabor. What about judicial restraint? It provides a convenient rationale for supporting state action when such action supports a Justice's economic attitudes. But does it evenhandedly guide judicial policy making? Hardly.

The same pattern prevailed in the regulatory commission decisions. In the 56 cases decided during the first seven terms of the Warren Court, the Justices again split their votes in a random fashion. Warren supported the agencies 63 percent of the time; Whittaker, at the other extreme, supported them only 42 percent of the time. Labor regulation is the province of only one of these commissions, the National Labor Relations Board. With regard to the NLRB, the Justices voted as follows:

Justice	NLRB Prounion			NLRB Antiunion		
	Pro	Con	Percent pro	Pro	Con	Percent pro
Frankfurter	2	5	29	7	1	88
Harlan	0	5	0	4	2	67
Whittaker	0	5	0	5	1	83
Black	6	1	86	0	8	0
Douglas	6	1	86	0	8	0
Warren	7	0	100	3	5	38

The Conservatives opposed the NLRB's prounion decisions and supported the agency's antiunion decisions. The Liberals voted to the contrary. With regard to the agencies regulating business (such as the Interstate Commerce Commission, the Federal Trade Commission, and the
Federal Power Commission), consistency is again manifest:

Justice	Agency Probusiness			Agency Antibusiness		
	Pro	Con	Percent pro	Pro	Con	Percent pro
Frankfurter	12	2	86	8	15	35
Harlan	10	2	83	7	11	39
Whittaker	5	2	71	1	10	9
Black	3	11	21	20	1	95
Douglas	2	12	14	16	7	70
Warren	3	11	21	20	3	87

The Liberals were antibusiness; the Conservatives were probusiness.
The patterns displayed in these tables obviously do not occur by chance.
The consistently selective pattern of support and nonsupport clearly
indicates that judicial restraint did not motivate the Justices' votes. Judicial restraint was merely a convenient cloak with which to conceal their
personal policy preferences.

Was Justice Frankfurter, the untiring proponent of judicial restraint,
then guilty of deliberate deception? Was he a hypocrite who counseled
his colleagues to do as he said, not as he did? Certainly not. Was he guilty
of self-deception? Did his right hand not know what his left hand was
doing? Most assuredly. Homo sapiens' capacity for rationalizing their
druthers is limitless. Judges are no more immune from this proclivity
than the rest of us. They too believe their own rhetoric. Their failure, if

indeed it is a failure, is their inability to segregate their biases and predispositions from the murky provisions of the Constitution and from the argot of legislation.

Strict Construction

The other term used to putatively assure judicial objectivity is strict construction. Popularized more recently than judicial restraint, it made its ascendance during the hegemony of Richard M. Nixon. Given the general uneasiness that greeted the increasingly Liberal decisions of the last years of the Warren Court, Nixon's phrase struck a comforting chord. Nixon wisely refrained from attempting to give a precise definition of the phrase; rather he used it only to characterize the type of person he wanted to place on the federal bench. The issue that Nixon capitalized on was crime and lawlessness. He stated the matter well in the national address in which he nominated Lewis Powell and William Rehnquist to the Supreme Court: "I believe some Court decisions have gone too far in weakening the peace forces against the criminal forces in our society. The police forces . . . must not be denied the legal tools they need to protect the innocent from criminal elements."[77]

But this concern has little to do with strict construction. The term has two well-defined meanings. It can mean literal adherence to the provisions of the Constitution. For example, the First Amendment says "no law" shall be made "abridging the freedom of speech, or of the press; or the right of the people peaceably to assemble. . . ." According to Justices Hugo Black and William Douglas, this means *no* law—period. Freedom of speech and of the press cannot be restricted because Congress or a city council are concerned about subversive activities or the dissemination of obscene movies or books. The other meaning of strict construction pertains to the interpretation and application of criminal laws. If there is any ambiguity in the provisions of such a law—and, given the imprecision of the English language, there invariably is—such doubts are to be resolved in the defendant's favor. The reason is twofold. First, when an action is defined as criminal, those subject to the law ought to be clearly informed of what their illicit activity is. Second, because criminal penalties are sometimes severe and because of the stigma attached to persons convicted of crime, the definition of crime should be the responsibility of lawmakers, not judges.[78]

As an example of strict construction in the criminal law context, reference may be made to *United States* v. *Bass*.[79] Bass was convicted of possessing firearms in violation of the Omnibus Crime Control Act of 1968, which, among other things, made it a felony for "any person who . . . has been convicted . . . of a felony . . . and who receives, possesses, or transports in interstate commerce . . . any firearm."[80] The critical question was whether the term "interstate commerce" applies only to "transports," or whether it applies to "receives" and "possesses" as well. The government contended that the former interpretation was correct and offered no evidence of any interstate transaction. The Court, however, ruled that the provision's wording lacked clarity and that the intent of Congress was also unclear. Hence, the term "interstate commerce" must be understood to modify all three verbs, not merely "transports."

Was Nixon accurate in faulting the Warren Court for lack of strict construction? Not at all. During its last 11 terms (1958–1968), 26 of 28 First Amendment cases upheld the contention that government regulation violated freedom of expression. During the same period, 36 of 47 obscenity decisions favored the accused. With regard to the interpretation of federal criminal statutes, ambiguity was resolved favorably to the defendant in 23 of 32 instances.

If Nixon's indictment of the Warren Court was not supportable, it is sensible to assume that he intended strict construction to have something other than a literal definition. His concern with rising crime rates, the law-and-order posture assumed by Vice-President Agnew and Attorney General Mitchell, and his Administration's espousal of a "Southern strategy" strongly suggested a lessening of judicial support for individual freedom and human equality. The states should be allowed to do their own thing in such areas as race relations, and state and federal law enforcement officials should be given relatively free rein.

It is, of course, impolitic for a President, or anyone else for that matter, to admit this in so many words. We need to view our judges as dispassionate, objective, and unconcerned with policy making. Though reality may be to the contrary, wish fulfillment dictates the formulation of myth to cloak the fact that judges play God with our lives. The rhetoric and the slogans may come and go, but the myth abides.

NOTES

1. See, for example, Martin Shapiro's suggestions in his "Stability and Change in Judicial Decision Making: Incrementalism or Stare Decisis," *Law in Transition Quarterly* 2 (1965): 134–157.

2. 347 U.S. 483, number 20 in Harold J. Spaeth, *Classic and Current Decisions of the United States Supreme Court* (San Francisco: W. H. Freeman and Company, 1977).

3. In *Plessy* v. *Ferguson*, 163 U.S. 537, number 12 in *ibid.*

4. The Court did cite as authority for its ruling a pair of cases decided four years earlier in which black graduate students were denied facilities equal to

those afforded whites. *Sweatt* v. *Painter,* 339 U.S. 629; and *McLaurin* v. *Oklahoma State Regents,* 339 U.S. 637 (1950). In neither of these cases, however, did the Court deem it necessary to reexamine the separate but equal doctrine in order to grant relief to the black students.

5. 370 U.S. 421. By a vote of 6 to 1, the Court ruled that New York State's program of daily classroom prayers violated the establishment of religion clause in the First Amendment. The prayer, to be recited at the start of each school day, was composed by the Board of Regents—the ultimate authority on educational matters in New York State—and read as follows: "Almighty God, we acknowledge our dependence upon thee, and we beg thy blessings upon us, our parents, our teachers and our country."

6. As an illustration, see the discussion of the decisions concerning Louisiana's illegitimates in the section of this chapter headed "Distinguishing a Precedent."

7. 295 U.S. 602.

8. *Myers* v. *United States,* 272 U.S. 52 (1926).

9. *Jacobellis* v. *Ohio,* 378 U.S. 184 (1964), is a good example. By a vote of 6 to 3, the Court reversed the conviction of the manager of a movie theater for showing an allegedly obscene movie. But the majority could not agree on an opinion to support their decision. Brennan and Goldberg stated that the "contemporary community standards" to be applied to determine whether material was obscene was a single national standard. (In *Miller* v. *California,* 413 U.S. 15 [1973], number 45 in *Classic and Current Decisions,* the Court overruled this precedent, saying that "People in different states vary in their tastes and attitudes, and this diversity is not to be strangled by the absolutism of imposed uniformity." 413 U.S. 15, at 33.) Black and Douglas stated that the conviction of anyone "for exhibiting a motion picture abridges freedom of the press. . . ." 378 U.S. 184, at 196. Stewart stated that criminal obscenity laws are constitutionally limited to hard-core pornography, which "perhaps I could never succeed in intelligibly [defining]. . . . But I know it when I see it, and the motion picture involved in this case is not that." 378 U.S. 184, at 197. White, the remaining member of the majority, did not even try to explain his reasons for his vote. He simply concurred in the result without opinion.

10. *Levy* v. *Louisiana,* 391 U.S. 68.

11. *Labine* v. *Vincent,* 401 U.S. 532 (1971).

12. 406 U.S. 164.

13. In four of its seven succeeding decisions concerning illegitimates—none of which involved Louisiana's laws—the Court used *Levy* and/or *Weber* to vindicate the rights of illegitimates: *Gomez* v. *Perez,* 409 U.S. 535 (1973); *New Jersey WRO* v. *Cahill,* 411 U.S. 619 (1973); *Jimenez* v. *Weinberger,* 417 U.S. 628 (1974); and *Trimble* v. *Gordon,* 45 LW 4395 (1977). It used *Labine* to deny the illegitimates' claims in the other three: *Mathews* v. *Lucas,* 427 U.S. 495 (1976); *Norton* v. *Mathews,* 427 U.S. 524 (1976); and *Fiallo* v. *Bell,* 45 LW 4402 (1977).

14. *Frothingham* v. *Mellon,* 262 U.S. 447. The plaintiff sought to block the application of an act of Congress that provided money to the states for programs aimed at reducing maternal and infant mortality. She alleged that the appropriations authorized by this act would increase her federal tax burden and thereby take her property without due process of law.

15. *Flast* v. *Cohen,* 392 U.S. 83.

16. 384 U.S. 436, number 29 in *Classic and Current Decisions.*

17. 401 U.S. 222. The accused, indicted for selling heroin, had been questioned by the police when taken into custody, but he had not been told that he had a right to have an attorney present before being questioned. During the questioning, the accused made statements to the police that contradicted the testimony he gave at this trial. The majority held that "the shield provided by Miranda cannot be perverted into a license to use perjury by way of a defense, free from the risk of confrontation with prior inconsistent utterances. We hold, therefore, that petitioner's credibility was appropriately impeached by use of his earlier conflicting statements." 401 U.S. 222, at 226.

18. 417 U.S. 433 (1974). The suspect, arrested on a charge of rape, was informed prior to police questioning that he understood the crime for which he was arrested, that he did not want an attorney, that he understood his rights, and that he realized that anything he said could be used against him in court. However, he was not informed of his right, as an indigent, to be furnished counsel free of charge. During interrogation, he named an alibi witness whose statements while on the witness stand discredited the suspect's account of where he had been the night of the crime.   •

19. One authority has counted 105 instances where the Court overruled itself between 1810 and 1974. Henry J. Abraham, *The Judicial Process,* 3rd ed. (New York: Oxford University Press, 1975), p. 330.

20. 163 U.S. 537, number 12 in *Classic and Current Decisions.*

21. *Mapp* v. *Ohio,* 367 U.S. 643 (1961), number 21 in *ibid. Mapp* overruled *Wolf* v. *Colorado,* 338 U.S. 25 (1949), on the basis of *Rogers* v. *Richmond,* 365 U.S. 534 (1961). A more recent example of overruling a precedent in the name of *stare decisis* is *Oregon* v. *Corvallis Sand & Gravel Co.,* 50 L Ed 2d 550 (1977), in which the Court ruled that state rather than federal law governs disputes over the extent of a state's ownership of riverbeds within its boundaries. In 1973, the Court had stated that such controversies must be resolved on the basis of federal law: *Bonelli Cattle Co.* v. *Arizona,* 414 U.S. 313. The majority justified overruling *Bonelli* on the basis that "since one system of resolution of property disputes has been adhered to from 1845 until 1973, and the other only for the past three years, a return to the former would more closely conform to the expectations of property owners than would adherence to the latter." 50 L Ed 2d 550, at 565.

22. 416 U.S. 600 (1974), at 627–628 (footnote omitted).

23. 347 U.S. 483 (1954), number 20 in *Classic and Current Decisions.*

24. *Hepburn* v. *Griswold,* 8 Wallace 603 (1870); *Knox* v. *Lee,* 12 Wallace 457 (1871); and *Parker* v. *Davis,* 12 Wallace 461 (1871). In order to finance the Civil War, Congress made paper money not backed by gold or silver legal tender in the payment of debts between private persons. Once issued, these greenbacks became worth less than gold or silver dollars. In *Hepburn,* the Court ruled the congressional action unconstitutional insofar as it applied to debts incurred before the law was passed. If the *Hepburn* decision had stood, many persons would have faced financial ruin if they had had to repay their borrowings in cold, hard cash.

25. See David W. Rohde and Harold J. Spaeth, *Supreme Court Decision Making* (San Francisco: W. H. Freeman and Company, 1976), pp. 140-145.

26. 370 U.S. 195.

27. 398 U.S. 235 (1970).

28. *Id.* at 240 (footnote omitted).

29. *Id.* at 241 (footnotes omitted).

30. *Id.*

31. *Id.* at 241–242.

32. *Id.* at 256.

33. *Id.* at 255.

34. 421 U.S. 397.

35. 407 U.S. 67, number 38 in *Classic and Current Decisions.*

36. *Mitchell* v. *W. T. Grant Co.,* 416 U.S. 600 (1974).

37. *Id.* at 635.

38. *North Georgia Finishing Inc.* v. *Di-Chem,* 419 U.S. 601.

39. *Id.* at 606.

40. *Id.* at 608.

41. *Id.* at 619.

42. *Wesberry* v. *Sanders,* 376 U.S. 1 (1964).

43. *Reynolds* v. *Sims,* 377 U.S. 533 (1964), number 24 in *Classic and Current Decisions.*

44. *Furman* v. *Georgia,* 408 U.S. 238. Cf. *Gregg* v. *Georgia,* 428 U.S. 153; and *Woodson* v. *North Carolina,* 428 U.S. 280 (1976)—number 52 in *Classic and Current Decisions.*

45. *Roe* v. *Wade,* 410 U.S. 113; and *Doe* v. *Bolton,* 410 U.S. 179 (1973)—number 42 in *Classic and Current Decisions.* As a result, no state may flatly prohibit abortions during the first six months of pregnancy.

46. *Bank of the United States* v. *Deveaux,* 5 Cranch 84.

47. *L C & C R. Co.* v. *Letson,* 2 Howard 497.

48. *Id.* at 554.

49. *Justice Daniel Dissenting* (Cambridge, Mass.: Harvard University Press, 1964), pp. 218–219.

50. 1 Cranch 137 (1803), number 2 in *Classic and Current Decisions.*

51. *Id.* at 177.

52. *Id.*

53. *Id.* at 177–178.

54. *Id.* at 180.

55. *Id.*

56. Quoted in Max Lerner, ed., *The Mind and Faith of Justice Holmes* (New York: Modern Library, 1943), pp. 51–52.

57. 4 Wheaton 316 (1819), at 407, 415, number 5 in *Classic and Current Decisions.*

58. *United States* v. *Foster Lumber Co.,* 50 L Ed 2d 199 (1976), at 212.

59. 36 Stat 825, 18 USCA §398, Section 2.

60. *Hoke* v. *United States,* 227 U.S. 308 (1913).

61. *Caminetti* v. *United States,* 242 U.S. 470 (1917).

62. *Mortensen* v. *United States,* 322 U.S. 369 (1944).

63. *Cleveland* v. *United States,* 329 U.S. 14 (1946), at 19, 26.

64. *Rosado* v. *Wyman,* 397 U.S. 397 (1970), at 412, 413.

65. 422 U.S. 454, 45 L Ed 2d 319 (1975).

66. 45 L Ed 2d 319, at 324, footnote 2.

67. *Id.* at 331.

68. *Id.*

69. *Id.* at 340.

70. The constitutionality of the Civil Rights Act of 1964 was upheld in *Heart of Atlanta Motel* v. *United States,* 379 U.S. 241 (1964); and *Katzenbach* v. *McClung,* 379 U.S. 294 (1964)—number 26 in *Classic and Current Decisions.*

71. *Hamm* v. *City of Rock Hill,* 379 U.S. 306 (1964), at 319, 320, 321.

72. *Constitutional Politics* (New York: Holt, Rinehart and Winston, 1960), p. 243.

73. *Justices Black and Frankfurter: Conflict in the Court* (Chicago: University of Chicago Press, 1961), pp. 130–131.

74. *United States Trust Co.* v. *New Jersey,* 52 L Ed 2d 92 (1977), at 130, footnote 17.

75. Mendelson, *op. cit.,* note 73 *supra,* p. 131.

76. These data and their analysis are taken from Harold J. Spaeth, "The Judicial Restraint of Mr. Justice Frankfurter—Myth or Reality?" *American Journal of Political Science* 8 (February 1964): 22-38.

77. *New York Times,* October 22, 1971.

78. In *Huddleston* v. *United States,* 415 U.S. 814 (1974), at 831, the Court stated the limit on the resolution of doubt in the accused's favor: "Zeal in forwarding these laudable policies, however, must not be permitted to shadow the understanding that 'sound rules of statutory construction exist to discover and not to direct the congressional will.' . . . Although penal laws are to be construed strictly, they 'ought not to be construed so strictly as to defeat the obvious intention of the legislature.' "

79. 404 U.S. 336 (1971).

80. 18 USC App. Sec. 1202(a).

The Representative Character of the Supreme Court

Does the Supreme Court, in the proverbial words of Mr. Dooley, follow the election returns? This important question remains the subject of an on-going debate.[1] The argument that the Court adjusts its policy making to conform with the objectives of the governing coalition has merit, as does the contrary view. But in one respect the question is inapposite. The Framers never intended any part of the governmental system to be purely representative, least of all the federal judiciary. Given this fact, no attempt is made here to ascertain the extent to which the Court has been in or out of touch with public wants. Rather the focus is on the question of whether the Court has *addressed* the major issues that have convulsed American society (not *how* the Court resolved the major controversies that it did confront). This chapter begins with a specification of some of the difficulties involved in attempting to determine how representative a decision-making body is. In estimating the extent to which the High Bench has grappled with the issues confronting American society, reference will be made to the record of the Roosevelt, Warren, Burger, and Taney Courts.

The choices Presidents make in filling the vacancies that occur on the High Bench determine the degree to which the Court will reflect public opinion. What characteristics do appointing Presidents look for in their nominees? What motivates Presidents to choose this person rather than that one? To what extent do the Justices reflect the wishes of the President who nominated them?

THE CONCEPT OF REPRESENTATION

Representation is a slippery concept. There are three different styles of representation. A representative can function as a delegate, or as a trustee, or as a symbol of the members of his constituency. Delegates act with a minimum of discretion; they merely do their constituents' bidding, as their constituents' instrument for getting things done. Trustees, by contrast, exercise discretion. They filter the opinions of their constituents through their own perception of the common good. Symbolic representation has as its goal the microcosmic re-creation of the larger society, so that its representative bodies mirror the characteristics of the body politic.

These styles of representation, however, are equivocal. Does the delegate respond to all his constituents, or only to those who voted for him? Is a campaign contributor entitled to more favorable treatment than a mere voter? What happens if constituent opinion is divided? By what criteria is the trustee's judgment superior to that of his constituents? Does the mere fact of election make him a philosopher king? How is the common good, the public interest, to be defined? What are to be the goals of symbolic representation? Why these and not others? Does possession of certain traits guarantee congruence with group interests? Which segment of the farming community should be represented: sharecroppers or agribusiness? Is the black representative a spokesperson for the black bourgeoisie or for the residents of the ghetto?

Beyond the matter of representative style, how can a representative know what the "public" wants? By studying public opinion polls? By listening to whoever hollers the loudest? A candidate's supporters do not speak with a single voice. Nor does the membership of even a sharply defined group. Assuming that the public's wants are clearly defined, should the criterion be "whatever Lola wants, Lola gets"? Don't minorities and dissenters have rights? What about those who have no opinion? What if today's desire is tomorrow's dislike? Is the resolution of a public policy issue like a theater ticket—good for Saturday's matinee performance only?

The answers to these and related questions are the business of political philosophers, constitution makers, and the representatives of the public. Though the questions (and their answers) are of major importance, they do not admit of objective resolution. As such, they are beyond the scope of this book. But within our range of concern is the effect the policy making of the Court has had upon the major issues confronting the nation at various points in time. The point of this discussion is not that the Court has or has not represented public sentiment. Given the nature of our constitutional system, that is not the Court's *raison d'être*. What is important is whether the Court has addressed the issues that, at a given point in time, were of major concern to Americans generally. On this score, the Court rates high marks, as the following paragraphs make clear.

The Roosevelt Court

Undoubtedly the most frequently cited instance of judicial resistance to public opinion is Franklin Delano Roosevelt's Court-packing proposal of 1937, which produced "the switch in time that saved nine." For four full years, FDR had watched his New Deal reforms go down the judicial tube. Four stern-faced guardians of the old order had stalwartly defended the principles of laissez-faire economics, of rugged individualism and unfettered free enterprise. These four—Justices Willis Van Devanter, James C. McReynolds, George Sutherland, and Pierce Butler—with like-minded compatriots, had held sway since the early 1920's. Beginning in 1930, their compatriots were Justice Owen J. Roberts and, on occasion, Chief Justice Charles Evans Hughes.

Roosevelt was unlucky. On the average a Supreme Court Justice dies, retires, or resigns every 22 months. But more than double that amount of time had elapsed during Roosevelt's first term without a vacancy. Every President before and since has appointed at least one Justice during his first term in office, except for James Monroe, who could not appoint anyone until his second term; William Henry Harrison, who lived only one month after his inauguration; and Zachary Taylor, who lived less than half a term after his election. At the other extreme, Taft appointed six Justices during his one term in office. Roosevelt eventually made a total of nine appointments, second only to Washington's eleven. But early in 1937, FDR's score was zero.[2]

The Four Horsemen and Roberts were clearly out of step with the general public. Roosevelt had ridden roughshod over his opponent in the 1936 election like no Presidential candidate had before or has since. Even George McGovern's 17 electoral votes in 1972 were more than double those received by Alf Landon. Huge Democratic majorities existed in both House and Senate. Roosevelt, increasingly frustrated, made his move in February 1937. His bill to "reorganize" the federal judiciary was a barefaced Court-packing scheme. Any federal judge with ten years' service who failed to resign at age 70 could be supplemented (not supplanted) by an additional appointee to the septuagenarian's court. FDR's plan was unquestionably constitutional—Congress had altered the Court's size on seven previous occasions—but it was thoroughly impolitic. The Senate Judiciary Committee reported the bill out unfavorably in June, and one month later the full Senate effectively rejected it by sending it back to the Judiciary Committee.[3]

But though FDR lost this battle, he won the war. Between March and June, five major New Deal reforms were upheld as a result of a switch by Roberts and Hughes.[4] Then, in May, at the end of the Court's term, 78-year-old Willis Van Devanter resigned after 27 years on the High Tribunal. The fight was over. During the next six years, Roosevelt completely reconstituted the Court with but a single exception: Justice Roberts.

The Court's refusal to accede to the New Deal reforms did not result from its refusal to come to grips with the issue of economic reform. The overwhelming preponderance of the Court's decisions throughout the 1930's concerned the right of government, state and federal, to regulate economic activities of one sort or another. At no other time did the Court demonstrate such a single-minded preoccupation with a particular matter. The fact that the Court locked horns with the Roosevelt Administration made it unrepresentative in one sense: it refused to knuckle under, to place its seal of approval on the New Deal. It did, however, address the issue; it neither ignored it, nor passed the buck to other decision makers. The Court, at least, was responsive, even though it played a tune discordant to the ears of FDR and his supporters.

The Warren Court

Changes in the Court's personnel since the late 1950's reveal another facet of the Court's representational character. In 1958, the Court was composed of three Liberals (Douglas, Warren, and Brennan), three Conservatives (Frankfurter, Whittaker, and Harlan), one New Dealer (Clark), one Populist (Black), and the Moderate Stewart.* Of the three major values, two were paramount: freedom and New Deal economics. With regard to freedom, no built-in majority existed. The three Liberals, plus Black, were supportive. Opposed were the three Conservatives and Tom Clark. The balance of power rested with Justice Stewart. Consequently, not much transpired. The burning freedom issue, internal security and alleged security risks, continued to flame as it had since the late 1940's. On this matter, the Court had waffled. Initially supportive, the Court turned hostile to governmental efforts to ease the Red Menace in the mid-1950's before reverting to its original posture.[5]

By contrast, with regard to the value of New Deal economics a built-in majority did exist: the three Liberals, plus Black and Clark, supported prounion, antibusiness, and procompetition policies. The third value, equality, was not the subject of substantial litigation. *Brown* v. *Board of Education* had been decided in 1954; its sequel, which enunciated the "with all deliberate speed" formula, was decided one year later.[6] The Court, of course, was still receiving flak for outlawing segregation, but it avoided additional criticism on this score by giving responsibility for the implementation of its decree to the federal district courts.

---

*The labels "Liberal," "Conservative," "Moderate," and so on are defined in Chapter 5, in the section headed "Value Systems." The terms "freedom" and "New Deal economics" are also defined in Chapter 5, in the section on "Values."

All in all, then, the Court of the late 1950's was not out of sync with society at large. His Cherubic Majesty, Dwight D. Eisenhower, presided over a placid people and a quiescent government—but not for long. In the spring of 1962 Whittaker resigned, and was followed by Frankfurter four months later. President Kennedy replaced them with Byron White and Arthur Goldberg. These changes in the line-up proved portentous; Justice Harlan was now alone in right field as the Court's only remaining Conservative. Goldberg gave the Liberals additional punch, while White doubled the Court's strength down the middle.

For the first time in history, the Court had a profreedom majority. A constitutional revolution, on a par with that of the late 1930's, was at hand. Whereas that of the 1930's fundamentally altered property rights, that of the 1960's virtually rewrote the First Amendment and increased the rights of persons accused of crime. Furthermore, whereas the New Deal upheaval legitimized governmental intrusions into what previously had been matters of purely private concern, that of the 1960's proved just the reverse: government could no longer trench upon the rights and liberties of its citizens. Accordingly, the right to counsel was extended to all persons accused of a felony;[7] law enforcement officials were made more subject to the rule of law;[8] many loyalty oaths and the compulsory disclosure of organizational affiliations were voided;[9] the major provisions of the Fourth, Fifth, Sixth, and Eighth Amendments were made binding upon the states, and the protections they afforded were defined more broadly;[10] freedom of expression became the rule and censorship the exception;[11] and additional bricks were added to the wall separating church and state.[12]

The Johnson landslide of 1964 pushed the Liberal tide to flood stage. The replacement of Goldberg with Abe Fortas in 1965 produced no alteration in the Court's policy-making orientation: Tweedledum superseded Tweedledee. Five Justices continued to support the value of freedom and six continued to support New Deal economics. But with the seating of Thurgood Marshall in place of Tom Clark at the start of the 1967 term, the Liberals commanded an absolute majority with regard to the value of equality as well. The fact that the first black member of the Court occupied so crucial a position is serendipitously symbolic. Although Stewart or White had provided a necessary fifth vote in a number of equality-based issues (such as sit-in demonstrations and reapportionment) before Marshall's appointment, a solid hard core of Liberals was now in the driver's seat.

The new regime lasted less than two years, from October 1967 to May 14, 1969, when Fortas resigned. One month later, the Court adjourned. Its last item of business was acceptance of the resignation of Earl Warren and the swearing in of his successor, Warren Burger. The Liberal tide had ebbed. A majority no longer existed on the Liberal side of any of the three major values. The three remaining Liberals (Douglas, Brennan, and Marshall) had Black's vote on freedom and New Deal economics. But four votes do not a majority make. The balance of power had shifted virtually overnight to White and Stewart. Out in right field, the beleaguered Harlan, who had been the lone Conservative voice for seven long years, now had the company of the new Chief Justice.

The Burger Court

Within six months of his inauguration, Nixon had successfully filled one vacancy, and there was still one to go. The replacement of Fortas proved no easy task, however. The Democrats controlled the Senate, and Nixon's nominees, Clement Haynsworth and G. Harrold Carswell, were too much for either Northern Democrats or liberal Republicans to stomach. They were fully aware of Haynsworth's impropriety in participating in cases in which he had a financial interest when he was a federal appeals court judge and Carswell's racist background and undistinguished judicial record. Not until May 12, 1970, was Fortas's seat occupied, thereby ending the longest vacancy since the Civil War. The new occupant, Harry Blackmun, brought the Conservatives into equal balance with the Liberals.

Illness forced Black and Harlan to resign within a week of one another in September 1971. A minimum of controversy, relative to that attending the nominations of Haynsworth and Carswell, surrounded the confirmation of Nixon's selections, Lewis Powell and William Rehnquist. When they took their seats in January 1972, the Court became four-ninths Nixonite: Nixonite not only in the sense that Nixon had placed four Justices on the Court (the first President to do so in his first term of office since Warren Harding), but more importantly, in the sense that these four persons espoused a value system that reflected that of their nominator.† In a span of two and one-half years, a controlling Liberal

---

† In a conversation we had several years ago, my colleague, Joseph A. Schlesinger, perceptively pointed out to me that the label "Burger Court" or "Nixon Court" is something of a misnomer. A more accurate label, he said, would be the "McCarthy Court," named after the erstwhile Minnesota Senator and perennial Presidential candidate. Schlesinger argued, quite correctly, that were it not for the bitterly divisive internecine warfare between the McCarthyites and the supporters of Hubert Humphrey for the Democratic Presidential nomination in 1968, which culminated in the disastrous Chicago Convention, Humphrey rather than Nixon would have won the Presidency. As it was, Nixon barely squeaked by with a popular-vote plurality of barely 500,000, compared with the winning candidate's average plurality of more than 6¾ million in the ten previous Presidential elections. Nixon, moreover, garnered only 43.4 percent of the popular vote, the lowest of any President since the three-cornered race of 1912. Accepting the accuracy of Schlesinger's analysis—and undoubtedly tens of thousands of idealistic liberal Democrats (righteously wrathful over the denouement that occurred inside as well as outside the convention hall) sat on their hands and/or undermined the efforts of the regular Democrats to unite the party against the law-and-order rhetoric of Nixon and the Republicans—the moral of this tale is that the best way to ensure the *least* preferable outcome in American politics is to take a rigidly dogmatic stance on an issue or candidate.

majority was replaced by one that fell only a single vote short of Conservative control.

This rapid shift in the Court's policy-making orientation arguably reflected public sensibilities reasonably well. Nixon ended eight years of Democratic occupancy of the White House, but the Republicans failed to win control of either the Senate or the House of Representatives. Even his landslide victory of 1972 did not carry with it a Republican majority in either house of Congress. This division of control also characterizes the Court. The Liberal policies of the Warren Court have not been overturned; nor have they been expanded. Rather, the overall approach of the Burger Court is best described as moderation, or moderate conservatism. But the moderation does not result from refusal to decide the policy issues of the day (with one exception: it declined to decide on the constitutionality of the Vietnam War). No more than its predecessors does the Burger Court shirk responsibility. Its moderation is rather a result of a balance between Liberal and Conservative policies: it upheld the First Amendment right of the press to publish classified government documents (the Pentagon Papers[13]), yet it also upheld suppression of pornography;[14] it upheld the prohibition of a jail sentence without representation by counsel,[15] but decided against a lessening of restrictions upon the activities of law enforcement officers;[16] it held the nondiscretionary use of capital punishment to be unconstitutional,[17] but restricted the indiscriminate use of cross-district busing.[18]

The Burger Court, moreover, has not hesitated to consider controversies largely or wholly alien to those that confronted the Warren Court: sex discrimination,[19] environmental protection,[20] the status of juveniles,[21] abortion,[22] debtors' rights,[23] and, by no means least, the Watergate Tapes controversy.[24]

The Taney Court

The willingness of the Court to address issues of major moment is not unique to the last half century. The manner in which the Court has resolved such issues may not have "represented public opinion" (whatever each of those words means), but most assuredly the Court has been responsive. There have undoubtedly been occasions when the Court might have been more politic—when discretion would have been the better part of valor. A notable example was the Dred Scott decision, by which the Justices hoped to resolve the constitutional controversy over slavery.[25] Instead, the Justices poured salt, not salve, on the open wound. The die was thereby cast. Ineluctably the nation moved toward civil war.

Even so, the value systems of the Justices who sat on the Court from the mid-1840's until the late 1850's were probably shared by the vast majority of their fellow citizens. What divided the Court then were various aspects of federalism—the power relationships that ought to prevail between the national government and the states—and various issues relating to property rights. These matters were of major concern to the Framers of the Constitution; they were the root of the political controversies of the first half of the nineteenth century. They were also matters that were systematically treated in the writings of Thomas Jefferson and Alexander Hamilton. Although other minds made signal contributions to the growth and development of the American constitutional system, "Hamiltonian" and "Jeffersonian" were and are the labels most commonly employed to distinguish the protagonists of the period 1787–1861.

On the basis of the theoretical framework and the methodological techniques discussed in Chapter 5, we can establish that the following were the major issues decided by the Court of the 1840's and 1850's (the Taney Court): the jurisdiction of the federal judiciary vis-à-vis that of the states; whether the federal government or the states ought to regulate various types of business activity; the scope of the contract clause of the Constitution, which forbids the states to enact any "law impairing the obligation of contracts"; the adjudication of titles to land in the public domain; patent claims; the scope of the Supreme Court's decisional authority; the compensation claims of employees of the federal government; and the finality of a jury's verdict.

Although other issues also divided the Court during the period preceding the Civil War—admiralty and tariff cases, rules of judicial procedure, and civil liberties—they were the subject of but a small proportion of the Court's decisions. Interestingly enough, during the entire history of the Taney Court, from 1837 to the beginning of the Civil War, only sixteen cases related even peripherally to the matter of slavery. And in nine of those cases the Court's decision was unanimous. The other civil liberties cases did not concern the First Amendment, about which Jefferson had written so eloquently. They pertained, rather, to the legal competence of women and governmental taking of property—matters that were as much (or as little, in the case of women) a part of the Jeffersonian tradition as they were of the Hamiltonian tradition.

The major issues, however, are interrelated and reveal a rather consistent pattern of voting on the part of the Taney Court Justices: nationalistic tendencies, coupled with support for business and vested property rights, as opposed to a states' rights, antibusiness, and anti-special privilege stance. The former posture comports with Hamiltonianism; the latter comports with Jeffersonianism. Accordingly, the Hamiltonian Justices supported expansion of the power of the federal judiciary, while opposing expansion of that of the states. They also supported federal rather than state regulation of business. The contract clause should be strictly construed; otherwise the states would be able to meddle with vested property rights. The Hamiltonians similarly regarded land titles as sacred. These cases involved Spanish or Mexican land grants in Texas,

California, and what had been the Louisiana Purchase. The Jeffersonians wanted these grants voided and the lands made part of the public domain. The yeomanry—God's chosen people, according to Jefferson—would thereby benefit rather than the speculators. With regard to patents, Hamilton himself founded the Society for Establishing Useful Manufactures so that patents and the economic benefits accruing therefrom would be assiduously protected. As for the authority of the Supreme Court, judicial review was championed by the Federalists, Hamilton's party, and was just as bitterly opposed by Jefferson and his friends. (The legacy of *Marbury* v. *Madison* was obviously still a live issue fifty years after Marshall's decision.)

The issues of the compensation claims of federal employees and the finality of a jury's verdict were less obviously part of the Hamiltonian-Jeffersonian conflict; but the voting of the Justices indicates that they were—and quite reasonably so. The elitist Hamiltonians considered public office the exclusive province of the "natural aristocracy" of persons of "proved competence." By contrast, Jefferson's political progeny, the Jacksonians, based appointments to federal office upon their belief in the competence of the common man. Nor should one expect a Hamiltonian Justice to be particularly respectful of the verdict of a group of locally empaneled jurors chosen more or less by lot.

Whether the Justices of the 1840's and 1850's were representative of the proportion of Hamiltonians and Jeffersonians in the country at large is anybody's guess. These proportions, like those of today's Liberals, Moderates, and Conservatives, undoubtedly changed from one day to the next, or at least from one issue to the next. Again, what is significant is that the Justices addressed themselves to resolution of the major issues that confronted society, and that they did so then, as the Justices do now, on the basis of value systems that were inherent in the culture, traditions, and society of which they were a part.

Judges as American Society's Professional Decision Makers

For better or for worse, apart from the judiciary, our government is basically a negative, do-nothing system. The fact that the Constitution is the world's longest-enduring national constitution is irrefutable evidence that the system has worked for the better. The frequent inability of Congress and the President to cooperate in steering the ship of state does not mean that decisions are not made. But the judges are able—and usually ready and willing as well. Consequently, they, more than the legislators or bureaucrats, are America's professional decision makers. Judges, of course, do depend on legislators for the enactment of statutes and on bureaucrats to make rules and to adjudicate matters that affect persons in myriad ways. But their decision making is subject to scrutiny at all levels of the judicial system, which scrutiny is most authoritative when exercised by the Supreme Court. Consequently, Harry Truman simply overstated his responsibilities when he placed on his desk the sign, "The Buck Stops Here." It does not. He had the right city, but the wrong address. Not 1600 Pennsylvania Avenue. Rather One First Street, NE.

The fact that the Justices are lifetime appointees making basic policies does not appear especially bothersome even to those who are supportive of participatory democracy. A recent example will suffice. People's Lobby is a California-based, Ralph Nader-type citizens' group. Among their current objectives is an amendment to the Constitution to incorporate a national initiative and recall provision. The purpose of the proposed amendment, according to People's Lobby, is to further self-government by allowing citizens, through the device of the petition, "to write and pass their own laws," and to "remove elected officials from office before their terms expire when those in power fail to respond to the needs of the people."

Note that recall is limited to "elected officials." Federal judges are thereby excluded. The proposed amendment also includes an equally significant restriction on the scope of the initiative process: "An initiative measure may not be submitted to alter or amend the Constitution of the United States." But whether a given initiative measure "alters or amends" the Constitution is not exactly self-evident. For example, Congress could abolish the income tax simply by repealing the provisions of the Internal Revenue Code. The banning of child labor, the subject of a proposed constitutional amendment during the 1920's, was eventually realized through an act of Congress—the Fair Labor Standards Act of 1938. Feminist efforts to outlaw sex discrimination through ratification of the Equal Rights Amendment could also be realized by the passage of state and federal legislation, some of which, such as the Equal Pay Act of 1964, is already on the statute books.

Consequently, if the People's Lobby proposal should become the Twenty-seventh or Twenty-eighth Amendment—a most unlikely prospect—it would not advance the cause of representative government very far. Whether or not an approved initiative measure altered or amended the Constitution would still require resolution. Who will make such a determination? The people? Their representatives?

Guess again.

WHOM SHOULD PRESIDENTS APPOINT TO THE COURT?

The extent to which the Supreme Court may reflect public opinion depends upon Presidential choice in filling the vacancies that occur on the High Bench. Even though the appointing President's nominees may reflect public sentiment—as appears to have been the case with those of Franklin Roosevelt—there is no guarantee that they will continue to be representative if the succeeding President pursues a different set of policies and goals. Presidents have a freer hand in filling vacancies on the Supreme Court than they do in filling other offices (except for Cabinet positions, where they have a very free hand). This does not necessarily mean that whomever the President wants, the President gets. Nixon wanted Clement Haynsworth, a federal court of appeals judge, to replace Abe Fortas, who had resigned in May 1969. But Nixon did not get Haynsworth, nor did he get G. Harrold Carswell, who was also a federal court of appeals judge, whom he nominated after the Senate rejected Haynsworth.[26]

The Senate must confirm the President's nominees to major federal offices, and on twenty-seven occasions—including the nominations of Haynsworth and Carswell—they have refused to do so. At an earlier point in time, Presidents had an additional weapon at their command: the recess appointment. When the Senate was not in session, a President could appoint an individual to office and the appointment would continue until the end of the next congressional session. Some fifteen Justices have been so appointed, but it was Dwight Eisenhower who raised the recess appointment to the level of a fine art. Prior to Eisenhower's Administration, only two recess appointees had actually taken their seats on the High Bench before confirmation, and one of these was rejected: John Rutledge in 1795. Three of Eisenhower's appointees did so, however: Chief Justice Warren in 1953, William Brennan in 1956, and Potter Stewart in 1958. All three, of course, were confirmed, but not without considerable grumbling amongst the senators about how the President was presenting them with a *fait accompli.* But the recess appointment is now a thing of the past. Since 1963, Congress has subscribed to one of Parkinson's Laws: work expands to fill available time. Accordingly, Congress remains in session virtually 365 days a year instead of only six months or so.[27]

Characteristics of Presidential Nominees

Party affiliation. The most obvious characteristics of Presidential appointees to the Supreme Court are that all of them have been men and all have been attorneys. However, nothing in the Constitution or federal statutes requires either characteristic. The next most obvious characteristic is political party affiliation. Through the appointment of John Paul Stevens, 89 of the 101 men who have sat on the Supreme Court have been of the same political party as the President who appointed them. The first President to cross party lines was Tyler, a Whig, who appointed Samuel Nelson, a Democrat, in 1845. Tyler may have crossed party lines in desperation. He tried five times to appoint Whigs, including one nominee whom he appointed twice, but because of conflict between himself and a majority of the senators, the Senate adamantly refused confirmation. Tyler thus goes down in history as the President who was most often rejected. Another Whig President, Millard Fillmore, fared almost as poorly: three of his four nominees bit the dust. The one Fillmore nominee who did pass muster, Benjamin Curtis, was the only Whig ever to sit on the High Bench.

Democrats have fared much better than Republicans in receiving appointments from Presidents of the opposite party. In addition to Tyler's appointment of Nelson, nine other Democrats have been appointed by Republican Presidents. Three were appointed by William Howard Taft. The Democrats appointed by Taft were all Southerners, however. Edward D. White, from Louisiana, was promoted to Chief Justice, and Horace Lurton and Joseph Lamar, from Tennessee and Georgia, respectively, became Associate Justices. The only Democrats to favor Republicans were Franklin Roosevelt, who promoted Harlan Stone to Chief Justice in 1941, and Harry Truman, who appointed his senatorial colleague, Harold Burton, in 1946.

Of the 27 persons who have been nominated but failed of senatorial confirmation, an even higher proportion have been of the same party as the President who nominated them: 26 of 27. The one exception was another poor Whig, John J. Crittenden, whom John Quincy Adams nominated shortly before his term of office expired. Accordingly, fully one-third of the rejected nominees were Whigs. The proportion of nominees, by party affiliation, that were confirmed is striking: Whigs, one of 10 (10 percent); Federalists, 13 of 15 (87 percent); Democrats, 50 of 57 (88 percent); Republicans, 38 of 47 (81 percent). Confirmations total 102 because Charles Evans Hughes, a Republican, was confirmed twice. He resigned in 1916 to accept his party's nomination for President. He returned to the Court fourteen years later as Chief Justice.

Other considerations.   Presidents, then, clearly prefer to appoint members of their own party to vacancies on the Supreme Court. But other considerations also play a part—geography, for example. As with American politics generally, where candidates for office hang their hats is a matter of some importance. It would not behoove a President to favor unduly one part of the country rather than another. A Court dominated by New Englanders would not find favor west of the Hudson. Nor would one packed with "good old boys" meet approbation north of the Mason-Dixon line. Some geographical spread is therefore desirable. Accordingly, 31 of the 50 states have been represented on the Court by one or more of their residents (that is, resident when appointed). New York leads with a dozen, followed by Ohio and Massachusetts with nine and eight, respectively. Indeed, New York has had at least one resident on the Court during all but twenty-eight years between 1789 and 1976. From February 1932 to July 1938, three of the nine Justices were New Yorkers. The years without a New Yorker would be only 25½ were it not for internecine warfare among New York Democrats. In 1893, Grover Cleveland nominated William Hornblower, who had previously crossed swords with the powerful senator from New York, David B. Hill. Hill persuaded his Senate colleagues to reject Hornblower. Cleveland then nominated Wheeler Peckham, an anti-Tammany Hall Democrat, who had figured prominently in the successful prosecution and conviction of Boss Tweed twenty years earlier. Hill again prevailed upon his colleagues to reject Peckham. Cleveland thereupon selected Edward White of Louisiana. The Senate confirmed him the same day he was nominated.

Regionally, the Northeast (New York, Massachusetts, Pennsylvania, New Jersey, Connecticut, Maine, and New Hampshire) has contributed 35 members. The South (all the states of the Confederacy except Arkansas and Florida) has contributed 25; the Midwest (Ohio, Illinois, Indiana, Iowa, Michigan, Minnesota, and Kansas), 22; the Border States (Kentucky, Maryland, and Missouri), 12; and the Far West (California, Wyoming, Colorado, Utah, and Arizona), 7.

Apart from geographical considerations, Presidents have paid some attention to religion, ethnicity, and race. Except for the period 1949 to 1956, there has been a Roman Catholic on the Court since 1898. The first Jew was appointed in 1916 and there was at least one on the Court until 1969, when Abe Fortas resigned. The one and only black, Thurgood Marshall, took his seat in 1967.

The foregoing considerations are essentially political, as were the following nominations. Abraham Lincoln nominated Stephen J. Field of California midway during the Civil War to help cement the ties of California and the Far West to the union. Franklin Roosevelt promoted the highly regarded Republican, Harlan Stone, to Chief Justice on the eve of World War II to promote national unity and to overcome the popular perception of himself as a partisan President. Richard Nixon, as part of his Southern strategy, nominated two Southerners, Clement Haynsworth and G. Harrold Carswell, to fill the Fortas vacancy. Nixon's efforts came to naught when the Senate rejected them both. Nixon, however, partially realized his objective when the appointment of Lewis Powell of Virginia was confirmed in 1971.

A *sine qua non* of all appointments to the Court is a measure of professional eminence, either as a lawyer, judge, or public servant. Nominees with less than distinguished credentials are carefully scrutinized by the Senate. A deficiency in this respect may be the basis for a vote against confirmation, as when the Senate rejected G. Harrold Carswell. Presidents, accordingly, nominate persons with distinguished backgrounds, especially in the public service. Indeed, all but three of the 101 Justices have had an extensive history of partisan political activity. The only exceptions were George Shiras at the end of the nineteenth century and Harry Blackmun and John Paul Stevens. Blackmun and Stevens, however, had spent eleven and five years, respectively, as federal appeals court judges before their elevation to the High Bench. Shiras had had no previous judicial experience.

Previous judicial experience. The criterion of previous judicial experience for appointment to the Court has been insisted upon by a number of Presidents (most recently Eisenhower), but others, such as FDR, could not have cared less. Some sentiment that nominees should have a modicum of previous judicial experience does exist. Bills are annually introduced in Congress to this effect. Invariably, they never see the light of day—and well it is that they do not. For the historical record shows no correlation between previous judicial experience and distinguished service on the Court.

Of the 101 men who have sat on the Court, 40 had no previous judicial experience whatever. Nine others had two years of experience or less. At the other extreme, 22 had 10 years or more. Among those with no judicial experience at the time of their appointment to the Court were 8 of the 15 Chief Justices: Marshall, Taney, Salmon P. Chase, Waite, Fuller, Hughes, Stone, and Warren—great names all. Compare these names with Jay, Rutledge, and Ellsworth, who were Marshall's predecessors, and White, Taft, Vinson, and Burger. The jury, of course, is still out on Burger. But the fact that he has had more prior judicial experience (14 years) than any of his predecessor Chief Justices does not bode well.

Pre-eminent among Associate Justices without prior judicial experience are: Joseph Story, Marshall's disciple; Peter V. Daniel, the greatest dissenter of them all;[28] Samuel Miller and Joseph Bradley, giants of the post-Civil War Courts; James McReynolds, the pristine troglodyte; and Brandeis, Frankfurter, Douglas, Robert Jackson, and Byron White. If those with less than two years' experience are added, the list includes both John Marshall Harlan's, each of whom came to the Court with a previous year on the bench, and Hugo Black, who early in his career served eighteen months as a municipal police court judge.

On the other side of the ledger, two names leap out: Oliver Wendell Holmes and Benjamin Cardozo, with 20 and 18 years of previous judicial experience, respectively. But they are the exceptions, as are William Johnson from the Marshall Court; Stephen J. Field from the post-Civil War Courts, whose addiction to the doctrines of laissez-faire economics caused him to make private property rights the alpha and omega of the Constitution; and Brennan and perhaps Stewart on the present Court.

On the whole, previous judicial experience suggests mediocrity rather than greatness, whether as Associate or Chief Justice. Mediocrity may be too harsh a term, considering its relative nature. Not every member of baseball's Hall of Fame was or is a Babe Ruth or a Cy Young. In that sense, the rest of the membership may be labeled "mediocre" perhaps. But these players constitute an eminently select group. So do the Justices.

The oft-quoted assertion of former Justice Frankfurter thus seems accurate:

> Apart from meaning that a man had sat on some court for some time, "judicial service" tells nothing that is relevant about the qualifications for the functions exercised by the Supreme Court. While it seems to carry meaning, it misleads. . . . The Supreme Court is a very special kind of court. "Judicial service" as such has no significant relation to the kinds of litigation that come before the Supreme Court, to the types of issues they raise, to qualities that these actualities require for wise decision.[29]

Frankfurter, of course, may have been blowing his own horn when he wrote these words. Because he was himself among those without previous judicial experience, his objectivity on this matter may properly be questioned. Nonetheless, this may be one instance where appearance is not deceiving.

The Fundamental Reasons for Presidential Choice

The record, then, indicates that Presidents prefer men of their own party who are lawyers and who have a lengthy record of public service that may or may not include prior judicial experience. Presidents may also pay attention to geographical dispersion and religious, racial, and ethnic considerations. But these concerns, quite obviously, are only the tip of the iceberg. The fundamental reasons for Presidential choice are purely political. One reason was mentioned in the discussion of Lincoln's nomination of Field midway through the Civil War and FDR's promotion of Stone to the Chief Justiceship on the eve of World War II. These and similar nominations were motivated by the desire of the appointing President to attain certain partisan objectives. The objective may have been nothing more than improving his chances for re-election. An example was Eisenhower's recess appointment of New Jersey Democrat William Brennan three weeks before the 1956 election. Not only was Brennan a Democrat, he was also a Catholic. The Court had been without a Catholic member since the death of Frank Murphy in 1949. The choice of Brennan could not but enhance Eisenhower's popularity in the metropolitan East and among Catholics. Eisenhower's nomination of Earl Warren for Chief Justice is thought by many also to have been dictated by partisan concerns. Warren, as Governor of California, had played a crucial role in the 1952 Republican National Convention. He had thrown his support to the Eisenhower forces in the credentials committee dispute over the seating of delegates committed to Robert Taft, thereby paving the way for Ike's nomination. Eisenhower, however, insistently denied that he selected Warren to pay off the debt that he had thereby incurred.

The other fundamental reason for Presidential choice is to populate the Court with persons who share the President's views on the major issues of the day, that is, whose personal policy preferences are identical to their own.[30] To accomplish this objective, Presidents will naturally look to members of their own political party who have had extensive experience in the affairs of state, and with whom they are personally acquainted. Such persons have a readily identifiable track record on major public policy questions. Presidents realize that their Administrations are of short duration. If a President's accomplishments are to outlast his Administration, his Supreme Court appointees should share his policy goals.

Presidential Misguesses

Presidents, of course, are not clairvoyant. Sometimes they misguess. The cure that the doctor has ordered then turns out to be worse than the malady. The liberal Woodrow Wilson certainly did not perceive James McReynolds as anything other than a dutiful trust-busting Democrat when he nominated him to the Court in 1914. Wilson's two other nominees, Brandeis and John Clarke, fully mirrored Wilson's views. But McReynolds turned out to be another story. Not only was he conservative, he was the Court's all-time leading reactionary. He had difficulty coming to terms with the nineteenth century, much less the twentieth. Did the leopard, then, change his spots? Not likely. It is more probable that a lifetime appointment brings out a Justice's true colors. Hence, the need to assay the *real* politics of a nominee rather than his nominal affiliations. Taft was quite confident that the three Southern Democrats he nominated—Lurton, Lamar, and White—would prove to be men after his own heart. History bore out the correctness of his judgment, notwithstanding the disgruntlement of leading Republicans at his crossing of party lines. But getting at a person's real politics is not an easy job, even when the candidate is well known to the President.

Truman, for example, put four of his friends and associates on the Court: Chief Justice Vinson, Harold Burton, Tom Clark, and Sherman Minton. Truman will probably be counted among the great Presidents of American history. But such a judgment, if made, will be in spite of his appointments to the Court. His four Justices rendered no more than undistinguished service on the High Bench. Moreover, as Justices they did not reflect the liberal, progressive stance that characterized the policies of the President who appointed them. Truman's own words, as reported by Merle Miller, are revealing:

What do you consider the biggest mistake you made as President?
"Tom Clark was my biggest mistake. No question about it."
"I'm sorry, sir. I'm not sure I understand.
"That damn fool from Texas that I first made Attorney General and then put on the Supreme Court. I don't know what got into me. He was no damn good as Attorney General, and on the Supreme Court . . . it doesn't seem possible, but he's been even worse. He hasn't made one right decision that I can think of. And so when you ask me what was my biggest mistake, that's it. Putting Tom Clark on the Supreme Court of the United States.

"I thought maybe when he got on the Court he'd improve, but of course, that isn't what's happened. I told you when we were discussing that other fellow [Nixon]. After a certain age it's hopeless to think people are going to change much."
How do you explain the fact that he's been such a bad Justice?
"The main thing is . . . well, it isn't so much that he's a *bad* man. It's just that he's such a dumb son of a bitch. He's about the dumbest man I think I've ever run across. And lots of times that's the case. Being dumb's just about the worst thing there is when it comes to holding high office, and that's especially true when it's on the Supreme Court of the United States.

"As I say, I never will know what got into me when I made that appointment, and I'm as sorry as I can be for doing it."[31]

This, mind you, was said by the man who ordered the dropping of the atomic bomb and the development of the hydrogen bomb, presided at Potsdam, oversaw the transition from a wartime to a peacetime economy, gave his blessing to the UN, NATO, and the Marshall Plan, sent American troops into Korea, and coped with the onset of the Cold War and the Communist conquest of mainland China. The fact that Truman did not consider one of his actions pertaining to world affairs as his biggest mistake (certainly he was the single most powerful person in the world at that time) does not mean that he made no mistakes as commander in chief or in his diplomatic role. It is rather a striking indication of the importance of the Supreme Court in the American scheme of things.

The Importance of Personal Policy Preferences

Many Presidents have found that previous judicial experience is the best guide to a potential nominee's real politics, especially if this experience has been obtained in the lower federal courts. Eisenhower is a case in point. Ike was quite obviously disappointed in the liberalism displayed by Warren after his appointment to the Court. He therefore decided to nominate to future vacancies only persons with judicial experience. And except for Brennan, Eisenhower's nominees—Harlan, Whittaker, and Stewart—closely reflected the Conservative-to-Moderate value system that was his own.

Occasionally, a President's choice of candidates will turn on a single policy issue rather than on his concern for a general similarity of views. The classic instance concerned the constitutionality of the Legal Tender Act of 1862. The Act made paper money ("greenbacks"), rather than gold, legal tender for the payment of debts. The financial stakes were high. On the one side were the bankers, mortgagees, and creditors. On the other side were the railroads, municipalities, land speculators, and debtors. In 1870, with two vacant seats on the Court, the Justices ruled the Act unconstitutional by a 4 to 3 vote. On the same day that the decision was announced, President Grant sent to the Senate the names of two supporters of the Act's constitutionality—William Strong and Joseph Bradley. Four days after their confirmation by the Senate, the Attorney General requested the Court to reconsider its decision. The request was duly granted, and one year later Strong and Bradley joined the three dissenters to produce a 5 to 4 decision that overturned the earlier result and upheld the Act's constitutionality.

More or less in the same vein were the concerns that guided Richard Nixon in his choice of nominees. Crime and lawlessness were defined by the American public as the chief issues in the election year of 1968. The Court's decisions in the criminal justice area were themselves a subject of considerable controversy. Nixon had articulated policies for dealing with the "breakdown" of law and order, and he viewed the Court's position as hostile to his own. He clearly stated his concern in the national address in which he nominated Powell and Rehnquist to the Court:

> As a judicial conservative, I believe some Court decisions have gone too far in the past in weakening the peace forces as against the criminal forces in our society.
>
> In maintaining—as it must be maintained—the delicate balance between the rights of society and defendants accused of crimes, I believe the peace forces must not be denied the legal tools they need to protect the innocent from criminal elements.[32]

In his appointments to the Court Nixon batted 1000 percent. His Justices closely reflect a Nixonian conservatism, not only with regard to criminal justice, but with regard to other issues as well. Approximately three-fourths of the votes of the Nixon appointees have been cast against the defendant in criminal cases. Even when the defendant has won, more than one-third of their votes have been cast against the defendant; and when a majority of the Court has voted against the criminal defendant, more than 99 percent of the votes of the Nixon Justices have also been in that direction.[33]

Nixon's success in populating the Court with persons whose personal policy preferences reflect his own is unsurpassed by any other President. Others may have done as well (Taft, for example). But notwithstanding the bitterness and rancor engendered by the defeat of Haynsworth and Carswell, Nixon remained steadfast in his commitment to appoint judicial conservatives. In so doing, he broke the Liberals' domination of the Court with his first appointment—Warren Burger. The succeeding appointments of Blackmun, Powell, and Rehnquist left the Court one short of a Conservative majority. All this occurred in a span of 2½ years.

This is not to say that the Nixon Justices have invariably hewed to the Nixonian line. Warrantless wiretapping, government aid to parochial schools, abortion reform, and, of course, the Watergate Tapes case, are paramount examples of instances where his troops left him in the lurch.[34] But on balance, his nominees reflected his policy preferences. He spoke truly when he said:

> By far the most important appointments [a President] makes are those to the Supreme Court of the United States. Presidents come and go, but the Supreme Court through its decisions goes on forever.[35]

History may well record Nixon as the nation's worst President. If so, he will have displaced Warren G. Harding. Harding, however, is the only other twentieth-century President who rivaled Nixon in his skill at choosing Justices whose political views reflected his own. He also batted four for four. Whatever else may be said about them, they most assuredly knew how to choose Justices of the Supreme Court.[36]

NOTES

1. Robert Dahl, "Decision Making in a Democracy: The Supreme Court as a National Policy Maker," *Journal of Public Law* 6 (1957): 279–295; David Adamany, "Legitimacy, Realigning Elections, and the Supreme Court," *Wisconsin Law Review* 73 (1973): 790–846; Richard Funston, "The Supreme Court and Critical Elections," *American Political Science Review* 69 (1975): 795–811; Jonathan D. Casper, "The Supreme Court and National Policy

Making," *American Political Science Review* 70 (1976): 50–63; Paul Allen Beck and Richard Funston, "Critical Elections and the Supreme Court: Putting the Cart after the Horse," *American Political Science Review* 70 (1976): 930–932; Bradley C. Canon and S. Sidney Ulmer, "The Supreme Court and Critical Elections: A Dissent," *American Political Science Review* 70 (1976): 1215–1218; and Richard Funston, "Funston Reply to Canon and Ulmer," *American Political Science Review* 70 (1976): 1218–1221. Also see Beverly B. Cook, "Public Opinion and Federal Judicial Policy," *American Journal of Political Science* 21 (1977): 567–600.

2. Lists of members of the Supreme Court may be found in the appendices of many constitutional law textbooks. For example, C. Herman Pritchett, *The American Constitution*, 3rd ed. (New York: McGraw-Hill, 1977), pp. 584–586.

3. An account of the Court-packing proposal may be found in any constitutional history text. For example, Carl Brent Swisher, *American Constitutional Development* (Boston: Houghton Mifflin, 1943); Alfred H. Kelly and Winfred A. Harbison, *The American Constitution* (New York: Norton, 1976).

4. State minimum wage laws were upheld in *West Coast Hotel Co.* v. *Parrish*, 300 U.S. 379, number 14 in Harold J. Spaeth, *Classic and Current Decisions of the United States Supreme Court* (San Francisco: W. H. Freeman and Company, 1977); the Farm Mortgage (Frazier-Lemke) Act was upheld in *Wright* v. *Vinton Branch*, 300 U.S. 440; the Railway Labor Act, which required railroads to bargain collectively with their employees, was upheld in *Virginian Railway* v. *System Federation*, 300 U.S. 515; the National Labor Relations Act was upheld in *National Labor Relations Board* v. *Jones and Laughlin Steel Corp.*, 301 U.S. 1, number 15 in *Classic and Current Decisions;* and the Social Security Act was upheld in *Steward Machine Co.* v. *Davis*, 301 U.S. 548.

5. See Walter F. Murphy, *Congress and the Court* (Chicago: University of Chicago, 1962), chaps. 6–10.

6. 347 U.S. 484 and 349 U.S. 294, number 20 in *Classic and Current Decisions.*

7. *Gideon* v. *Wainwright*, 372 U.S. 335 (1963), number 22 in *Classic and Current Decisions.*

8. *Mapp* v. *Ohio*, 367 U.S. 643 (1961); *Miranda* v. *Arizona*, 384 U.S. 436 (1966); and *Katz* v. *United States*, 389 U.S. 347 (1967)—numbers 21, 29, and 30 in *Classic and Current Decisions.*

9. *Cramp* v. *Board of Public Instruction*, 368 U.S. 278 (1961); *Baggett* v. *Bullitt*, 377 U.S. 360 (1964); *Keyishian* v. *Board of Regents*, 385 U.S. 589 (1967); and *Whitehill* v. *Elkins*, 389 U.S. 54 (1967).

10. Pritchett, *op. cit.,* note 2 *supra,* chap. 26.

11. *Ibid.,* chaps. 19–21; *Memoirs* v. *Massachusetts Attorney General*, 383 U.S. 413 (1966); and *Redrup* v. *New York*, 386 U.S. 767 (1967)—number 28 in *Classic and Current Decisions.*

12. *Engel* v. *Vitale*, 370 U.S. 421 (1962); and *Abington School District* v. *Schempp*, 374 U.S. 203 (1963)—number 23 in *Classic and Current Decisions.*

13. *New York Times* v. *United States*, 403 U.S. 713 (1971), number 36 in *Classic and Current Decisions.*

14. *Miller* v. *California*, 413 U.S. 15 (1973); and *Paris Adult Theatre* v. *Slaton*, 413 U.S. 49 (1973)—number 45 in *Classic and Current Decisions.*

15. *Argersinger* v. *Hamlin*, 407 U.S. 25 (1972), number 37 in *Classic and Current Decisions*.

16. *Stone* v. *Powell*, 428 U.S. 465 (1976), number 53 in *Classic and Current Decisions*.

17. *Gregg* v. *Georgia*, 428 U.S. 153 (1976); and *Woodson* v. *North Carolina*, 428 U.S. 280 (1976)—number 52 in *Classic and Current Decisions*.

18. *Milliken* v. *Bradley*, 418 U.S. 717 (1974), number 48 in *Classic and Current Decisions*.

19. For example, *Frontiero* v. *Richardson*, 411 U.S. 677 (1973), number 44 in *Classic and Current Decisions*.

20. For example, *Citizens to Preserve Overton Park* v. *Volpe*, 401 U.S. 402 (1971); *Lake Carriers'* v. *MacMullan*, 406 U.S. 498 (1972); *A. & R. R. Co.* v. *SCRAP*, 422 U.S. 289 (1975); *Union Electric* v. *EPA*, 427 U.S. 246 (1976); *Kleppe* v. *Sierra Club*, 427 U.S. 390 (1976); *duPont* v. *Train*, 51 L Ed 2d 204 (1977).

21. For example, *Goss* v. *Lopez*, 419 U.S. 565 (1975); and *Wood* v. *Strickland*, 420 U.S. 308 (1975)—number 49 in *Classic and Current Decisions*.

22. *Roe* v. *Wade*, 410 U.S. 113 (1973); and *Doe* v. *Bolton*, 410 U.S. 179 (1973)—number 42 in *Classic and Current Decisions*.

23. For example, *Fuentes* v. *Shevin*, 407 U.S. 67 (1972), number 38 in *Classic and Current Decisions*.

24. *United States* v. *Nixon*, 418 U.S. 683 (1974), number 47 in *Classic and Current Decisions*.

25. *Scott* v. *Sandford*, 19 Howard 393 (1857), number 9 in *Classic and Current Decisions*.

26. A brief history of these episodes may be found in *The Supreme Court: Justice and the Law*, 1st ed. (Washington, D.C.: Congressional Quarterly, 1973), pp. 19–24. Not since 1894 had a President failed to secure confirmation of two successive nominees.

27. But not without frequent recesses—that is, days off. According to one source, "in the first five months of 1975, Congress had already taken twenty days off and was getting ready for a third ten-dayer." William Miller and Frances S. Leighton, *Fishbait: The Memoirs of the Congressional Doorkeeper* (Englewood Cliffs, N.J.: Prentice-Hall, 1977), p. 53.

28. John P. Frank, *Justice Daniel Dissenting* (Cambridge, Mass.: Harvard University Press, 1964).

29. Felix Frankfurter, "The Supreme Court in the Mirror of Justices," reprinted in Walter F. Murphy and C. Herman Pritchett, *Courts, Judges, and Politics*, 2d ed. (New York: Random House, 1974), p. 180.

30. Nixon's nominees—Burger, Blackmun, Powell, and Rehnquist—are classic examples. Considerations governing Presidential nominations to the lower federal courts may be found in three articles by Sheldon Goldman, "Characteristics of Eisenhower and Kennedy Appointees to the Lower Federal Courts," *Western Political Quarterly* 18 (1965): 755–762; "Johnson and Nixon Appointees to the Lower Federal Courts, *Journal of Politics* 34 (1972): 934–942; and "Judicial Backgrounds, Recruitment, and the Party Variable," *Arizona Law Review* 1974 (1974): 211–222.

31. Merle Miller, *Plain Speaking* (New York: Berkley, 1973), pp. 225–226.

32. *New York Times,* October 22, 1971.

33. David W. Rohde and Harold J. Spaeth, *Supreme Court Decision Making* (San Francisco: W.H. Freeman and Company, 1976), pp. 109-111.

34. *United States* v. *District Court,* 407 U.S. 297 (1972); *Lemon* v. *Kurtzman,* 403 U.S. 602 (1971); *Roe* v. *Wade,* 410 U.S. 113 (1973); and *United States* v. *Nixon,* 418 U.S. 683 (1974)—numbers 40, 35, 42, and 47 in *Classic and Current Decisions.*

35. *New York Times,* October 22, 1971.

36. A skillfully formulated methodology to enable an appointing President to judge the effect of membership change on the Court's policy making is given in Stuart Teger, "Presidential Strategy for the Appointment of Supreme Court Justices," *Public Choice* 31 (1977): 1–22.

CHAPTER

5

Why the Justices Decide as They Do

The decisions that people make depend on their goals, and in deciding on goals, people must also decide which course of action will best enable them to attain the desired result. In this chapter, we assume that the goals the Justices desire to achieve are their personal policy preferences. This assumption is tested by an analysis of the Justices' votes in the cases decided by the Warren and Burger Courts. Such an analysis allows us to identify a number of "attitudes" that enable us to explain why the individual Justices vote as they do. Many of these "attitudes," in turn, correlate closely enough that we can discern three "values"—freedom, equality, and New Deal economics—that enable us to further explain why the Justices decide as they do. An analysis of the individual Justice's patterns of response with regard to these three values also permits us to describe each Justice's overall voting in terms of a distinctive "value system."

This analytical focus on the personal policy preferences of the Justices is possible because the constraints under which the Justices decide their cases do not inhibit them from expressing their preferences insofar as voting on the cases before them is concerned. The reasons why a Justice may allow his votes to be guided by his personal policy preferences are presented in this chapter in the section headed "The Dominance of Personal Policy Preferences." Our focus on the Justices' attitudes and values, however, does not mean that their perceptions of what their role as a Justice should be has no bearing on their decisions. As is pointed out in this chapter, in the section headed "The Measure of Motivation," our identification of a Justice's personal policy preferences does not tell us *why* a Justice prefers one course of action rather than another. A likely explanation is his perception of what a judge's role should be.[1] He may, for example, believe that a judge ought to be especially supportive of those whom society has disadvantaged. If so, his voting will likely categorize him as a Liberal as that term is defined in this chapter. Or he may perceive a judge's role as being limited, with the result that he will approve almost all actions of the other branches of government, state as well as federal. His voting behavior will reflect the policy-making orientation of these nonjudicial decision makers. Finally, he may view a judge's role as one that should support the agencies of law enforcement. If he does, his votes will show that he has adopted a law-and-order stance.

The fact that the Justices have certain role expectations and orientations does not, however, refute the utility of the approach adopted in this chapter. The theory and methods used to identify the Justices' personal policy preferences—although they do not explain why a Justice is Liberal, Conservative, and whatever—do enable us to predict how he will vote and how the Court will decide cases that have been accepted for review. The predictive accuracy that my methods have achieved is detailed in Chapter 6.

THE NATURE OF DECISION MAKING

High on the list of humanist heresies is the belief that human activity is predictable. Those who believe in the dignity and worth of the individual tend to view each person as unique and to believe that the resulting individuality precludes predictability. Allegations that people are programmable are derided, and efforts to elicit Pavlovian responses are deemed reprehensible. But uniqueness and predictability are not mutually exclusive. No two snowflakes are identical; yet all snowflakes are of a common color and melt at the same temperature. To associate uniqueness with unpredictability is a pietistic myth that undoubtedly serves salutary purposes, but myth it remains.

The best evidence that mankind acts predictably is the fact that we are creatures of habit. We need to be so because we cannot function in an overly dynamic environment. Indeed, the very reason for the existence of criminal laws is humankind's need for predictable behavior in important kinds of interpersonal activity. Consider a matter as mundane as the use of automobiles. If laws were not passed to regulate traffic flow, chaos would result. A weekly trip to the supermarket would be fraught with danger to life and limb. Traveling salespersons would have the life expectancy of a June bug. Consequently, humankind has devised a *quid pro quo* arrangement: to some extent and within certain degrees of freedom, I demand predictable behavior from you and, in turn, I will accord you the same. To ensure such predictability, lawmakers enact laws governing important kinds of interpersonal activity, the violation of which is a crime.

Purely formalistic arrangements produce highly uniform behavior; when altered, they produce chaos. Consider the effect of a quickly passed law that states that beginning tomorrow, motorized vehicles must travel on the left side of the road rather than on the right. Or the effect of a system of traffic signals that mandates that a red light means go, a green light means stop. Not only would traffic accidents increase horrendously, so also would psychological stress. The incidence of nervous breakdowns among drivers would skyrocket well beyond the price of oil and gas. Ingrained habit thus becomes a powerful force for consistency of conduct. Changing such habits, even if the change has no substantive effect upon the activity involved, is psychically painful. When government considers such changes, the time required to educate the public is at least as important as the legislation itself. Current plans to introduce the metric system of weights and measures are a prime example.

Personal Policy Preferences

If people generally behave predictably as law, custom, tradition, or habit dictates, is it not likely that consistent behavior may also occur in areas of activity not so governed? We commonly characterize people on the basis of their individual traits: cheerful, friendly, stingy, kind, aggressive, candid, deceitful. No less is this true of political view or orientation: liberal, conservative, moderate, racist, dictatorial. The reasons why a person manifests certain characteristics are not part of our concern, however. Whether trait possession is inherited, acquired, or both, is a question best left to geneticists and learning theorists.

Inasmuch as people do act consistently, one may assume that human behavior is goal oriented. Individuals desire certain objectives, and in seeking these objectives they act in a purposeful, not an aimless, fashion. With respect to political and governmental affairs, the preferences that an individual has for this or that objective may be labeled personal policy preferences.

More often than not, more than a single means is available to attain an objective. (If we wish to go to Rome, and if it is true that all roads lead thereto, which one shall we take?) Accordingly, to achieve a goal, a choice must be made from among alternative courses of action.

The Rules of the Game

But not all means are equally appropriate. Some are permissible, others are not. Some are inefficient; others entail great costs. We may wish to dispatch an opponent with aplomb, but we had better be careful that the method we choose is socially acceptable. For example, it is one thing to wring the neck of the proposed entree for Thanksgiving dinner, and quite another to do so to an obstreperous next-door neighbor. Accordingly, the means one chooses to attain an objective will depend on what may be called the rules of the game. These rules consist of the various sets of formal and informal regulations and norms within the framework of which decisions are made. They specify what kinds of actions are permitted and what kinds are prohibited, as well as the circumstances and conditions under which choice may be exercised.

In football, a player may score by carrying the ball. But in volleyball, soccer, and basketball, carrying the ball is strictly forbidden. In baseball, there is no penalty for failure to strike the ball at the first opportunity; in golf, there is. A pole vaulter must clear the crossbar; a hurdler need not. Each game tends to have a distinctive playing surface and equipment. Chess and checkers, for example, are played on an identical board; yet chess uses more pieces that, as a group, may be moved much more freely than in checkers. Innumerable card games, each with its distinctive set of rules, employ a common 52-card deck.

Politics, too, is a game, played according to rules that vary from one community and institution to another. The choices that a politically active person makes will be directly affected by these rules. Thus, the same individual will act differently, even though his goals remain fixed, as he moves from one institution or community to another. Congress is a good illustration. Its members' objectives are governed by the formal rules of the House of Representatives and the Senate, the provisions of the Constitution that pertain to Congress, various election laws, and the criminal statutes that are applicable to congressional behavior. Informal rules and norms include the custom of senatorial courtesy, certain aspects of the seniority and committee systems, and the expectations of congressmen, public officials, and constituents about what sorts of behavior are "proper."

Furthermore, rules may be so structured that they significantly affect decisional outcomes. Rules are never neutral. Furthermore, some participants, by reason of their previously acquired skills and talents, or because of their objectives, will be advantaged or hindered in the contest. A photographic memory is an advantage in a bridge game, as are a powerful serve in tennis and an unerring eye in target practice. Similarly, members of Congress who communicate persuasively, who face minimal opposition from their constituencies, who have mastered the intricacies of parliamentary procedure, who are liked and respected by their colleagues, and who support the status quo are more likely to attain their objectives. Because Congress is composed of two autonomous units, the passage of legislation is considerably more difficult than it would be if Congress were a unicameral body. Those who desire change and reform consequently have a more difficult row to hoe than those who do not. In addition, some rules benefit those who are supportive of existing conditions; for example, the Senate's unlimited debate rule, which permits filibusters, and the seniority system, according to which uninterrupted longevity on a given committee correlates rather directly with power and influence.

Rules may also allow certain decision makers to alter the rules of the game. A committee chairperson usually sets the agenda and time of the committee's meetings, and the speaker of the House of Representatives rules on disputed points of parliamentary procedure.

The Supreme Court also operates under a set of rules. Some are distinctive to that body; others control activity throughout the federal and state judicial systems. For example, no judge may initiate litigation; courts may respond only to cases that are brought to their attention.[2] Only bona fide legal disputes may be heard (except in some state supreme courts); advisory opinions are forbidden. Judges may decide only those cases that lie within the geographical and subject matter jurisdiction of their court; an offense defined as criminal under Kansas law may not be tried in Nebraska; a court of common pleas may not try a charge of first-degree murder.

THE DOMINANCE OF
PERSONAL POLICY PREFERENCES

The distinctive rules under which the Supreme Court operates include the procedures and norms that govern the Court's decision-making process. It is significant that the Court's rules do not preclude any Justice from voting compatibly with his personal policy preferences. There are three underlying reasons for this freedom (in addition to the discretion inherent in judges' decisions): (1) the Justices are not electorally accountable; (2) they lack ambition for higher office; and (3) the Supreme Court is the court of last resort.

Electoral Unaccountability

Federal judges, according to the Constitution, "shall hold their offices during good behavior." Once appointed and confirmed, they serve until death, resignation, or retirement. They are beholden to no one—not the President who appointed them, nor to the senators who confirmed them, and certainly not to the voters. The Justices' lack of accountability can also be traced to the absence of an effective removal power. Only once, in 1804, has a member of the Supreme Court been impeached—Samuel Chase, an irascible Federalist, whose partisanship on the High Bench was matched by that of the Jeffersonians in Congress. The House of

Representatives voted articles of impeachment, but the Senate failed to convict by a margin of four votes.

Other Justices have been the subject of impeachment resolutions, but the House has never approved them. The most recent action concerned Justice William O. Douglas. In the spring of 1970, one Gerald R. Ford, then a Michigan congressman, spearheaded the resolution, which was signed by 52 Republicans and an equal number of Democrats. The action was precipitated by the publication in the *Evergreen Review*[3] of excerpts from one of Douglas's recently published books, *Points of Rebellion*. The excerpts appeared cheek by jowl with a seven-page photographic display of oral-genital sex. Ford said that the magazine was full of "hard-core pornography"; that Douglas espoused the "hippie-yippie style revolution"; that he was "unfit and should be removed" from the bench; and that he (Ford) "would vote to impeach him right now."* However, saner heads prevailed. The resolution was referred to a special subcommittee of the House Judiciary Committee, which quietly buried the proposal on the ground that no basis for impeachment existed. The controversy may also have occasioned Ford's major contribution to posterity during his 25 years as a Congressman—his statement that an "impeachable offense is whatever a majority of the House of Representatives considers [it] to be at a given moment in history."

The absence of an effective removal power differentiates Justices from such officials as Cabinet officers who, like federal judges, are not elected, but serve only at the pleasure of the President who appoints them. Also unelected are the members of the various federal regulatory agencies (such as the Securities and Exchange Commission, the National Labor Relations Board, and the Federal Communications Commission). These commissioners, unlike members of the President's Cabinet, may not be removed from office at the President's discretion, but only for cause. They serve staggered terms of office ranging from five to seven years, depending on the agency to which they are appointed.

Lack of electoral accountability and absence of an effective removal power mean that judges are much freer than other decision makers to voice their personal policy preferences. Elected officials must face the voters every two, four, or six years. Appointees depend upon their appointers for continuation in office. Either condition requires that discretion be exercised within a relatively narrow range. The desire for re-election or reappointment is totally absent from Supreme Court policy making.

---

*President Ford is also known for other equally intelligent solecisms, such as "If Lincoln were living today, he would turn over in his grave." Reported in Sydney J. Harris's syndicated column of July 28, 1977.

Contrast the freedom allowed federal judges with the pressures commonly felt by members of Congress. The following scenario is typical. Congressman Z narrowly wins election in a campaign in which he sharply criticized "needless defense spending." He wrangles membership on the House Armed Services Committee. The Army cancels a truck-purchase contract with a manufacturer in the congressman's district, saying that it does not need the trucks. The congressman writes letters and makes speeches protesting the loss of jobs. (Labor funded and staffed his campaign effort.) The manufacturer is a major employer. Its management made substantial contributions to the congressman's opponent in the last campaign and has influence in circles the congressman would like to tap. Do we dismiss the congressman as a hypocrite and his campaign pledge as so much rhetoric? This, of course, is the sort of dissimulation that leaves people with a bad taste and a low regard for politicians. But to castigate the official as hypocritical is unwarranted. He may conscientiously believe in the Burkean tenet that he ought to represent all his constituents, not only those who elected him. He probably did not realize that he would have to make some difficult choices because legislative issues are rarely black or white. And most assuredly, his vanity, if not his intellect, tells him that he is more deserving of the office than his opponent or any likely future opponent.

Lack of Ambition for Higher Office

Lack of ambition for a higher office also enhances the play of personal policy preferences.[4] It can be argued that most officeholders desire an office more prestigious than the one they currently occupy. Such desire will obviously affect the causes they espouse and the issues they attempt to resolve. Consequently, such individuals may well make decisions not on the basis of their own personal policy preferences, but on the basis of how their decisions will affect the likelihood of attaining that higher office.

For at least a century, such ambition appears not to have motivated any Justice of the Supreme Court, with perhaps an exception or two. The Justices seem to view service on the Supreme Court as the pinnacle of their political careers, rather than as a way station to other offices. The only office that carries higher prestige is that of the President (and some people may not have held this view—even before Watergate). Charles Evans Hughes did resign as an Associate Justice in 1916 to accept the Republican nomination for President. He did, however, return fourteen years later as Chief Justice. One might say that he merely took a leave of absence. Salmon P. Chase, Lincoln's rival for the Presidency, stated that the only office he "heartedly desired" was that of Chief Justice, a goal he realized in 1864. William Howard Taft, when asked whether he liked being President, replied, "on the whole, yes." But, he added, "I would rather be Chief Justice of the United States."[5]

Other than Hughes, only two twentieth-century Justices resigned to accept other offices. After barely a year on the Court, James Byrnes resigned in 1942 at the urging of President Roosevelt to accept the position of Director of Economic Stabilization, or "Assistant President" (Roosevelt's term). Byrnes made the move only because of the exigencies of World War II. Arthur Goldberg resigned in 1965, after three years on the Court, to become Ambassador to the United Nations. Not only was this appointment not a promotion, it was not even a credible boot upstairs. What prompted Lyndon Johnson to make the appointment, and why Goldberg accepted, have never been ascertained.†

Most officeholders also share a desire for increased power in the institution of which they are a part. A congressman, for example, may be satisfied to remain in the House of Representatives for the rest of his life, but he may also wish to increase his power and influence by securing a position of leadership in his party or a particular committee assignment. Attainment of either of these objectives depends on the approbation of his colleagues. Hence, his decisions on matters of interest to those capable of smoothing his path will be affected to some extent by the preferences of these colleagues.

This sort of ambition also seems to be absent from the Marble Palace, if only because of lack of evidence to the contrary. A marked difference between the Court and many other governmental bodies is that there is no division of labor within the Court. Except for an occasional instance of self-disqualification, all the Justices participate in every decision. Consequently, the only higher office available within the Court is that of Chief Justice. But the existence of only one higher office does not preclude the possibility that some Associate Justices have coveted that position.

A case in point, probably the only one, is that of Justice Robert Jackson. Following the death of Chief Justice Harlan Stone in 1946, Jackson, then serving as Chief Prosecutor at the Nuremberg Trials in Germany, precipitated what many consider the ugliest feud in the Court's history. In the late 1930's and in 1940, Jackson gained deserved recognition first as Solicitor General and then as Attorney General, in

---

† Goldberg has stated that he accepted the position because Johnson persuaded him that it was in the national interest for him to go to the United Nations. Goldberg reportedly thought he could alter American policy in Vietnam by beginning peace negotiations in the United Nations. Johnson, on the other hand, said that Goldberg was "bored" with his service on the Court, a judgment that Goldberg said was "highly inaccurate" and "not the truth." See Neil Sheehan, "Goldberg Disputes Johnson Memoirs on U.N. Post," *New York Times*, October 27, 1971.

consequence of which he was considered a likely candidate for President if Roosevelt decided not to run for a third term. He was also acclaimed as the leading candidate for the Chief Justiceship when Charles Evans Hughes announced his resignation in 1941. But Roosevelt passed him over in favor of Stone and instead made him Stone's replacement as Associate Justice. Upon Stone's death in 1946, Jackson unwisely expressed his frustration and disappointment in a lengthy cable addressed to the judiciary committees of both the House and the Senate, in which he told all concerned his view of the "feud" that he claimed had racked and split the Supreme Court.[6] He attributed President Truman's nomination of Fred Vinson as Chief Justice to the politicking of other members of the Court, particularly Justice Black, with whom he had not been on the best of terms before he left for Nuremberg.

But even if such a feud actually existed (it seemed more a figment of Jackson's imagination than anything else), vacancies in the office of Chief Justice simply do not occur very often. From 1789 to the appointment of Chief Justice Burger, 14 persons served as Chief Justice and had an average tenure of 13 years. If we exclude John Jay, the first Chief Justice, and his two successors (one of whom presided over only two cases), the average tenure becomes 15 years. Given the infrequency of a vacancy, an Associate Justice's ambition for the center chair is wholly unrealistic, assuming he wants it in the first place.

The Court of Last Resort

The third and final reason for the free play of personal policy preferences in Supreme Court policy making is the Court's position as the court of last resort. The buck stops here. No other court can overrule the Supreme Court. It is thereby differentiated from other courts, state and federal. Even though lower-court judges may occasionally be disinclined to follow precedent, they must nonetheless take into account the fact that higher courts can reverse their decisions.

To be sure, Congress can overrule the Court in matters of statutory interpretation. This, however, rarely happens. And when it does, the last word is still the Court's, because when all is said and done, the Court determines the meaning of the revised legislation, of the reworded statute. Especially is the Court supreme in matters of constitutional interpretation. Reversal of decisions in these matters can occur only if the Court overrules itself or if a constitutional amendment is adopted. The latter check is negligible, having happened only four times: the Eleventh Amendment in 1798 reversed the 1793 decision in *Chisholm v. Georgia*,[7] which permitted an individual to sue a state in federal court; the Fourteenth Amendment in 1868 reversed the 1857 decision in *Dred Scott v. Sandford*,[8] which held blacks not to be American citizens; the Sixteenth

Amendment in 1913 reversed the 1895 decision in *Pollock* v. *Farmers' Loan and Trust Co.*,[9] which prohibited a federal income tax; and the Twenty-sixth Amendment in 1971 reversed part of the 1970 decision in *Oregon* v. *Mitchell*,[10] which denied Congress's power to enfranchise 18- to 20-year-olds in state elections.

For the reasons given, the Justices are free to decide cases as they see fit. But one should not deduce that the Justices actually do as they damn well please. They greatly desire that their decisions be obeyed, and they are cognizant of the fact that they have no means by which to coerce compliance (see Chapter 8). Accordingly, they need to maintain public confidence, and to have the respect of both bench and bar. They must not provoke Congress to retaliate by altering the Court's appellate jurisdiction, size, or budget. Even a Justice's desire to fulfill the role inculcated in him during his early legal training should be seen as a factor limiting his personal policy preferences.

What, then, are these personal policy preferences, and how do we really know that they constitute the bases of the Justices' decisions? To these matters we now turn.

THE MEASURE OF MOTIVATION

Why does a person prefer candidate x to candidate y? Why did Carrie Nation go about chopping up saloons? Why did Thomas Jefferson consider farmers to be God's chosen people? Is there something Godlike about slopping hogs and shoveling manure? Short of psychoanalysis, we may answer by saying that a person acts the way he does because of his beliefs, attitudes, and values. The relevant beliefs, attitudes, and values that motivate political decision makers (and this includes judges) are described as personal policy preferences.

Accurate identification of a decision maker's personal policy preferences will not tell us *why* he or she prefers this course of action to that. We simply do not know enough about the effects of heredity and environment upon the human organism. Two peas from the same pod may be no more different than Tweedledum and Tweedledee. But if the "peas" are human beings, the difference between them may well be the difference between daylight and darkness. Therefore, identification of decision makers' personal policy preferences may explain *what* they do, but it tells us nothing about *why* they do it. Such identification, however, is not unimportant. If a decision maker's attitudes and values are reliably and validly identified, we can make a judgment about whether or not these are the attitudes and values we want such decision makers to have—that is, whether we ought to applaud or disapprove their actions.

Political decision makers have at their disposal effective means of cloaking their policy preferences. Speeches, press releases, and (in the case of judges) opinions transmute bias into impartiality. Absent an ability to distinguish truth from fiction, delusion and deceit reign supreme. Finally, knowledge of a decision maker's preferences enables us to gauge the future course of his or her conduct. Judges, especially, remain true unto themselves. Inconsistency is not their bag, although waffling sometimes occurs.[11] The vagaries of public opinion cannot justify an altered course for a judge, as they may for other public officials.

Before the Justices' personal policy preferences can be identified, the constructs of belief, attitude, and value must be defined. Note the use of the word "construct" with reference to belief, attitude, and value. These psychological determinants of behavior cannot be seen, smelled, tasted, heard, or felt. They are abstractions—wholly artificial creations whose existence can in no way be demonstrated. Nonetheless, the use of constructs is basic to the analysis, explanation, and prediction of human behavior.

In view of my intention to present the realities of judicial policy making, it may appear more than passing strange, indeed ironic, that myths should be exploded by means of an *imaginary* device. The observation is valid. My only defense is that the proof of the pudding is in the eating.

Beliefs

Social psychologists consider beliefs the most basic and elemental of the psychological determinants of behavior. *A belief is commonly defined as any simple proposition, conscious or unconscious, that may be inferred from what a person says or does, and that is capable of being preceded by the phrase, "I believe that. . . ."* The content of a belief, then, may describe the object of belief as true or false, good or bad, desirable or undesirable. Because beliefs are the basic determinant of behavior, we can assume that the average person has tens (or perhaps hundreds) of thousands of them. But so elemental a construct is not likely to be useful in the explanation and prediction of judicial decision making; the issues judges are called upon to decide are not that simplistic.

Attitudes

Consequently, attitude is the key construct. Unfortunately, there are about as many definitions of attitude as there are social psychologists. Rather than add to the clutter, the essence of the definition formulated by Milton Rokeach, a well-known social psychologist, will be used. *An attitude is a relatively enduring set of interrelated beliefs that describe, evaluate, and advocate action with regard to some object or situation.*[12] Two aspects of this definition are crucial. First, attitudes are not ephemeral—at least, not among adults whose status and occupational pattern are relatively stable. Second, the activation of an attitude involves both an *object* and the *situation* in which that object is encountered.

The major deficiency of opinion polling and other attitudinal research is that they tend to focus upon persons, places, and things without any reference to the context with which the person, place, or thing is associated. In order to explain and predict a person's behavior, one needs to know more than his or her attitude toward such "objects" as blacks, students, indigents, business, and labor unions. It is also necessary to know what the "object" is *doing*. Students studying and students rioting will not likely evoke the same response. A white person's attitude toward a black sitting next to him at a lunch counter may be markedly different from the same person's attitude toward a black who moves in next door, or a black who is employed as his boss.

To a greater extent than the attitudes of the average person, the attitudes of Supreme Court Justices are likely to be "relatively enduring." First, their decisions are a matter of public record. They are published, commented upon, and subjected to close scrutiny by the communications media and the legal profession. Second, all judges, not merely those on the Supreme Court, are expected to decide cases compatibly with what has previously been decided—to adhere to precedent. As a result, judges perforce commit themselves to consistency to a greater extent than they would if their choices and decisions were private.

Apart from the obvious fact that people's actions result from the interplay of their attitudes toward an object and their attitudes toward the situation in which that object is encountered is the norm of judicial blindness: justice is supposed to be blind. Who the litigants are is irrelevant; what the litigants have done is paramount. Though the judicial blindfold may slip occasionally, with results that are less than even-handed, only a cynic would deny that the norm is without a measure of force and effect.[13] Consequently, we may simply assume that the Justices are motivated more by the situations in which litigants find themselves (what they have or have not done) than by the personal characteristics of the litigants.

Rokeach's definition of attitude is purely conceptual. What is now needed is a means to apply it to the Justices' policy making. Such a means exists: cumulative scale analysis.

The measurement of attitudes. Toward the end of World War II, a group of Defense Department scientists successfully solved a problem that had long bedeviled social science research: consistency. How, for example, can one know if each of the questions on a test or questionnaire actually bears on the matter being studied? A survey of public attitudes toward crime may be measuring public concerns about violence instead. A test of academic achievement may really be measuring a person's aptitude for learning rather than his or her knowledge of some specific subject. Related to the problem of consistency is ambiguity. Does each question have the same meaning for every respondent? English, after all, is not the most precise language. Clearly, the problem of consistency is basic to a great deal of social science research: aptitude and achievement testing, social status, neurotic behavior, census data, public opinion, and voting behavior.

Cumulative scaling postulates that one way to solve the problem of consistency is to rank order respondents on the basis of how favorable or unfavorable each of them is to the matter being investigated. Consider three questions, to which 75, 50, and 25 percent, respectively, respond favorably. Cumulative scaling simply assumes that if a person endorses an extreme question or statement, that person must also endorse all less extreme statements for the questions to constitute a scale. This merely means that the 25 percent who responded favorably to the one question must be among the 50 and 75 percent who supported the other two statements. The reverse is also necessarily true: a person who replies "no" to the question to which 75 percent said "yes" must also reply "no" to the questions that elicited a less favorable response.

This is the sense in which cumulative scaling solves the problem of consistency. Consistency does not mean that a particular respondent must answer each statement with the same response; rather, it means that once he responds negatively, he must continue to respond negatively to all statements that were supported by a smaller proportion than supported the most extreme statement that he did support. Accordingly, a person may respond "yes" to the statement that was supported by 75 percent of the respondents, and "no" to the other two. He may not, however, say "yes" to the 75 percent statement, "no" to the 50 percent statement, and then reverse himself with a "yes" to the statement that was supported by only 25 percent of the respondents. The pattern must be consistent: yes-yes-yes, yes-yes-no, yes-no-no, or no-no-no.

Now let us apply cumulative scaling to the Supreme Court. Assume that the 10 cases in the table on p. 122 concern federal regulation of public utilities. A "+" signifies a vote favorable to the government and against the utility. A "−" signifies the opposite: an antigovernment, proutility vote. All the Justices supported the government in the least extreme case (Case 1)—the case that was decided 9 to 0. Justice *I* voted against the government in Case 2. He remained consistent, however, by voting against the government and in favor of the utilities in all the other more extremely decided cases. A similar pattern prevails for all the other

Case	Justices									Vote
	A	B	C	D	E	F	G	H	I	
1	+	+	+	+	+	+	+	+	+	9–0
2	+	+	+	+	+	+	+	+	−	8–1
3	+	+	+	+	+	+	+	−	−	7–2
4	+	+	+	+	+	+	−	−	−	6–3
5	+	+	+	+	+	+	−	−	−	6–3
6	+	+	+	+	+	−	−	−	−	5–4
7	+	+	+	+	−	−	−	−	−	4–5
8	+	+	+	+	−	−	−	−	−	4–5
9	+	+	−	−	−	−	−	−	−	2–7
10	+	−	−	−	−	−	−	−	−	1–8

Justices: once a Justice supports a utility, he continues to do so in each of the more extremely decided cases.

Two things should be noted about the table. First, the cases are ordered solely and simply on the basis of the decreasing proportion of the Justices who voted "+": progovernment and antiutility. Thus, Case 6 is less extreme than Case 7 because 5 Justices voted "+" in 6, 4 voted "+" in 7. Case 7, then, is more extreme than Case 6 because fewer Justices voted "+," and not because in some ideal world it ought to be less extreme, or because an expert thinks it should be less extreme. Note that extremeness can be justified just as logically in terms of "−" votes: Case 10 is the least extreme, Case 1 is the most extreme. The order of the cases and the proportion of the Justices remain the same either way.

Second, the voting pattern is not one that is likely to occur by chance. The Supreme Court is a 9-member body and a simple majority of the Justices determines who wins and who loses. Consequently, the Justices may combine in 256 different voting alignments. A unanimous vote can occur in only one way; each of the 9 Justices can dissent alone to produce an 8 to 1 decision; 36 different pairs may dissent to provide a 7 to 2 margin; 84 distinct combinations of 3 dissenters will produce a 6 to 3 vote; and 4 Justices may combine in 126 different ways to provide a 5 to 4 result.[14] But in constructing a cumulative scale, this sum of 256 different combinations must be doubled. The reason for this is that "directionality" is assigned. Each of the decisions in the table, for example, is classified as either progovernment and antiutility or, alternatively, as antigovernment and proutility. Therefore, each of the 9 Justices may dissent alone in an 8 to 1 decision *upholding* the government, and each correspondingly may be the solo dissenter in an 8 to 1 decision *opposing* the government. The result, then, is 512 different combinations (256 × 2).

Given the perfectly consistent pattern of votes displayed in the table, we may reliably infer that the Justices voted as they did in these cases because of their individual attitudes toward federal regulation of public utilities. We need not find an absolutely consistent voting pattern to make such an inference. Assume, for instance, that Justice G had voted "–" in Case 2 and that Justice E had voted " + " in Case 9. These two votes would be "inconsistencies" or nonscale responses. Too many such votes will destroy the consistent pattern of response, which, as noted, is crucial to cumulative scale construction. How much is too many? To allow us to explain and predict Supreme Court voting, at least 95 percent of the votes in a scale should be consistent; 95 percent, that is, of the votes cast in cases in which there were two or more dissents. Cases decided unanimously and those with only one dissent are excluded from calculation. The former are, by definition, the most extreme items in a scale, and cannot possibly have any inconsistent votes. Solo dissent cases can never have more than one inconsistent vote. Hence, one starts with at least 8 of 9 consistent votes—88.9 percent. This percentage is too close to 95 percent for comfort.

We are now in a position to formulate an operational definition of our basic construct, attitude. *An attitude is a set of cumulatively scaled cases, determined as precisely as the nature of the Court's decisions permit.* What is meant by the phrase "determined as precisely as the nature of the Court's decisions permit"? Inasmuch as explanation and prediction are a function of precise measurement, apples must not be mixed with oranges, nor even cucumbers with pickles. We must not stack the deck in favor of either overly complex or unduly simplistic explanation. Concern that the deck not be stacked is warranted. Law professors and legal scholars never tire of pontificating that each and every case is unique. Social scientists, on the other hand, have a penchant for glib overgeneralization. Consequently, the Court's decisions are categorized on the basis of their legal and semantic content. Compatibly with the conceptual definition of attitude, each cumulative scale must include a designated attitude object and a designated attitude situation. The result is a tedious trial-and-error, question-and-answer process. Do all First Amendment freedom cases belong in a single scale? Or are obscenity and establishment of religion separate issues based on the First Amendment? The equal protection clause prohibits unreasonable discrimination. Should race and sex discrimination be included in one scale, then, or do the Justices treat them differently? What about a penniless defendant who cannot afford an attorney, as opposed to the indigent convict who cannot appeal his conviction unless he is given a transcript of the record of his trial? Or a single parent applying for welfare benefits? They are all indigents. Is a tax case simply that and no more? Does the situation in which a business or a labor union finds itself make any difference to the Justices? Is there a difference between a police officer who stops and frisks a suspicious person and one who bugs a person's home? The Fourth Amendment's prohibition of unreasonable searches and seizures pertains to both situations.

The objective of this trial-and-error process is fourfold: (1) to categorize as large a proportion of the Court's decisions as possible; (2) to construct cumulative scales whose content is as specific as possible; (3) to base each scale on an attitude object and an attitude situation; (4) to approximate a perfectly consistent pattern of votes in each scale.

The last 11 terms of the Warren Court (1958–1968) elicited 73 cumulative scales encompassing 96 percent of that Court's decisions. By comparison, the first 8 terms of the Burger Court (1969–1976) yielded 63 cumulative scales that included 94 percent of that Court's decisions. The 2 percent difference in the proportion of decisions scaled undoubtedly results from the Burger Court's shorter life span. Most issues crop up only a few times per term; some are brought even less frequently. The infrequency of a given issue, plus the fact that those decided may have been unanimous or nearly so, precludes scale construction. For example, the Burger Court decided 7 state regulation of business cases during its first 5 terms, 6 of which had a unanimous pro-state/anti-business outcome. These 7 cases are consequently part of the 6 percent of the Burger Court's decisions that are not scalable.

Unfortunately, the attitude objects and the attitude situations that describe the content of each of the scales are not as specific as might ideally be desired. In a number of scales, for example, the attitude "object" cannot be specified more precisely than "criminal defendants" or "litigants negatively sanctioned by the judicial system." Similarly with regard to the attitude situation: "federal regulation" is perhaps the grossest example of an attempt at categorization. Although many of the attitude objects and attitude situations (particularly the attitude situations) are quite specific, the content of the typical scale is less than refined. For example, the self-incrimination scale contains 4 distinguishable subsets, all of which are too few in number or too badly skewed to allow for the construction of separate scales. A good example of a skewed set of decisions is school desegregation. Seventeen of the nineteen Warren Court cases were decided unanimously. Consequently, school desegregation must be grouped with other forms of racial discrimination—transportation, housing, recreation, and jury selection—to form an acceptable cumulative scale. That the content of the scales cannot be thoroughly refined is indeed unfortunate. It is the price one pays to analyze data that are not self-generated. (The Justices obviously are not amenable to deciding sets of hypothetical cases.) On the other hand, the data constitute the actual decisions of real decision makers.

Application of the operational definition of attitude has produced several dozen scales that explain well over 90 percent of the Court's decisions. On each of these scales, the participating Justices are rank ordered from most to least favorable to the attitude that the scale presumably taps. And so we have a fairly precise indication of each Justice's attitudes toward the various issues with which the Court has dealt. But to list each Justice's degree of support or nonsupport of each of the several dozen issues is hardly parsimonious. Might there not be some similarity in the way the Justices vote from one issue to another? It is a matter well worth probing.

Values

Attitudes were conceptually defined—in part—as an interrelated set of beliefs. Proceeding in the same vein, *a value may be conceptually defined as simply an interrelated set of attitudes*. This definition arguably accords with a commonsensical understanding of the term "value." Whereas an individual may have tens of thousands of beliefs, he may have only a few hundred attitudes, and perhaps but a few dozen values.

What is needed, then, is a measure of interrelatedness among attitudes. Such a measure exists: the rank-order correlation coefficient, which measures the similarity of the rank order of the Justices on any given pair of scales.[15] Each scale constitutes an attitude, and on each scale the Justices are ranked from most to least favorable. If a Justice's rank order on one scale is identical to that on another, the resulting correlation coefficient is +1.00. If the rank order on one scale is the exact opposite of that on another, the coefficient is –1.00. The measure of interrelatedness is set at or above +.60. Why +.60? Because two rankings of nine Justices that produce a correlation coefficient this similar are likely to occur by chance only once in a hundred instances—a more than minimally rigorous criterion.

Even so, this measure of interrelatedness is not wholly adequate. The correlation coefficient measures the degree of similarity between the rank order of the Justices on only a *pair* of scales. We certainly hope that the major values that motivate the Justices' decisions are comprised of more than two attitudes each. The solution to this shortcoming is the use of a variety of computer-dependent techniques of analysis that gauge the similarity among the Justices' rank orders on all the scales simultaneously, not merely two at a time.[16] The output from these computer-dependent analytical techniques indicates which of our scales are most similar. But the computer's output is not revealed truth. Spurious relationships can and do result, and real relationships may be overlooked. Hence, the computerized results must be checked against the rank-order correlation coefficients.

Assume that the computer reports that scales A, B, C, D, and E cluster closely together. Further assume that the correlation coefficients between each pair of scales are as displayed in Table 1. The five scales intercorrelate highly, at +.71. But each scale also correlates with at least one of the others at a level less than +. 60: A with B, B with C, C with D, and D with E. If we discard each scale that has a correlation less than +. 60, we have no value whatsoever. What to do? The best solution is simply to relax the measure of interrelatedness between a pair of scales. Instead of concentrating upon the correlation between a pair of scales, we focus upon the interrelatedness among all the scales that putatively form a value. If the sum total of all the correlation coefficients between all the pairs of scales that the computer analyses identify as closely associated averages +.60 or above, then a value exists. The five hypothetical scales in Table 1 meet this definition.

A supplemental criterion is also needed, however. Each scale should also show an average and (just to be safe) a median correlation at or above +.60 with the other scales that form the value. The scales in Table 1 meet this requirement: Scale A produces an average correlation of +.71 (.40 + .90 + .85 + .70 ÷ 4 = .71); scales B and C, +.68; D, +.71; and E, +.75. This criterion is added to the operational definition of value to avoid including a scale that correlates only marginally with the other scales that form the value.

The operational definition of value, then, is a set of cumulative scales (each of which meets the operational definition of attitude) in which (1) the sum total of all the correlation coefficients between all the pairs of scales averages and produces a

TABLE 1

Hypothetical Set of Rank-Order Correlation
Coefficients between Pairs of Cumulative Scales

	A	B	C	D	E
A		.40	.90	.85	.70
B			.45	.95	.90
C				.50	.85
D					.55
E					

Note: Average correlation = +. 71.

median of at least +.60; and (2) each scale (attitude) has an average and a median correlation with the others of at least +.60.

Value Systems

Utilization of this definition of value should reduce the several dozen attitudes to a manageable number. It would, however, be especially nice if a final construct could be invented that would enable us to describe in a word or two a Justice's response to *all* the relevant values that explain his decisions. (As the matter now stands, a Justice's response to each relevant value can be described only if that response is isolated from the others.) For this purpose, the construct "value system" has been formulated. It is conceptually defined as the peculiar configuration, or pattern, of a Justice's values. Consider, for example, a decision maker whose votes can be explained by his response to three values. Further assume that these three values are dichotomous—that the decision maker either supports or opposes each of them. (This is the case with regard to judicial voting. A Justice must vote either for or against the party whose case is being reviewed.) A Justice's value system, then, can have one of 8 possible response patterns—he has two choices with respect to three separate values ($2 \times 2 \times 2 = 8$). Similarly, if 4 dichotomous values explain behavior, his value system has one of 16 possible response patterns ($2 \times 2 \times 2 \times 2$). Conceptually, then, *a value system is simply the pattern of support or nonsupport of the relevant values that explain a person's decisions.*

Operationalization of the definition of value system need not detain us. All that is needed is a measure of the extent to which a Justice does or does not support any given value. Such a measure exists: the scale score. It is simply a numerical specification, between +1.00 and –1.00, of a Justice's position on a cumulative scale. Scale position is the midpoint between a Justice's last consistent "+" vote and his first consistent "–" vote. Thus, in the hypothetical scale on page 122, Justice C's scale position is 8; that of Justice G is 3. To calculate a scale score (S), scale position (P) is multiplied by 2, divided by the number of cases in the scale (n), and 1 is subtracted from this number: $S = (2P/n) - 1$. The multiplication and subtraction provide the range from +1.00 to - 1.00. The average of a Justice's scale scores on the scales that constitute the value roughly indicates his support or nonsupport of the value in question. Accordingly, *the operational definition of a value system is a Justice's combination of support (between +1.00 and .00) or nonsupport (between −1.00 and .00), as determined by the average of his scale scores, on the cumulative scales that constitute each value that explains his voting behavior.*

The methods whereby the Justices' voting may be explained and predicted have now been specified. The next step is to apply them to the behavior of the individual Justices.

THE JUSTICES' VALUES
AND THEIR VALUE SYSTEMS

The content of the attitude scales that measure the votes of the Justices clearly indicates—as we shall see in Chapter 6—that they vote the way they do because of their attitudes toward public policy issues, rather than because of purely legalistic considerations. The Justices, then, are full-fledged political decision makers. Their decisions resolve various issues that affect significant segments of American society. In other words, they engage in the authoritative allocation of resources, which is what politics is all about.

To be sure, the Justices verbalize their decisions in a legalistic manner. This is good form, and it effectively softens disagreements that otherwise might become strident and rancorous. But the manner in which the Justices reach their decisions must be distinguished from what they say in their opinions. Our measures of motivation do not preclude an identity of word and deed. On the other hand, neither do they portend such an identity. And as we shall see, in this as well as later chapters, the Justices' decisions result from their political attitudes and values.

In no sense is it intimated that a political motivation produces an unprincipled decision. The Justices do not respond to partisan political pressure. They do not hew to any party line; rather, each Justice marches to the beat of his own drum. It has been asserted that the Court follows the election returns; that, however, is a half-truth at best.[17] Presidents do, more often than not, appoint to the Court persons whom they think will reflect their policy preferences. Consequently, a series of Conservative Presidents may replace, over time, a formerly Liberal majority, or vice versa. Only in this sense does the Court follow the election returns. But the time lapse is frequently such that the pendulum has begun its swing in the opposite direction before the new majority has replaced the old. Moreover, the new Justices do not invariably reflect the policy preferences of the appointing President. They may on many issues, but they sometimes deviate from the expected course—and more often than not on a matter of especially major moment. A prime example is the Watergate Tapes case.

The political attitudes and values to which the Justices respond are those that guide the activities of government—the human concerns that mediate the accommodation of conflicting interests and outlooks. The attitudes and values are principled because they are applied in a consistent, evenhanded fashion. They encapsulate each Justice's vision of what American society should be—his personal political philosophy.

The Warren and Burger Courts provide ample data for the analysis of the attitudes and values of the Justices. The 1958 term of the Court is a convenient starting point, for this term ushered in a period of 3½ years during which the Court's personnel remained constant. If too many Justices are here today and gone tomorrow, an accurate analysis of their voting behavior is prevented because a given Justice does not participate in a substantial proportion of the Court's decisions.

Eighteen Justices sat on the High Bench between 1958 and 1977. Six held membership during the last eleven years of the Warren Court: Chief Justice Warren, Hugo Black, John Marshall Harlan, William O. Douglas, Potter Stewart, and William Brennan. The last two have also served throughout the Burger Court period. Black and Douglas were appointed by Roosevelt before World War II. Warren, Harlan, Stewart, and Brennan were Eisenhower appointees. Byron White replaced Charles Whittaker at the beginning of the 1962 term and has served ever since. Arthur Goldberg replaced Felix Frankfurter at the same time and sat for three years. White and Goldberg were both Kennedy appointees; Whittaker and Frankfurter were appointed by Eisenhower and Roosevelt, respectively. Abe Fortas replaced Goldberg at the start of the 1965 term and served throughout the four remaining years of the Warren Court. Tom Clark served through the end of the 1966 term and was then replaced by Thurgood Marshall, whose service spans the remaining terms being analyzed. Fortas and Marshall were Johnson appointees; Clark was a Truman appointee. Four of the remaining Justices are Nixon appointees: Burger in 1969; Harry Blackmun, who replaced Fortas in 1970; and Lewis Powell and William Rehnquist, who replaced Black and Harlan midway through the 1971 term. Douglas was replaced by John Paul Stevens in December 1975.

The Values That Explain the Justices' Votes

The cumulative scales that constitute the attitudes that explain the votes of the Justices in both the Warren and Burger Court periods can be divided into three clusters. Each of these clusters is a value, and the three together account for approximately 85 percent of the Court's decisions. Let us examine the contents of each of them.

In the first cluster are the scales that tap such attitudes as those toward involuntary confessions, the right to counsel, double jeopardy, due process of law, freedom of communication, the rights of persons alleged to be security risks, protest demonstrations, the right to confront one's accusers, establishment of religion, trial by jury, self-incrimination, the retroactive application of newly enunciated constitutional guarantees, the rights of debtors and military personnel, abortions, subconstitutional fair procedures, and the Federal Rules of Civil Procedure.

What do these issues have in common? First, many pertain to specific provisions in the Bill of Rights: freedom of speech and press, the establishment of religion clause, due process of law, the right to counsel, double jeopardy, self-incrimination, and the right to trial by jury. Second, these are typically considered civil liberties issues. Third, most of the litigants are persons accused of crime—criminal defendants—or political offenders of one sort or another—security risks and persons expressing unpopular and unconventional points of view. All told, these are situations where individuals are protesting alleged governmental infringements upon their liberty. In a word, what is fundamentally at stake is freedom. This, then, is the label assigned the various attitudes that motivate the Justices' behavior in these sets of cases: the value of *freedom*.

The second cluster of attitude scales taps such attitudes as those toward cruel and unusual punishment (more specifically, the constitutionality of capital punishment); the extralegal influences to which jurors may be subject; the rights of indigent convicts, illegitimates, and juveniles; poverty law; desegregation of schools and other public facilities; sex discrimination; searches and seizures; plea bargaining; the willingness of federal courts to step into allegedly biased state judicial and administrative proceedings; moot questions; the availability of the writ of habeas corpus; and the length of time persons must reside in a state in order to vote, run for public office, or secure state-provided benefits.

What do these attitude scales have in common? First, most of them concern persons who allege discrimination on the basis of race, economic condition, or age, or for political reasons. Second, many of these attitude scales turn on the legal issue of equal protection of the laws: race and sex discrimination; indigent convicts, illegitimates, and juveniles; and residency requirements. This being so, a second label best describes behavior in these sets of cases: the value of *equality*.

In the remaining cluster are attitude scales such as antitrust, mergers, bankruptcy, worker's compensation, state regulation of business, public utilities, federal regulation of securities, the reapportionment and districting of voting districts, natural resources, libel actions alleging defamation of character, the legal rights of unions vis-à-vis business, antitrust activities of unions, the rights of Indians, and the jurisdiction of the federal courts.

The characteristic common to this cluster is economic activity.‡ It is, moreover, economic activity in the context of governmental regulation. Because of this regulatory aspect, it is perhaps most appropriate to label this value *New Deal economics* or New Dealism. This label aptly describes the issues that were raised by the transformation of an agricultural

---

‡The merits of most of the Indian cases, as well as the merits of cases involving the jurisdiction of the federal courts, concern economic matters. The defamation cases are all tort actions in which the plaintiff sues for monetary damages. Arguably, the reapportionment cases affect economic interests as much as they do political and racial voting strength.

economy into an industrialized economy. For better or for worse, the resolution of most of these issues was the work of the Court of the 1930's and 1940's.§ The criteria and formulae of those decades still undergird our attitudes and affect our behavior in matters economic.

These, then, are the three values. They explain slightly more than 85 percent of the decisions of both the Warren and Burger Courts. The content of the three values has changed somewhat between the two periods, however. Trial by jury and military personnel, for example, shifted from New Deal economics on the Warren Court to freedom on the Burger Court. This movement of an attitude scale from one value to another can be explained by differences in the content of the cases in these two scales. During the Warren Court, well over one-half of the jury trial cases were civil proceedings in which economic interests were at stake. During the Burger Court, however, three-fourths of the controversies were criminal cases. Similarly, during the Warren Court, many of the cases involving military personnel concerned veterans' benefits. But during the Burger Court, these pertained exclusively to provisions of the selective service statutes—such as draft exemption and conscientious objection—matters that semantically suggest freedom rather than economics.

But not all shifts of an attitude scale from one value to another are as readily explainable. Establishment of religion was part of New Deal economics during the Warren Court; it is now located where one would expect: with the value of freedom. Similarly, transportation, patents and copyrights, and the rights of business vis-à-vis unions were all appropriately part of New Deal economics during the Warren Court era. Now, however, they are off on their own tangents. Each is unique unto itself, far distant from any other attitude scale.

Furthermore, some attitude scales associate with two of the values. Statutory construction, which concerns the meaning of various criminal laws, was part of the value of freedom during the Warren Court. It now clusters with equality as well as freedom. The probable explanation is that the criminal laws construed by the Burger Court have a substantial civil rights focus that was absent during the Warren Court. Less explicable are voting and employment discrimination. Both associate with equality, but voting also associates with New Deal economics and employment discrimination also associates with freedom. Also puzzling is state regulation of obscenity, an issue that has wracked the Court since the mid-1950's. Federal regulation of obscenity is part of the value of freedom, where it properly belongs both legally and semantically; but state regulation, on the other hand, associates with the value of equality.

---

§ Defamation, natural resources, and reapportionment were not addressed by the Court until the 1960's, however.

The point of the foregoing discussion is that the analytical techniques neither inhibit nor compel the movement of attitude scales from one value to another, or to no value at all if that be the situation. It would indeed be nice if all issues that legally and semantically pertained to freedom, equality, and New Deal economics clustered together in a distinctive fashion; if all economic issues without exception correlated highly with one another; and if all issues that pertained to freedom and equality could be similarly depended upon. Unfortunately, human decisions cannot be displayed in as neat and tidy a fashion as rings in a jeweler's showcase. So, the Justices' decisions must be allowed to speak for themselves. If the rank order of the Justices on one attitude scale correlates closely with their ordering on other scales, then that scale is considered part of the value with which it associates, even though, from a legal or semantic standpoint, it ought to locate elsewhere. It is, of course, possible that the rank-order correlation between a pair of scales may be spurious. Nonetheless, if the rank order of the Justices on an economic issue produces an average correlation of $+.80$ with the scales that form the value of equality, but correlates much less with New Deal economics, should it be excluded from the value of equality simply because it has no relationship, legally or semantically, with what is conventionally considered equality? Perhaps. On the other hand, the Justices do vote on this issue in substantially the same fashion as they do on the other equality issues. These anomalous correlations, although they weaken the legal and semantic purity of the three values, do not destroy the descriptive value of the labels given to each of these three clusters. Debtors is the only scale that does not properly pertain to the value of freedom; only extralegal jury influences and state regulation of obscenity appear to have no connection with the definition of equality, and only reapportionment bears little resemblance to what may appropriately be considered New Deal economics.

Of most significance is the fact that three values explain more than 85 percent of the Court's decisions. These three values have motivated the Justices' votes for the better part of two decades. That the content of each of the values is not identical from the Warren Court to the Burger Court is not unexpected. In addition to the factors already mentioned, personnel changes have also occurred. The Nixon appointees to the Burger Court did not serve under Earl Warren. It is quite likely that one or more of these Justices perceive a given attitude to pertain to a value other than that perceived by his predecessor. Burger and Blackmun are not cut from the same mold as their predecessors, Warren and Fortas. Nor is Justice Powell a pea from the same pod as his predecessor, Justice Black. And though William Rehnquist shares many of John Marshall Harlan's predispositions, differences between them are nonetheless marked.

The Justices' Value Systems

A value system was previously defined as the pattern of support or nonsupport of the relevant values that explain a person's decisions. Scores were computed, ranging from $+1.00$ to -1.00, for each of the Justices on each of the attitude scales that constitute a given value. These scores were then averaged to provide an overall indication of that Justice's support ($+1.00$ to $.00$) or nonsupport (-1.00 to $.00$) of the value in question. Note should be made that most of the Justices did not serve the entirety of the periods under analysis. Consequently, not every Justice participated in enough decisions in every scale to allow us to rank order him and thereby calculate his score on that scale. Therefore, scores are calculated only for those Justices who can be rank ordered on a given scale. Thus, a Justice who was rank ordered on 15 of the 20 scales that constitute a value would have his degree of support or nonsupport determined on the basis of the average of his scores for the 15 scales on which he was rank ordered.

As has been noted, analysis has revealed the existence of three major values, each of which a Justice may support or oppose. Eight combinations of support ($+$) or nonsupport ($-$) are possible. Each such combination represents a value system. Table 2 lists the eight possible combinations.

One may quarrel with the value system descriptions given in Table 2. But for the most part they accord with common usage. Liberals support the exercise of civil liberties and an expansion of the rights of persons

TABLE 2

Values and Value Systems

Value System	Values		
	Freedom	Equality	New Dealism
Liberal	+	+	+
Civil Libertarian	+	+	−
Individualist	+	−	−
Populist	+	−	+
Utopian Collectivist	−	+	−
Benevolent Authoritarian	−	+	+
New Dealer	−	−	+
Conservative	−	−	−

NOTE: A "+" indicates support of the value in question; a "–" indicates nonsupport.

accused of crime; they also support the demise of racial, social, and political discrimination, and improvement of the economic status of the poor. Liberals also support New Deal economics; that is, they are pro-union, antibusiness, and procompetition, and they favor compensation for injured persons. The value system of Conservatives is opposite that of Liberals. | | Civil Libertarians support the noneconomic values of freedom and equality. Individualists are the classic nineteenth-century-type liberals—they believe that that government is best that governs least. Government should keep its hands off the economic system, should avoid social engineering regardless of "humanitarian" considerations, and should allow the individual to do his own thing with but a minimum of constraint. Populists are the agrarian reformers of an earlier era. Supportive of personal freedom and economic reform, they had an impact in the West and South from the 1890's to the 1930's.

The next two types, the Utopian Collectivists and the Benevolent Authoritarians, are furthest removed from the mainstream of American politics. (I apologize for the exotic labels, but other existing referents for these types are decidedly uncomplimentary.) Neither supports freedom for others, but both are high on equality. Various Marxist groups, the New Left, student radicals, and some anti-Establishment types might possibly personify them. The New Dealer supports economic reform to the exclusion of personal freedom and political, social, and racial equality. Presumably, the heyday of this type was the Great Depression of the 1930's.

Now that the eight possible value systems that describe the pattern of support or nonsupport of the values of freedom, equality, and New Deal economics have been identified, the voting behavior of the individual

---

| | The statement that a Conservative Justice does not support the values of freedom, equality, or New Deal economics is not meant to be pejorative. Support or nonsupport is a matter of degree—a measure of *comparative* support or non-support. In a set of 30 First Amendment freedom cases, for example, a Justice may have voted to support freedom of communication in 10, but may have voted against the First Amendment claim in the other 20, along with all but one of his colleagues, on the basis that these 20 cases incited mob violence. Our hypothetical Justice accordingly scores −.33 with regard to First Amendment freedoms. Is it accurate to say that he does not support the First Amendment in any absolute sense? Certainly not.

Moreover, a Justice may well believe that other considerations outweigh support for such values as freedom and equality. He may strongly believe that individuals must bear full responsibility for their own actions and that the government must not engage in social engineering regardless of "humanitarian" considerations. Such a Justice would likely appear hostile to equality as it has been described in this chapter. Similarly, a Justice who was strongly supportive of states' rights and who thus believed that primary responsibility for enforcement of the criminal laws rested with the states. Such a Justice would likely be tolerant of state efforts to cope with crime, with the result that he would appear to be antifreedom.

Justices can be analyzed. This has been done in Table 3. The table lists all eighteen Justices and specifies what part of the 1958–1977 period each served on the Court. The period of membership is presented in terms rather than years. Thus, Chief Justice Warren served from the beginning of the period being analyzed until the end of the 1968 term, which was June of 1969. The period of service of those Justices who left the Court at a time other than the end of a term is given as the beginning or the end of the term closest to their appointment or departure. The two Justices without a date next to their names held membership throughout 1958–1977.

The three middle columns of Table 3 numerically represent the extent of each Justice's support of or opposition to each of the three values. The scores can range from +1.00 to −1.00. The scores for Douglas, Brennan, Marshall, Stewart, and White are based upon their votes in Burger Court decisions only. This was done in order to specify as accu-

TABLE 3

The Justices and Their Value Systems

Justice	Values and Average Scale Scores			Value System
	Freedom	Equality	New Dealism	
Douglas (through 1974)	.73	.76	.73	Liberal
Warren (through 1968)	.65	.61	.43	Liberal
Fortas (1965–1968)	.63	.64	.24	Liberal
Goldberg (1962–1964)	.63	.63	.18	Liberal
Brennan	.38	.58	.37	Liberal
Marshall (from 1967)	.45	.57	.23	Liberal
Black (through 1970)	.53	−.55	.43	Populist
Stevens (from 1975)	.05	.31	−.15	Moderate
Stewart	.09	−.08	−.32	Moderate
White (from 1962)	−.40	−.07	−.02	Moderate
Clark (through 1966)	−.51	−.20	.25	New Dealer
Blackmun (from 1970)	−.34	−.27	−.22	Conservative
Powell (from 1971)	−.26	−.26	−.49	Conservative
Whittaker (through 1961)	−.38	−.67*	−.06	Conservative
Frankfurter (through 1961)	−.12	−.81*	−.36	Conservative
Burger (from 1969)	−.49	−.42	−.38	Conservative
Harlan (through 1970)	−.30	−.36	−.64	Conservative
Rehnquist (from 1971)	−.58	−.58	−.55	Conservative

*Based on two scale scores.

rately as possible their current response to the values of freedom, equality, and New Deal economics. The scores of all the other Justices, however, pertain to the part of the 1958–1977 period during which they were members of the Court.

The last column of the table lists each Justice's value system. This column includes a value system not heretofore described: Moderate. Convention decrees that scores occupying the midpoint of a measure that ranges from +1.00 to –1.00 lie in a zone of indifference or neutrality with regard to the underlying variables. Persons having such scores are neither pro nor con. Because the scores of Stevens, Stewart, and White (with one exception for each of them) lie in this middle zone between +.20 and −.20, an additional value system had to be established. The label "Moderate" aptly describes those whose scores fall in that zone.

The ordering of the Justices on Table 3 is from most to least Liberal and from least to most Conservative. This ordering was established simply by totaling each Justice's scores across the three values. Douglas, accordingly, appears most Liberal; Marshall appears the least so. Similarly, Blackmun is the least Conservative; Rehnquist is the most.

All but 5 of the Justices (that is, 13 of 18) have either a Liberal or a Conservative value system. Each group is of approximately equal size— six Liberals, seven Conservatives. Three Justices are neither fish nor fowl—the Moderates (Stevens, Stewart, and White). Justice Clark was apparently the last of the New Dealers, whereas Justice Black, true to his poor rural Southern origins, was very much a Populist.

The identification of Black as a Populist runs counter to the judgment of other observers.[#] During the 1950's, the heyday of McCarthyism, when dirty linen invariably carried Red stains, Black, along with Douglas, was the judicial champion of the Liberal community. But Black did not wax Conservative with age. Prior to the 1960's, the value of equality was not pertinent to the Justices' decision making. Except for the Court's decisions in *Brown* v. *Board of Education*, race relations was not an issue in the Court's deliberations. Concerns that bear on equality, such as sit-in demonstrations; sex discrimination; the rights of juveniles, indigents, and illegitimates; and poverty law did not figure prominently in the Court's decisions until the 1960's. Black simply did not have an opportunity to reveal his true colors until then.

No perceptible shift occurs in the value systems of the Justices who served during both the Warren and Burger Court periods, with the possible exception of Justice White. If separate scores are calculated for

---

[#] Even some who should know better. Seven years after he left the Court, and a decade after he clearly revealed his true colors, the mislabeling of Black continues. See, for example, the "Letters" column of the *New York Times Book Review* of June 19, 1977.

the two periods, White appears to be growing slowly more opposed to the values of freedom and equality, especially the former. If this trend continues, he may not qualify in the future as a Moderate but rather may be classified as a marginal Conservative.

The classification of 16 of the 18 Justices as Liberal, Conservative, or Moderate comports with the value systems that the vast majority of Americans possess. These value systems are commonplace, as even a cursory reading of editorial pages and journals of opinion will reveal. Nor is the New Dealism of Justice Clark, or the Populism of Justice Black, discordant. Clark and Black espoused value systems that were prominent, though at an earlier point in time. On the other hand, who is to say that the economic conditions of the 1980's might not spawn another generation of New Dealers? Especially if freedom and equality become concerns of minor moment, as they already have in some circles?

Be that as it may, these eighteen individuals respond neither to alien nor to inscrutable influences. Their decisions are not dictated by whim, nor by the side of the bed they got up on. The Justices are not motivated by venality or personal aggrandizement. They respond rather to values that are an integral part of our heritage, that touch Americans generally, and that have a fundamental impact upon the character of American life. If we must entrust our fate to others, we could do a lot worse.

NOTES

1. Studies of judicial roles are numerous. See Charles H. Sheldon, *The American Judicial Process: Models and Approaches* (New York: Dodd, Mead, 1974), pp. 73–98, and the works cited therein; Joel B. Grossman, "Role Playing and the Analysis of Judicial Behavior," *Journal of Public Law* 11 (1962): 285–309; and Joel B. Grossman, "Dissenting Blocs on the Warren Court," *Journal of Politics* 30 (1968): 1068; Henry R. Glick, *Supreme Courts in State Politics* (New York: Basic Books, 1971); Henry R. Glick and Kenneth N. Vines, "Law Making in the State Judiciary," *Polity* 2 (1969): 142–159; J. Woodford Howard, "Role Perceptions on the U.S. Courts of Appeals," *Research Report No. 2* (Washington, D.C.: Federal Judicial Center, 1974); Stuart S. Nagel, "Political Party Affiliation and Judges' Decisions," *American Political Science Review* 55 (1961): 843–850; Theodore L. Becker, "A Survey Study of Hawaiian Judges: The Effect on Decisions of Judicial Role Variations," *American Political Science Review* 60 (1966): 677–680; Beverly Blair Cook, "Sentencing Behavior of Federal Judges: Draft Cases—1972," *University of Cincinnati Law Review* 42 (1973): 597–633; Sheldon Goldman, "Behavioral Approaches to Judicial Decision Making," *Jurimetrics Journal* 11 (1971): 156–160; Thomas D. Ungs and Larry R. Baas, "Judicial Role Perceptions," *Law and Society Review* 6 (1972): 343–366; Kenneth N. Vines, "The Judicial Role in the American

States," in Joel B. Grossman and Joseph Tanenhaus, eds., *Frontiers of Judicial Research* (New York: Wiley, 1969); S. Sidney Ulmer, *Courts as Small and Not So Small Groups* (New York: General Learning Press, 1971); Dean Jaros and Robert Mendelson, "The Judicial Role and Sentencing Behavior," *American Journal of Political Science* 11 (1967): 471–488; Dorothy B. James, "Role Theory and the Supreme Court," *Journal of Politics* 30 (1968): 160–186; Victor E. Flango, Lettie McSpadden Wenner, and Manfred Wenner, "The Concept of Judicial Role," *American Journal of Political Science* 19 (1975): 277–290; and James L. Gibson, "Judges' Role Orientations, Attitudes, and Decisions," *American Political Science Review* 72 (1978): 911–924.

In addition to his role orientation and expectations, a Justice's votes may well depend upon his background and socialization, or may be a response to a multiplicity of intracourt influences. In these regards, see the classic studies by John R. Schmidhauser, "The Justices of the Supreme Court—A Collective Portrait," *American Journal of Political Science* 3 (1959): 1–57; Walter F. Murphy, *Elements of Judicial Strategy* (Chicago: University of Chicago Press, 1964); and J. Woodford Howard, "On the Fluidity of Judicial Choice," *American Political Science Review* 62 (1968): 43–56.

Treating social background in particular are Joel B. Grossman, "Social Backgrounds and Judicial Decision Making," *Harvard Law Review* 79 (1966): 1551–1564; Joel B. Grossman, "Social Backgrounds and Judicial Decisions: Notes for a Theory," *Journal of Politics* 29 (1967): 334–351; Sheldon Goldman, "Backgrounds, Attitudes, and the Voting Behavior of Judges: A Comment on Joel Grossman's 'Social Backgrounds and Judicial Decisions,'" *Journal of Politics* 31 (1969): 214–222; Joel B. Grossman, "Further Thoughts on Consensus and Conversion: A Reply to Professor Goldman," *Journal of Politics* 31 (1969): 223–229; and S. Sidney Ulmer, "Dissent Behavior and the Social Background of Supreme Court Justices," *Journal of Politics* 32 (1970): 580–598.

2. See the discussion on access in Chapter 2.

3. Vol. 14, No. 77 (April 1970), pp. 41–43, 81.

4. See Joseph A. Schlesinger, *Ambition and Politics* (Chicago: Rand McNally, 1966).

5. Alpheus T. Mason, "The Chief Justice of the United States: Primus inter Pares," *Journal of Public Law* 17 (1968): 25.

6. See Glendon Schubert, *Dispassionate Justice: A Synthesis of the Judicial Opinions of Robert H. Jackson* (Indianapolis: Bobbs-Merrill, 1969), pp. 15–17.

7. 2 Dallas 419.

8. 19 Howard 393, number 9 in Harold J. Spaeth, *Classic and Current Decisions of the United States Supreme Court* (San Francisco: W. H. Freeman and Company, 1977).

9. 157 U.S. 429, 158 U.S. 601.

10. 400 U.S. 112.

11. For examples, see the sections in Chapter 3 headed "Distinguishing a Precedent" and "Overruling Precedent," and, in Chapter 6, the section headed "Deviation from Past Performance."

12. *Beliefs, Attitudes, and Values* (San Francisco: Jossey-Bass, 1968), pp. 112–122.

13. See Chapter 7.

14. The formula is

$$\frac{N!}{R! \times (N - R)!} \; .$$

Thus, in the case of a 5 to 4 vote:

$$\frac{9!}{4! \times (9 - 4)!} \;=\; \frac{362880}{24 \times 120} \;=\; \frac{362880}{2880} \;=\; 126.$$

15. Maurice G. Kendall, *Rank Correlation Methods*, 2d ed. (New York: Hafner, 1955), pp. 34–48; Sidney Siegel, *Nonparametric Statistics* (New York: McGraw-Hill, 1956), pp. 213–219.

16. A description of these techniques is found in David W. Rohde and Harold J. Spaeth, *Supreme Court Decision Making* (San Francisco: W. H. Freeman and Company, 1976), pp. 93–95.

17. Robert A. Dahl, "Decision Making in a Democracy: The Supreme Court as a National Policy Maker," *Journal of Public Law* 6 (1957): 279.

The Predictability
of Justice

In the introduction to Chapter 5, note was made that the focus on the personal policy preferences of the Justices does not explain why a Justice has one set of such preferences rather than another. This failure not only reduces the explanatory power of the analysis provided in Chapter 5; it also makes such an analysis somewhat suspect. The best way to test the validity of an analysis of personal policy preferences as an explanation of Supreme Court decision making is to use it to predict how the Justices will vote and how the Court will decide cases that it has accepted for review. That is the focus of this chapter.

The *sine qua non* of accurate prediction is a good bit of knowledge about that which one wishes to predict. The best theory in the world is of little help if one is ignorant of the facts. Although theory is not essential to prediction (of the tides, of the force of gravity), it is essential to explanation.

PROBLEMS ENCOUNTERED IN PREDICTION

Unfortunately, the Supreme Court is not the most co-operative of institutions when it comes to the dissemination of information. True, once a decision has been made, it is duly reported along with the votes and opinions of the individual Justices. But during the deliberations, the velvet curtains rarely part. What goes on at the weekly conference, when the Justices decide which cases to review and cast their votes in the cases that they have heard, is Washington's best-kept secret. Nobody but the Justices themselves is present, not even the Justices' law clerks. Leaks are

virtually unheard of though the stakes are often high, as in cases involving the application of antitrust laws, when millions of dollars may ride
on the outcome of the litigation.*

Limited Sources of Information

The Justices, however, do not labor totally away from the public spot-
light. Attorneys orally argue their cases before the Court with spectators
and reporters present. The attorneys also prepare written briefs, and the
opinions of the lower courts that previously heard the case are also
available. But unless one is present in the courtroom during oral argument or is sufficiently involved with the litigation to secure a copy of the
briefs, one is largely dependent upon the media for information.

Unfortunately, the media rarely report the facts of a case in advance
of its decision in anything but a cursory manner. The *United States Law
Week*, a specialized publication,[1] reports in some detail the oral argument
in 15 to 20 cases per year. The cases selected tend to be few in number,
however, and of interest to only a small legal readership. *Preview* is

---

*A recently reported leak concerned the convictions of three Nixon aides, John Mitchell,
John D. Erlichman, and J. R. Haldeman, for their part in the Watergate cover-up, which
the Court had been requested to review. Mitchell and Haldeman were convicted of conspiracy, obstruction of justice, and two counts of perjury. On April 21, 1977, National
Public Radio reported that in their secret conference the Justices, by a vote of 5 to 3, had
refused to review the convictions. NPR's report said that Burger, Blackmun, and Powell—
all Nixon appointees—were the three Justices who voted for review, and that Justice
Rehnquist, an official in the Department of Justice prior to his appointment to the Court,
was not participating. Whether a "leak" actually occurred has not been confirmed. It may
well have been that the story was planted in hopes that (1) the Court might be sufficiently
embarrassed to cause a fourth Justice to vote to grant certiorari (only four votes are needed
for the Court to accept a case for review, as is explained in Chapter 2); or (2) the way would
be paved for a rehearing if the Court did deny review—the basis being that denial was
tainted by the report of the initial vote.

Neither objective (if they were objectives) was realized, for on May 23, the Court unanimously denied the petitions for review: *Erlichman* v. *United States* and *Mitchell and Haldeman*
v. *United States*, 53 L Ed 2d 250. Eight days later, the Court, again unanimously, denied an
application for suspension of the order denying review: *Mitchell and Haldeman* v. *United
States*, 53 L Ed 2d 253. It may be noted that Rehnquist, not unexpectedly, did not participate in either of these actions.

Although the "leak" received extensive news and editorial coverage (for example, "High
Court Reported to Oppose a Review of Nixon Aides' Case," *New York Times*, April 22,
1977; T. R. Reid, "High Court Dilemma Over Leak," *Washington Post*, April 27, 1977;
Lesley Oelsner, "Disclosure Viewed as Embarrassment to High Court," *New York Times*,
April 30, 1977; Nick Thimmesch, "The High Court Should Explain How the Leak Occurred," *Chicago Tribune*, May 10, 1977), it should be emphasized that though the media
seemed to accept the fact that a "leak" did occur, the denouement of the litigation, plus
the lack of confirmation, rather persuasively suggests the "leak" was an effort to embar-
rass the Court, not just the work of a gossipy clerk or Court employee.

another specialized publication[2] that includes memoranda describing the background and significance of, and the issues in, all cases accepted by the Court for review. The lack of information is a serious problem because the typical case has several issues, any one of which may be the basis of the Court's decision. Which basis for decision the Court chooses will affect how the individual Justices vote and thus the final decision.

Consider the matter of the death penalty. In 1968, the Court agreed to review an Arkansas decision. Two issues were to be considered: (1) Is it a violation of due process to allow a jury to impose a sentence of death at its own discretion? (2) Does self-incrimination result when a jury simultaneously determines guilt and punishment, thereby forcing the defendant to make a Hobson's choice—maintain innocence and risk more severe punishment, or admit guilt and present mitigating evidence?[3] I predicted that the Court would answer "no" to these questions and would do so by a 4 to 4 vote. (Only eight Justices were members of the Court at the time.) But when the Court announced its decision in June 1970, it clearly had decided neither issue: "In the action we take today, we express no view whatever with respect to the two questions originally specified in our grant of certiorari."[4] Instead, by a 6 to 1 vote, Marshall not participating, it sent the case back to the federal district court for a determination of whether persons opposed to capital punishment had been unconstitutionally excluded from the jury. The outcome of the case and the votes of three of the seven participating Justices had thus been wrongly predicted. Some measure of comfort was realized one year later when the Court finally resolved these questions. The outcome was as predicted, with only Justice Stewart voting differently than as expected.[5]

If the theory presented in the preceding chapter were a complete one—if it told us how the Justices would view each case that they accepted for review, instead of telling us only how they will vote if they view the case as pertaining to issue x rather than issue y—information as to the issue or issues in a given case would not be essential to an accurate prediction. The initial task thus becomes one of identifying these issues and then judging which will be the most likely bases for decision. The ideal situation is a case with a single, sharply defined issue that bears directly upon one of the cumulative scales into which the Court's decisions have been apportioned. Sometimes this ideal situation exists; often it does not. When it does exist, the next step is to ascertain the proportion of pro and con decisions in the relevant cumulative scale and the scale scores of the participating Justices. If there is a subset of the cumulative scale that bears especially directly upon the case to be predicted, the votes of the Justices in those decisions are also scrutinized. After such data have been obtained, the scores of the Justices on the value of which the cumulative scale is a part are evaluated.

Single Issue Decisions

Thus, in the school desegregation cases of 1971,[6] which raised the question of whether busing and other means could be used to require Southern schools to desegregate, 90 percent of the cases in the desegregation scale supported black litigants; 25 of 26 decisions favored them in cases concerning school desegregation. Accordingly, a prodesegregation result was highly probable. And because more than 92 percent of the Justices' votes supported school desegregation, a unanimous vote on most of the issues was likely. On the other hand, only three of the participating Justices—Douglas, Marshall, and Brennan—strongly supported the value of equality, to which desegregation pertained. The prediction that black litigants would win, and that the Court would continue to support Southern school desegregation (but not unequivocally) turned out to be correct. The outcomes of all the cases were as predicted. Douglas, the Justice most supportive of the value of equality, was expected to require, and not merely permit, the use of busing, and to oppose retention of neighborhood schools. He and Marshall were also expected to vote to eliminate all-black schools. Neither of them did so. Instead, they joined with all their colleagues in the opinion of the Court.

Another example of a case in which there was a single, sharply defined issue was a 1972 decision that posed the question whether the Constitution shields newspersons from having to disclose their sources of information.[7] Even though the Court had never before had an opportunity to consider this question, the issue was clear-cut, bearing directly on the First Amendment. Both the Warren and Burger Courts were supportive of freedom of the press, but only the Court's three Liberals—Douglas, Marshall, and Brennan—supported the value of freedom, to which the First Amendment cases pertain. This fact, plus the unwillingness of the Burger Court to expand the sphere of freedom beyond the bounds set by the Warren Court, dictated a judgment that journalists would lose by a 6 to 3 vote. Lose they did, but by 5 to 4.

The fourth vote supporting confidentiality of news sources was cast by Justice Stewart. During oral argument he had asked, "Why does this question of privilege arise after more than 200 years?" His query suggested opposition to the journalists' claim. But the tone of a Justice's questions is a most unreliable indicator of his vote; to base prediction thereon is fraught with danger. Instead, the prediction that Stewart would vote against the newspersons was based on his moderate stance toward the value of freedom and his reluctance to expand the scope of the protection afforded by the First Amendment. He is, to be sure, more supportive of First Amendment freedoms than the Nixon appointees or his fellow Moderate, Byron White. On the other hand, his support is also much less than that shown by Douglas, Marshall, and Brennan.

Multiple Bases for Decision

There have been many cases where the issue was less than cut and dried. For example, the Court has considered Muhammad Ali's draft appeal, the Pentagon Papers controversy, and the constitutionality of using property taxes to finance public education.

Ali had applied for conscientious objector status and been rejected by his draft board and by the lower federal courts. Three related issues were present, each of which pertained to the same cumulative scale—armed forces: (1) Did he conscientiously oppose war in general? (2) Was this opposition based upon religious belief? (3) Or was he only a "selective" conscientious objector who opposed some wars (Vietnam)? The fact that three distinct questions bore on a single scale indicates that specification of the attitudes that motivate the Justices' voting behavior is not as refined as is ideally desirable. Unfortunately, the Justices are not in the habit of sitting for interviews or answering lengthy questionnaires. Consequently, the Justices' track records are not as detailed as they might otherwise be.

The decisions in the pertinent scale indicated that if Ali simply opposed war in general he would lose by reason of a tie vote. A tie in his case would uphold the ruling of the court of appeals. Justice Marshall abstained because he had been Solicitor General when the case first arose. If Ali could show that he opposed all war on religious grounds, he would win by a unanimous vote; but if his objection was shown to be selective, only Justice Douglas would support his claim. The Court found that Ali's beliefs were based on the tenets of the Muslim religion and that his understanding of these beliefs caused him to object to all wars not sanctioned by the Koran. The vote, as predicted, was unanimous.[8]

In the Pentagon Papers case there were two possible and independent bases for decision: First Amendment freedoms and federal internal security legislation. A unanimous vote in support of publication was predicted, and it was noted that Burger and Blackmun were the most likely to dissent, along with Byron White, who strongly supported the government in cases concerning national security. But the Court, with barely a passing nod in the direction of national security, based its decision squarely on the First Amendment, ruling that "any system of prior restraints of expression comes to this Court bearing a heavy presumption against its constitutional validity," and that "the government thus carries a heavy burden of showing justification for the imposition of such a restraint."[9] No such justification, the majority said, was shown.

The vote was 6 to 3, with each of the nine Justices writing a separate opinion. The three dissenters—Burger, Blackmun, and Harlan—objected to the "almost irresponsibly feverish" haste with which the Court decided the case,[10] a factor that had never entered into the predictive calculations. The dissenters clarified their position five days after the decision was announced when Chief Justice Burger stated in a television interview that "the Court was actually unanimous on the basic problem of First Amendment rights of newspapers."[11] This statement tempted a prediction score of 9 votes right, none wrong. But Burger's remark was off the record, and the pages of the *United States Reports* will forever show that the vote, for better or for worse, was indeed 6 to 3.

A final example of a case in which any one of several issues could have been the basis of the Court's ruling concerned the constitutionality of the use of property taxes to finance public education.[12] An action had been initiated by Mexican-American parents in Texas whose children attended schools that had a low property tax base. The parents claimed that disparities in the value of taxable property from one school district to another violated the equal protection of the laws clause because districts with a low tax base were predominantly either black or Chicano. Three possible bases for decision suggested themselves: poverty law, comity, and desegregation. Cases in the poverty law scale pertain primarily to welfare and Social Security benefits, but they do so in the context of the equal protection clause. The comity scale measures the Court's willingness to allow state courts first crack at deciding constitutional issues affecting state and local government. The state courts had not been afforded such an opportunity in this case. And although desegregation does not pertain to school financing as such, the facts that public schools were involved and that poorer school districts have a larger minority population than wealthy districts suggested that the desegregation scale might help predict the outcome.

All three of these scales did, however, relate to the value of equality, even though the proportion of pro- and antiequality decisions varied markedly among the three scales: 82 percent of the Burger Court desegregation decisions and 62 percent of its poverty law decisions were proequality, but only 18 percent of the decisions that concerned comity were proequality. Given that only three Justices supported greater equality, a prediction was made that the Court would not outlaw the property tax as a method of financing public education, with the three Liberals in dissent. The outcome was as predicted, but by a slender 5 to 4 margin, with White joining the three Liberals. If the decision had been otherwise, the method of financing public education in 49 of the 50 states—Hawaii alone excepted—would have been changed, and the residents of richer districts would have been constitutionally required to provide a common financial foundation for all of a state's schools.

The "Extremeness" of a Case

Apart from the problem of determining which of the issues raised in a given case the Court is likely to base its decision on is the problem of gauging the "extremeness" of a case. Will it be decided 9 to 0, 0 to 9, or by a vote that is in between these extremes? The answer depends directly on the individual Justices' past voting behavior as indicated by the cumulative scale or scales and the value of which such scales are a part. Determination of how each Justice will vote is as much a matter of judgment as it is statistical probability. Underlying the judgment of a case's extremeness is the assumption that the attitudes and values of each of the Justices are relatively fixed and stable—that Justices neither change their spots nor cast their votes at random.

Consider the matter of obscenity. In its last eleven terms the Warren Court upheld convictions for violation of state and federal obscenity laws in only 19 percent of its decisions. During the first three terms of the Burger Court, 41 percent of the decisions upheld such convictions. Why had the rate more than doubled? One possible explanation is the votes of Byron White. President Kennedy had nominated him to the High Bench in 1962 when he was serving as Deputy Attorney General. During his years on the Warren Court, White, an All-American football star from the University of Colorado, who was also Phi Beta Kappa and a Rhodes Scholar, had voted with the majority on 43 of 44 occasions. Only Douglas, Black, and Stewart among the holdover Warren Court Justices were more liberal than he. But on the Burger Court he slipped to fifth rank as of 1973, supporting obscenity convictions not only more frequently than Douglas and Stewart (Black having resigned), but also more frequently than Brennan and Marshall.

Thus in 1973, when the Court agreed to consider whether the states ought to be given more latitude to curb pornography,[13] its decision was likely to hinge on the vote of Byron White. Douglas, Brennan, Stewart, and Marshall had stalwartly resisted watering down the language of the First Amendment to allow for increased regulation. Equally insistent that state and local governments be allowed to curb the dissemination of such material were the four Nixon appointees. A prediction that White would side with the four Conservatives in loosening the ties that bound the states was on the money.

Did Byron White, then, change his tune? Not necessarily. The issues on which the Court was passing judgment in the 1960's were not those of the 1970's. Books the genre of John Cleland's *Memoirs of a Woman of Pleasure* are too tame for today's adult bookstores. Nor are the films of Russ Meyer nearly as explicit as *Deep Throat* or *Behind the Green Door*. The evidence is strong that the world, and not Justice White, had changed.

In the next seven months, the Court summarily decided 66 state obscenity cases on the basis of its 1973 decision. None of these cases was orally argued, and all of them, with two exceptions, produced the same 5 to 4 alignment. The two exceptions were 5 to 3 decisions, Douglas not participating. Then, in April 1974, the Court agreed to formally consider another case dealing with the authority of state and local officialdom to regulate alleged pornography. The question for decision was whether a theater manager in Albany, Georgia, could be convicted for showing the movie *Carnal Knowledge*. Would this be another victory for those whose vision ends at the tips of their blue noses? Would it be a further encouragement to self-anointed and officially appointed censors and fig-leafers? By this time the Burger Court's conviction rate in obscenity cases had climbed to more than 83 percent. Was another 5 to 4 vote in the offing? Superficially, it seemed so.

In its 1973 decision, the majority had made frequent reference to "hard core pornography." *Carnal Knowledge*, however, was not even X-rated. Reputable critics ranked it among the ten best films of 1971, and the female lead had received an Oscar nomination for her performance. Nor did the Court's authorization of tighter state control over pornography mean that the provincial standards of Yahoo Gulch were to be the moral law of the land. If obscenity were to be defined that broadly, almost anything could be suppressed—even *Little Women* or some of the productions of Walt Disney. Even before the great social to-do over toplessness or the controversy over *Lady Chatterley's Lover,* the Court had unanimously thrown out a law that made it a crime to make available to the public materials found "to have a potentially deleterious influence upon youth." To quarantine adults to protect juvenile innocence, the Court intoned, "is to burn the house to roast the pig."[14] The Georgia law at issue in the *Carnal Knowledge* case was of the same ilk; that law made it a crime to show in a movie conduct that could be prosecuted if done publicly. So what is so bad about that? If taken literally, the law meant that grade B murder mysteries could be proscribed. But can Perry Mason and James Bond rationally be classed in the same category as the likes of Linda Lovelace? Obviously not. A unanimous vote that *Carnal Knowledge* was not obscene was therefore accurately predicted. The Court decided that the standards of *Miller* v. *California* would remain unchanged,[15] and that the states could regulate pornography—but only if it were hard core.[16]

The Need for Judicial Track Records

Identification of the most likely basis for decision and determination of which litigant will win and by what vote are not the only problems of prediction. It is equally important to determine each Justice's track record—his previous votes in cases related to the one being predicted. The theory and methods of analysis assume that past performance is the guide to future behavior. Sometimes, though, a Justice's past performance is sufficiently ambiguous that no prediction can be assayed. An example is the parochiaid cases of 1971, which raised the question of whether the states could reimburse parochial schools for the costs of instruction in secular subjects.[17] The relevant cumulative scale, establishment of religion, showed that five of the nine Justices had a score of precisely zero. They neither supported nor opposed such programs. Only the votes of Black and Douglas could be predicted with any degree of assurance. But the Justices' voting patterns in these 1971 decisions and several others that were subsequently decided were clear enough to allow a prediction of the results of the parochiaid conflict of 1975: the provision of textbooks would be declared constitutional; the provision of professional staff and supportive materials would be declared unconstitutional. Both outcomes were correct, and 16 of the 18 votes were cast as predicted.[18]

Inscrutable track records are very much the exception. Much more troublesome is the absence of track records *in toto,* a situation encountered whenever a new member takes his seat. Fortunately, no changes in personnel occurred during the 1972–1974 terms of the Court. The absence of any new Justices may well account, at least in part, for an improvement in predictive accuracy during these three years. When predictions were begun in the spring of 1970, Warren Burger was midway through his first term as Chief Justice and Harry Blackmun had not yet been nominated. The resignations of Earl Warren and Abe Fortas in the spring of 1969 had ended Liberal domination of the Court's policy making. No longer did a built-in majority exist with regard to any of the three major values that explain the bulk of the Justices' votes—freedom, equality, and New Deal economics. Instead, Justices Stewart and White held the balance of power between the Liberal and Conservative extremes. Hence, Burger Court decisions had to be predicted on the basis of Warren Court data. This was a risky undertaking indeed.

How does one predict the votes of those newly ensconced on the High Bench? One hopes that they possess a set of background characteristics that provide some reliable indication of how they are likely to vote. These attributes, however, are soft predictors. Furthermore, a Justice may have a set of characteristics that cancel one another out: some may indicate a Liberal bent; others may suggest Conservatism. Whether a given characteristic indicates predictable tendencies is determined from the voting behavior of previous Justices who have possessed that attribute. The best predictor, not surprisingly, is political party affiliation. Republicans tend to be Conservative, Democrats tend to be Liberal. Previous judicial experience is also a good indicator, especially if such experience was on a lower federal court. Such Justices have tended to be Conservative and, as a group, a rather undistinguished lot.[19] Ethnicity and place of residence can also be indicative. Four of the five Jewish members of the Court, for example, have been Liberals—Frankfurter was the deviant. A rural or Southern background suggests Conservative leanings to a greater extent than does an urban or Northern upbringing.

Fortunately, Richard Nixon's nominees were not of mixed blood. All indicators pointed in a staunchly Conservative direction. Burger and Blackmun were Republicans; Blackmun, however, was much less partisanly active than Burger. Both had served on a federal court of appeals prior to their appointment to the High Bench. Blackmun had graduated from a nationally renowned law school; Burger had graduated from a local proprietary institution. This fact, plus Blackmun's negligible involvement in partisan politics, indicated that Blackmun's intellectual horizons should be a bit broader—and hence less Conservative—than that of his fellow Minnesotan. So far, this prediction has proven accurate.

Powell and Rehnquist were also from the same mold. Though a Democrat, Powell is a Virginian; and Virginia Democrats are usually not much different from Republicans. Powell was not. He had endorsed Republican candidates for office and had contributed $500 to Nixon's 1968 election campaign. He was, moreover, very active in bar association politics at both the state and national levels, rising to the presidency of the American Bar Association in 1964. Persons who hold such offices are not boat rockers. Rehnquist, like Powell, had never been a judge before taking his seat on the Court. He was, however, Conservative born and bred—so much so that he actively supported Barry Goldwater in his 1964 Presidential campaign. At the time of his nomination Rehnquist was an Assistant United States Attorney General. Attorneys general and their staff, with some exceptions, are not known for dedication to civil rights and liberties. Given these factors, it could be predicted that Rehnquist would be the most staunchly Conservative of his colleagues. This proved to be an accurate assessment.

But what undoubtedly made Nixon's appointees eminently predictable from the day they took their seats was not the set of background characteristics that each brought with him, but simply the fact that Nixon himself had selected them. To perhaps a greater extent than any President in history, Nixon took pains to nominate to the Court persons who reflected his personal policy preferences. At least on occasion, most Presidents have either been rather blasé about whom they appointed, guessed wrong in their estimation of their nominees' value system, or filled vacancies on the basis of political friendship or to gain electoral advantage. Not so Richard Nixon. He suffered two costly defeats when the Senate rejected his nominations of Clement Haynsworth and G. Harrold Carswell to fill the vacancy occasioned by the resignation of Abe Fortas.

Not since 1894 had the Senate rejected a President's nominees twice in succession. These rejections occurred because of defections in the senatorial ranks of the President's own party. Nixon could have knuckled under and nominated candidates who, in his words, would have "brought the country together." But he stuck to his guns. When Black and Harlan announced their resignations in September 1971, editorial writers demanded that Nixon replace them with individuals of equal stature. The names that subsequently surfaced did not exactly meet with universal approbation, if only because they were so little known: a Virginia congressman; Senator Robert Byrd of West Virginia, who had never practiced law nor even passed a bar exam; an Arkansas attorney primarily known for his skill in keeping black children out of white schools; two Southern federal court of appeals judges who had one and a half years' judicial experience between them; and a pair of otherwise unremarkable woman judges. Whether Nixon actually intended to nominate persons from this list or whether their nomination was a diversionary tactic is debatable. In any event, when Nixon did disclose the names of his nominees on nationwide television, they were not those that had previously surfaced. In comparison to the latter, Lewis Powell and William Rehnquist were professional giants. Their credentials, at least, were impeccable. Both had graduated first in their law school class. Both had distinguished reputations—Powell especially. Rehnquist, who had been Phi Beta Kappa as an undergraduate, had served as law clerk to former Justice Robert Jackson, an honor accorded to only a select handful of top law school graduates.

Upon Senate confirmation of Powell and Rehnquist, the Supreme Court was four-ninths Nixonite. This was not a mean accomplishment for someone who had been President less than three years. Though the record of his Administration may be tarnished by Watergate, it will nonetheless show that no President surpassed Nixon in fashioning a Court that reflected his policies. Four-ninths does not a majority make, but given his four opportunities, Nixon batted 1000 percent.

Deviation from Past Performance

A final difficulty bedeviling the prediction of justice is the fact that the occupants of the Marble Palace do occasionally deviate from their past performances, and there are instances when they do not adhere to what has previously been decided. A set of poverty law cases that came before the Court in the spring of 1971 provides a good example. Poverty law is a relatively new area of judicial policy making.[20] The Court did not become concerned with it until the later years of the Warren Court. From a single poverty law decision in the 1963 term, the Court's output rose to four in 1967, eight in 1968, and eleven in 1969. Poverty law pertains to welfare benefits, such as Social Security and Aid to Dependent Children. It includes the determination of eligibility and the standards and conditions under which such assistance is to be provided. The 1971 cases presented typical, clear-cut poverty law questions: Is a person who is receiving unemployment compensation entitled to a hearing before his benefits are terminated? May a state deny welfare to resident aliens? Is it constitutional to give a community's voters the right to block construction of low-rent public housing?

A prediction was made that the Court, by a 5 to 4 vote, would require a hearing before unemployment compensation was terminated and would, by a 6 to 3 vote, rule that states could not deny welfare to resident aliens. Both outcomes were as predicted, but the actual vote was unanimous in both cases.[21] None of the eleven poverty law decisions of the first term of the Burger Court had been unanimous, and only three of the thirteen decided by the Warren Court had been unanimous. Indeed, in all but four of the decisions of the Warren and Burger Courts, at least two votes were cast in opposition to the claims of the indigent litigant. Furthermore, the case concerning unemployment compensation was closely related to one that had been decided the previous year in which the Court had ruled, by a 5 to 3 vote, that due process had been violated by failure to provide persons notice and hearing prior to cutting off their ADC benefits.[22] In arriving at its decision the Court, however, ducked the constitutional question—the provision of notice and hearing—and instead merely construed the relevant section of the Social Security Act—that unemployment compensation must be paid promptly upon a determination of eligibility, and not withheld until after the employer has exhausted his appeals.

But the most startling of these three poverty law decisions was the one that concerned the constitutionality of the referendum requirement for low-rent public housing.[23] By a 5 to 3 vote, Douglas not participating, the Court upheld the constitutionality of the provision. On the basis of a seemingly relevant precedent from the last term of the Warren Court,[24] a prediction was made that the referendum requirement would be declared void with only Justice Black dissenting. The basis for this prediction was not only the 1969 precedent, but also the racial character of much public housing and the Court's strong opposition to sophisticated as well as simple-minded methods of officially sanctioned racial discrimination. In its 1969 decision, the Court had held that an amendment to the city charter of Akron, Ohio, discriminated against minorities by requiring that any ordinance enacted by the city council that dealt with racial discrimination in housing had to be approved by a majority of the city's voters before it became effective. The Court thereby limited the authority to repeal fair housing laws through popular referenda. Only Justice Black dissented. But in 1971, it was Black who wrote the Court's opinion:

> Unlike the Akron referendum provision, it cannot be said that California's Article 34 rests on "distinctions based on race." The Article requires referendum approval for any low-rent public housing project, not only for projects which will be occupied by a racial minority. And the record here would not support any claim that a law seemingly neutral on its face is in fact aimed at a racial minority. . . .
> . . . Provisions for referendums demonstrate devotion to democracy, not to bias, discrimination, or prejudice.[25]

By simple assertion, Tweedledum was thus distinguished from Tweedledee.

Unfortunately, the foregoing are not the only examples of deviation from past performance. How a Potter Stewart and a Byron White (especially White) could find a practice as ancient and widespread as the death penalty to constitute cruel and unusual punishment remains unfathomable.[26] Or how such pious pillars of Conservative rectitude as Warren Burger, Harry Blackmun, and Lewis Powell could void, at one fell swoop, the abortion laws of 49 of the 50 states on the basis of a right nowhere mentioned in the Constitution—the right to privacy.[27] Not only did they void these laws, they also found in this nebulous "right to privacy" a precisely detailed and comprehensive answer to the whole abortion controversy: during the first 3 months of pregnancy a woman has an absolute right to an abortion; during the second trimester the states can regulate the abortion procedure only to the extent that such regulation relates to the preservation and protection of maternal health; and only during the last trimester, when the procedure is at its most hazardous for the pregnant woman, can the states, if they wish, prohibit abortions altogether.

As examples of the Court as moral arbiter, these decisions are unsurpassed. That issues so deeply controversial—socially, politically, and religiously—as the death penalty and abortion should be resolved by a court speaks volumes on the authoritative policy-making capacity of the Supreme Court. I, for one, do not disapprove of such policy making. It has been a fact of American life for the better part of two centuries. And a truly dysfunctional institution could not have survived for two centuries. If time is a test of power, the Supreme Court has passed it well. And if the Court did not have this power, interest in its decisions today would be minimal. Attention would focus instead upon the legislative and executive branches of the state and federal governments. The basic issues confronting American society would have to be resolved here rather than in the nation's courtrooms.†

The Court is no less likely to deviate from past performance in cases that have a low emotional quotient. As a final example, consider the issue of whether the antitrust laws apply to major league baseball. In 1972, the Court agreed to consider that question.[28] Fifty years earlier, the Court had decided that baseball was not the sort of business antitrust laws were intended to cover.[29] And in 1953 the Court had decided precisely the same issue that would be before it in 1972: that baseball's reserve clause, which gives the employer outright ownership of his employees by denying a player any choice of which club he plays for, does not violate the antitrust laws.[30] Following its 1953 decision, the Court required other professional sports to abide by the antitrust laws, with the result that by 1972 baseball was the only major sport not specifically covered.[31]

During the 15 years prior to 1972, the Court had decided 79 antitrust cases, exclusive of mergers between businesses. Only 8 of these decisions supported the businesses in question. Among these 79 cases were 6 decided by the Burger Court, each of which was not only antibusiness, but unanimously so. The Court does not lack cases. If it wished to reaffirm what had been decided in 1922 and 1952, it could have refused to consider the matter. This is standard procedure given the demands on the Court's time. Therefore, it was predicted—with complete assurance—that by an 8 to 1 vote, Rehnquist dissenting, the Court would subject baseball, as it had other sports, to the operation of the antitrust laws, and that as a consequence the reserve clause would be illegal. Instead, by a 5 to 3 vote, Powell not participating, the Court merely reaffirmed its previous position. It did so in an opinion by Justice

---

† Although I was less than overjoyed at the inaccuracy of my predictions with regard to the 1972 death penalty decision and the Court's ruling on abortion, any dismay did not extend to my personal views of the rightness or wrongness of these decisions. In predicting the Court's decisions, nothing could be more fatal than to allow my own attitudes and values to enter the equation. Given the emotional nature of many of the issues presented to the Court for decision, it is not easy to remain personally unconcerned about their outcome. Yet it must be done. The data alone, and not wishful thinking, must guide the prediction. Even so, I am frequently accused by those who have read or heard my predictions that because I have predicted a certain outcome I personally approve of it as well. Such accusations are not uniformly unfavorable. I am currently on several organizations' mailing lists solely because one or another of my predictions convinced those organizations that I was on their side. Although I point out to all who are interested that I am not in the business of writing editorials, I fear that I make no more impression than a kamikaze flea upon a brick wall.

Blackmun, which, to be charitable, can be called a cop-out.‡ To rationalize baseball's special status would have been difficult, if not impossible; so Blackmun did not even try. The 1922 and 1952 decisions were, he said "an anomaly" and "an aberration."[32] The assumption that courts have a responsibility to correct anomalies and aberrations is not necessarily a valid one, for the very simple reason that "there is merit in consistency even though some might claim that beneath that consistency is a layer of inconsistency."[33] And if there is (as indeed there is) "any inconsistency or illogic in all this, it is an inconsistency and illogic of long standing that is to be remedied by the Congress and not by this Court."[34] Why, pray tell, by Congress? Because "we continue to be loath, 50 years after *Federal Baseball* and almost two decades after *Toolson,* to overturn those cases judicially when Congress, by its positive inaction, has allowed those decisions to stand for so long."[35] So it all boiled down to "positive inaction"—a lovely phrase, and one of the Court's more notable contributions to Orwell's dictionary of Doublespeak. The fact that it was not Congress that provided baseball with its antitrust exemption but rather those distinguished denizens of the Marble Palace merely attests to the utility of gobbledygook. But these comments are perhaps overly critical. To expect reasonable decisions to result from legal reasoning is, after all, to counsel perfection.§

APPLICATIONS OF THE PREDICTIVE PROCESS

The entirety of the considerations that go into making a prediction can perhaps be best understood by reference to two of the more momentous cases decided during the 1970's. Certainly they were the two biggest

---

‡ Blackmun began his opinion with a brief adulatory history of baseball, more akin to a press release than a judicial opinion. It listed 88 "celebrated" names "that have sparked [*sic*] the diamond . . . and provided tinder for recaptured thrills. . . ." 407 U.S. 258, at 262–263. The list included many nicknames: Goose, Rube, Big Ed, Wahoo Sam, Wee Willie, Iron Man, Three-Finger, Smokey Joe, Sad Sam, Stuffy, Dizzy, Old Hoss, Rabbit. Blackmun even included two bits of verse in this portion of his opinion. *Id.* at 263, 264. Interestingly, two of the five majority Justices—Burger and White—refused to join this part of Blackmun's opinion.

§ In view of the difficulties previously reported and the Court's not infrequent deviation from past performance, predictive accuracy has not been all that bad. Between 1970 and 1977, 105 predictions have been made, 92 (87.6 percent) of which have been accurate. Accuracy has improved since the start of the 1972 term (61 of 66 correct, or 92.4 percent), compared with the first years of the Burger Court. As for the votes of the Justices, 84.7 percent have been correctly predicted overall; 86.2 percent have been correctly predicted since the beginning of the 1972 term. The votes of Justices Stewart and White—the Court's

decisions of 1974: the Detroit cross-district busing case and the Watergate Tapes case.[36]

The outcome of both cases was predicted, as were the votes of each of the participating Justices. As was pointed out in Chapter 5, when all 9 Justices participate, they may combine in 512 different voting alignments, ranging from 9 to 0 in favor of one of the litigants to 0 to 9 in support of that party. The odds against hitting the nail on the head are thus 511 to 1. When only 8 Justices take part in the decision, as in the Watergate Tapes case, the odds improve to 186 to 1—still somewhat more than the usual long shot.

The two cases differed most markedly with regard to the issues they raised. Those that the Watergate Tapes case raised were soft, in the sense that there were a number of them, each of which was rather ill-defined. The Detroit case, by comparison, presented a single, sharply defined issue, on which each of the Justices had a detailed voting record.

The Detroit Cross-District Busing Case

At issue in this case was the constitutionality of busing school children between Detroit and 53 suburban school districts. All parties agreed that Detroit's schools were illegally segregated. The precise question was, what should be done about it? Is desegregation to end at the city limits, or may surrounding suburban districts be included to achieve a more equal balance of black and white students? Detroit's schools, like those of most of the nation's major cities, are predominantly black. In 1970, blacks constituted 63.6 percent of Detroit's public school population; by 1973, the proportion had risen to 71.2 percent. Desegregation limited to schools within city boundaries would not accomplish much. Indeed, it boded to be counterproductive, for it would probably cause a greater exodus to the suburbs and/or a transfer by white parents of their children to private schools. If the Court ruled that cross-district busing was not required by the Constitution, desegregation of Northern schools would be strangled by a noose of white suburban housing, and the specter of a resurrected Jim Crow would be cast over the landscape of American public education.

---

balance of power—have been hardest to predict (79.5 percent and 79.3 percent, respectively). Easiest to predict have been the votes of Rehnquist (89.1 percent), Blackmun (89.0 percent), and Douglas 88.6 (percent). Rates of accuracy in predicting the votes of the others have been: Powell (86.7 percent), Brennan (85.7 percent), Burger (84.3 percent), Marshall (82.9 percent), Black (82.4 percent), and Harlan (76.5 percent). Thus far, the votes of Stevens have been predicted with 100 percent accuracy.

The cumulative scale to which the Detroit case pertained was desegregation. Although the issue of school desegregation is arguably distinct from other forms of segregation, not enough variation had occurred in the voting of the Justices to allow for the formation of a separate school desegregation scale. The Justices had made no distinction between school desegregation and other sorts of desegregation—public accommodations, recreational facilities, housing, transportation, jobs, and so on.

Analysis showed that the Burger Court had decided 35 desegregation cases in which the votes of the Justices had been reported. Twenty-nine cases (83 percent) had produced a prodesegregation result. Indeed, more than two-thirds of these decisions were unanimously prodesegregation. In these 35 cases more than 84 percent of the Justices' votes supported a desegregated outcome. The Burger Court's 17 school desegregation decisions were even more lopsided. Each outcome supported desegregation, as did 92 percent of the Justices' votes, as the following table shows:

Justice	Vote on School Desegregation		
	Yes	No	Percent Yes
Douglas	17	0	100
Brennan	17	0	100
Marshall	16	0	100
White	16	0	100
Blackmun	8	1	89
Stewart	15	2	88
Burger	14	3	82
Powell	3	1	75
Rehnquist	2	2	50
TOTAL	108	9	92

These data, then, strongly indicated a desegregationist result, one that should have been unanimous. But prediction is not so simple. Insofar as cross-district busing was concerned, the raw data obscured more than they revealed.

Desegregation is an issue that clusters with a number of others[37] to form the value of equality. On a scale ranging from +1.00 (always votes in favor of equality) to −1.00 (always votes against equality), the Justices scored as follows:

Justice	Equality Score
Douglas	+.85
Brennan	+.62
Marshall	+.59
White	+.03
Stewart	+.03
Blackmun	−.34
Powell	−.51
Burger	−.54
Rehnquist	−.65

Three of the Justices rather strongly supported equality; the four Nixon appointees opposed it. White and Stewart were neutral and, theoretically at least, could have gone either way. Because of the extremeness of the desegregation proposed by the lower federal courts, a judgment was made that the Justices' responses to the value of equality would be a better predictor of the outcome than the voting pattern displayed in the school desegregation decisions. To desegregate a school system by ordering busing within the confines of that district is one thing (and was much in keeping with remedies that the Court had upheld in a number of previous decisions). But to order 53 neighboring districts to help atone for the sins of a district of which they are not a part is a remedy of an altogether different color. The lower courts had made no finding that any of the 53 suburban districts had ever been guilty of illegal discrimination. Only the Detroit school system was.

The extremeness of the cross-district busing order was not likely to faze the Court's three Liberals—Douglas, Brennan, and Marshall. Their support for the value of equality, plus the fact that they had not voted against desegregation in any Burger Court decision, made it unlikely that they would alter their course. On the other hand, the Nixon appointees—Burger, Blackmun, Powell, and Rehnquist—would find the relief ordered by the lower courts too much to stomach. Of the nine Justices, they supported equality the least. News reports that Powell's vote was critical was clearly wrong. He ranked seventh in support of equality, and only Rehnquist was more reluctant to vote in favor of school desegregation. The key to the outcome turned rather on the votes of White and Stewart. Both were fence sitters with regard to equality. White, however, had had an unblemished record in support of school desegregation. He had never voted against school desegregation either as a member of the Burger Court or during his seven years on the Warren Court. He could have broken his record in the Detroit case, but in the face of such consistency he was judged more likely to align himself with the Liberals. Unlike White, Stewart had voted against school desegregation three times, twice as a member of the Burger Court and once as a member of the Warren Court.[38]

The Justices' overall voting patterns, then, indicated a 5 to 4 vote *against* cross-district busing; Stewart and the Nixon appointees would constitute the majority, with White and the three Liberals dissenting. This prediction was supported by two previous decisions that bore most directly on the Detroit controversy.

The first of these cases was *Wright* v. *Emporia*, decided in June 1972. The Court ruled (the Nixon appointees dissenting) that a Virginia city, which was under a court order to desegregate, could not separate itself from the county school district of which it was a part. The combined school-age population of the town and county was 34 percent white and 66 percent black. If the town were allowed to form its own school district, the racial mix would have been 48 percent white and 52 percent black; the remainder of the county would have been 28 percent white and 72 percent black. Speaking through Chief Justice Burger, the dissenters agreed that a white enclave could not secede from the town if desegregation would thereby be thwarted. But, argued Burger, that would not happen as the schools of both the town and the county would be thoroughly desegregated. He contended that all that the Constitution required was that racially separate schools be dismantled, and that to equate desegregation with racial balance is a "gravely mistaken view."[39] Once school officials have eliminated segregation, Burger said, judges should not be free to concoct and impose their own plans in order to increase the ratio of black to white students.

The other case, decided in May 1973, also originated in Virginia.[40] A federal court of appeals had reversed the ruling of the trial court judge, which had required two suburban counties to merge their schools with those of the City of Richmond. Blacks constituted 70 percent of Richmond's school population, but less than 10 percent of that of the two surrounding counties. By a 4 to 4 vote the Supreme Court upheld the decision of the court of appeals that federal judges had no power to order such mergers. Justice Powell did not participate in the case because he had formerly been a member of the school boards of both Richmond and the State of Virginia. A prediction was made that the Court would void the merger and would do so by a 4 to 4 vote. And although the Court does not report who voted which way when the result is a tied vote, doubtless the three remaining Nixon appointees were joined by Justice Stewart, with the three Liberals and Byron White in opposition.

These two decisions, supplemented by the overall voting patterns of the Justices, strongly supported the predicted outcome of the Detroit case. If four of the Justices opposed racial balancing in Southern schools, most assuredly they would oppose it in Northern cities. And if massive cross-district busing could not be ordered in the South, the likelihood of its being permissible in the North (especially in suburban districts that were not parties to the unconstitutional segregation in which Detroit's officials had engaged) was nil.

On July 25, 1974, the Court voided cross-district busing between Detroit and the 53 surrounding school districts. Vote for vote, the decision was as predicted.

The Watergate Tapes Case

Predicting the outcome of the Watergate Tapes case was an entirely different matter. The issues were numerous, novel, and nebulous. Projections as to how the Justices would respond to them would require rather drastic inferential leaps. Furthermore, a decision was possible within a day or two after oral argument was heard. Consequently, the reports of those arguments, which would have been beneficial, would not be available before a prediction had to be made. Although oral argument rarely indicates *how* a Justice will vote, it frequently does provide an indication of the issue that the Justices perceive as central to the controversy. Given the novelty of a case in which a federal prosecutor subpoenaed the President of the United States to produce certain records of his conversations with personal aides and advisers, such information would have markedly shortened the limb out on which it was necessary to climb.

The President's lawyer, James St. Clair, had put forth a three-pronged defense of Nixon's refusal to comply with Special Prosecutor Leon Jaworski's subpoena of 64 conversations taped by the White House, which Federal District Court Judge John Sirica had ordered Nixon to turn over to the grand jury investigating the Watergate break-in. In order of importance, the arguments in Nixon's defense were as follows:

1. That the constitutional principle of separation of powers exists for the purpose of preserving the independence and autonomy of each of the branches of the federal government. In order to enable the President to maintain his independence from the dictates of Congress or the courts, he may claim executive privilege against those who demand disclosure of confidential matters. The confidentiality of Presidential communications is crucial to the operation of separation of powers.

2. That the special prosecutor is himself a member of the executive branch of the federal government. As such, he is an agent of the Presi-

dent and can perform only those duties delegated to him by the President. Because the President had not given Mr. Jaworski the authority to determine whether White House conversations are privileged, the dispute is not one with which the federal courts may properly concern themselves, but is only a squabble internal to the executive branch.

3. That the Watergate grand jury acted unconstitutionally when it named Nixon as an "unindicted co-conspirator" in February 1974. A President is immune from indictment and prosecution unless and until he has been impeached and removed from office.

To the extent that these arguments have a common focus, it is separation of powers. Separation of powers, however, is not a cumulatively scalable category because it has not been the basis for any Warren or Burger Court decisions. Consequently, none of the Justices had a track record that bore directly on the matters at issue. But a search did reveal two decisions that were peripherally related, as well as one decided in 1807 that could be counted as more or less of a precedent. In that year, Chief Justice Marshall, sitting as a federal circuit judge (a responsibility borne by Justices of the Supreme Court until the end of the nineteenth century), ordered President Jefferson to produce certain documents requested by Aaron Burr for his defense against charges of treason. Although Jefferson blustered indignantly at Marshall's effrontery in serving him with a subpoena, he nonetheless quietly produced the requested documents.[41]

As for the two peripheral decisions, one dated from June 1972 and the other from April 1974. In the 1972 decision Justice White, speaking for himself and the four Nixon appointees, quoted approvingly "the longstanding principle" that "the public . . . has a right to every man's evidence." He did add a qualification, however: "except for those persons protected by a constitutional, common-law, or statutory privilege."[42] Whether a President was covered by such an exception was not addressed by the Court. The issue, rather, was whether the First Amendment shielded reporters from disclosing to a grand jury their sources of confidential information. The Court said that they had no such protection and that they could be subpoenaed and ordered to supply information in criminal investigations. To equate Presidential prerogatives with those of journalists might be stretching things a bit, but it was at least a straw in the wind that was worth grasping for.

The April 1974 decision was perhaps a bit more pertinent. In a unanimous opinion, Chief Justice Burger stated quite emphatically that the Constitution and *not* the dictates of public officials is the Law of the Land, and that it is the responsibility of the *courts* to determine what materials must be produced and to what extent, if any, executive privilege applies. This case concerned the Kent State killings in 1970;

the issue was whether the Governor of Ohio and National Guard officers had immunity for their actions. The Court held that these persons did have some degree of immunity, but that its scope was not so broad as to preclude the parents of the deceased students from filing a suit for damages.[43]

Apart from these cases, clues to the Court's decision would have to be sought among underlying principles that, it was hoped, would point the way to a correct prediction. But such "principles" do not lend themselves to quantification, and, like precedents, at least one is always found on each side of every issue. Nonetheless, there was no alternative. How would the Court—a political institution, jealous of its own power—lean? If the Court were to accept the claim of executive privilege advanced by Nixon's attorneys, it would curb its own power to judge the legality of Presidential actions. By so limiting its decision-making capacity, the Court would seriously undermine the long-standing principle of judicial review. It would at the same time strengthen the principle of separation of powers, according to which each branch—especially Congress and President—remained independent and autonomous of the others. There was little doubt as to which one of these competing principles the Court would choose. Since *Marbury* v. *Madison*,[44] American judges have never failed to voice their support for the doctrine of judicial review. Consequently, if there is any fixed star in the constitutional firmament, it is, to hear judges tell it, the authority of courts to determine the legality of the actions of the other branches of government—legislative as well as executive.

The second of the arguments advanced in Nixon's behalf—that Special Prosecutor Jaworski was an agent of the President—held little water by the summer of 1974. Such an argument would be credible only if it were proven that the special prosecutor was merely an executive official. Then Nixon would emerge victorious. For nothing could be more anomalous than for a court to rule that a mere agent of a principal could compel the principal to perform actions against his will. That would be akin to a real estate broker determining to whom and at what price a householder must sell his home, or an attorney compelling his client to disclose incriminating evidence or to plead guilty to a crime.

But Jaworski, it turned out, was not a mere agent of the President. The Constitution gives Congress the power to delegate the appointment of "inferior officers" to "the heads of departments." Acting under this power, Congress gave the Attorney General power to appoint a new Special Prosecutor. When Nixon sought to fire Jaworski's predecessor, Archibald Cox, in the fall of 1973, he had to request the Attorney General to do so. When the Attorney General and his deputy both refused, Nixon promptly fired them and appointed Robert Bork as Acting Attorney General. Bork duly complied with Nixon's request and fired Cox.

When Jaworski replaced Cox in December, Attorney General William Saxbe not only pledged to Congress that he would not fire Jaworski for plunging further into Watergate, he reaffirmed Jaworski's independence and supported his right to go to court, if necessary, to secure additional White House evidence. Nixon himself had stated on numerous occasions that Jaworski was an independent official. Thus, it was established that Jaworski was not a purely executive official.

The third argument in Nixon's defense—that a grand jury may not consider a President an unindicted co-conspirator—appeared to be merely an attempt to muddy Watergate further. Although the Supreme Court agreed to consider this issue, it was not likely to affect the outcome of the case. Naming Nixon as an unindicted co-conspirator had no practical effect upon his ability to conduct affairs of state; nor did it subject him to criminal prosecution.

Aside from the arguments presented in Nixon's defense were two subliminal issues that likely would affect the Court's disposition of the case. Neither was raised either in oral argument or in the written briefs submitted by the parties' attorneys. Consequently, neither was likely to be considered by the Justices. Nonetheless, they should be deemed relevant.

The first was the matter of self-incrimination. In October 1973, Nixon did release edited portions of some of his Watergate conversations. He subsequently claimed that the "national interest" precluded his releasing other conversations on the same subject. Although Nixon never defended his refusal to release his tapes on the basis of self-incrimination, his use of "national interest" and "national security" to justify his refusals amounted to the same thing. Nixon's posture, therefore, was akin to that of a person who begins to testify on a subject and then asserts that he will answer no more questions because further answers on that subject may incriminate him. The law has established that proper invocation of the Fifth Amendment requires that a person refuse to answer *all* questions on a given subject. To choose among the questions asked is not permitted. Furthermore, the Burger Court certainly has not bent over backward in support of those pleading the Fifth Amendment. Of 23 self-incrimination decisions, only 4 supported the claim (17 percent), and only Justice Douglas had a Liberal voting record.

The other subliminal issue was the matter of criminal procedure. Protection against self-incrimination, of course, is one of the rights of persons accused of crime. It is an important one to be sure, but it is only a part of a much bigger picture. When Nixon nominated Lewis Powell and William Rehnquist to replace Black and Harlan in the fall of 1971, he made a statement that proved to be an accurate characterization of his nominees to the Supreme Court:

As a judicial conservative, I believe some Court decisions have gone too far in the past in weakening the peace forces as against the criminal forces in our society.

In maintaining—as it must be maintained—the delicate balance between the rights of society and defendants accused of crime, I believe the peace forces must not be denied the legal tools they need to protect the innocent from criminal elements.[45]

Would Watergate be an instance of the chickens coming home to roost? Or would Nixon's "judicial conservatives" rescue him from a morass of his own making? The data suggested an unequivocal answer. On issues pertaining to criminal procedures, Nixon's appointees had indeed been faithful to his position. Between January 1972, when Powell and Rehnquist took their seats, and July 1974, when the Watergate Tapes case was decided, the four Nixon justices cast approximately 75 percent of their votes in support of the "peace forces" and against "criminal elements."[46] Given this record, plus their position as the most Conservative members of the Court, it was not likely that they would change their spots and muzzle their fangs merely because their patron was in the dock.

What about the Liberals? Their sentiments clearly lay with the so-called criminal elements. Would the fact that the chief spokesman for law and order incongruously found the tables turned affect their votes? Their concern was not likely to be with criminal procedure, but rather with the matter of executive prerogative. They would take their cue from Douglas who was suspicious, if not paranoid, on the subject. In the famous steel seizure case of 1952,[47] Douglas had coupled his vote against Truman's assertion of implied executive powers with an unqualified statement that the only powers possessed by the President are those specified in the Constitution and these do not include the exercise of arbitrary power.

The Court's two Moderates, Byron White and Potter Stewart, frequently align themselves with the Nixon appointees to produce Conservative decisions—notably when considering various aspects of criminal procedure. It is also pertinent to note that in the 1100 cases decided by the Burger Court through the spring of 1974, White had dissented alone only eight times, Stewart seven. Hence, it was safe to assume that neither of them would steer their own course through Watergate.

The final factor entering into the calculation was that the Watergate Tapes case constituted a threat to the Court. The Justices tend to unite behind a single opinion when they perceive that their decision may not be complied with or if Congress is threatening to sanction the Court by limiting its jurisdiction or changing its size.[48] On several occasions, Nixon and his spokespeople had asserted that he might not comply with a decision ordering the surrender of the tapes unless it was considered "definitive." Presumably Nixon himself would be the one to determine what was or was not "definitive." These rumblings met the definition of a threat situation and thus markedly decreased the likelihood that a minimum winning coalition would form, that is, five Justices joining in a single opinion. (This is the usual result in the sense that, to a statistically significant extent, five-member coalitions are formed more frequently than would be expected on a purely random basis.) The probability of unanimity was therefore considerably enhanced. On the basis of this and the other indicators, all of which boded ill for the President, it was predicted that Nixon would lose by a unanimous vote. This was the result. The rest is history.

CAN COMPUTERS REPLACE COURTS?

By 1984 or thereabouts, the fifth and sixth generations of computers will be in production. Some say that these machines will be able to think. They visualize computers being asked philosophical questions that have stymied thinkers since the beginning of time, such as "Does God exist?" And the computers will answer, "He does now."

This vision of the brave new world in which computers are omnicompetent may make good science fiction; most assuredly it is not grounded in reality. Computers can make complex calculations with incredible speed and complete accuracy. Virtually unlimited amounts of information can be stored and retrieved almost instantaneously. Computers can monitor the activities of other machines and direct the operation of an assembly line or an entire mechanical process. Nonetheless, computers are robots. They experience no emotion—no love, kindness, hope, or fear. They lack creativity and are unable to exercise wisdom, imagination, or initiative—to say nothing of common sense. They can do only what they are told: to solve a small set of formal problems. And though what they are told to do may involve an exceedingly complex activity, without a human being to tell them what to do they cannot operate at all. In short, a computer is but another piece of machinery. They herald the dawn of a lobotomized world no more than an eclipse marks the transformation of the sun into a burned-out cinder.[49]

To the prophets of doom and gloom who have bemoaned the spread of the use of computers and the development of computer technology, the ubiquitous Hollerith card, with its warning not to fold, spindle, mutilate, or bend, may be unwelcome proof that events are in the saddle and ride humankind. But such querulousness seems not to have accompanied the invention of other sorts of labor-saving devices—except among Luddites. Farmers are not begrudging the fact that they no longer need to push their plows; a few romantics doubtlessly went into extended mourning when the Pony Express gave way to the telegraph, and when the telegraph gave way to the telephone. Perhaps a few of the more troglodytic male chauvinists attribute the demise of female domestication to the invention of home appliances. But almost everyone agrees that to travel long distances in a short time, riding—on, below, or above the surface of the earth—is preferable to walking and that refrigerators are useful for storing beer as well as yesterday's leftovers.

Computers are a means of easing mental, rather than physical, labor. As long as labor-saving devices made it easier to dig ditches, cut trees, or build bridges, they were welcomed. But when they began to intrude into the realm of nonphysical activity and to perform tasks that only the human brain had theretofore performed, reactions varied. The process whereby these tasks were performed was unobservable, hence mysterious. Unlike the typewriter or the adding machine, whose keys are hit to produce results mechanically, the computer is viewed as a proverbial black box—fascinating yet worrisome. A certain magic is at work, and those who have mastered its secrets can perform feats that are beyond the capability or the understanding of us poor mortals.

So, can computers replace courts or not? If the judicial function is what judges asserted it to be in the nineteenth and early twentieth centuries, that is, if the declaratory, or phonographic, theory is an accurate description of what judges do, the answer is an unqualified "yes." According to this perception of the judge's role, judges exercised no discretion whatsoever; decision making was a wholly automatic process. In the words of Sir William Blackstone, the eighteenth-century English jurist whose *Commentaries* have influenced and continue to influence American lawyers and judges, judges "are the depositaries of the laws; the living oracles, who must decide in all cases of doubt, and who are bound by an oath to decide according to the law of the land." Once a matter has been decided, it is "a permanent rule which it is not in the breast of any subsequent judge to alter or vary from according to his private sentiments." He must decide "not according to his private judgment, but according to the known laws and customs of the land." He must not "pronounce a new law, but . . . maintain and expound the old one." But what about those instances where judges did change their decisions? Even then the process entails no exercise of discretion: "In such cases the subsequent judges do not pretend to make new law, but to vindicate the old one from misrepresentation as manifestly absurd or unjust." When this happens, "it is declared, not that such a sentence was *bad law*, but that it was *not law*."[50]

If the foregoing were an accurate assessment of the complexity of the judicial decision-making process, then judges would be superfluous. A computer could be programmed with all previously decided cases, legislative enactments, and constitutional provisions, and new controversies would be plugged in as they occurred. The computer would then be instructed to compare the facts of the present case with those of cases previously decided and output those precedents that were factually compatible with the case before the court. These data would be coded and a computer with a very large "memory," or storage capacity, would be secured. Once a program was written and "debugged," judges and lawyers would be needed merely to hear evidence and take testimony in new cases.

Fortunately, or unfortunately, judicial decision making is not as described by Blackstone or by the apologists for the declaratory, or phonographic, theory. Judges really do exercise a great deal of discretion, as has been pointed out earlier in this book. The human factor cannot be excised by resorting to a computer. A computer cannot answer the questions, present in all cases, civil as well as criminal, trial and appellate, that are of necessity matters of judgment. Somebody has to program the beast. And that somebody or group of somebodies will determine which handful among all the facts in a previously decided controversy were crucial to a court's decision. Did the court decide as it did because it read the words of a law to mean this rather than that? Or because the words related to some constitutional provision? Was the fact that the defendant was a minor considered relevant? Did the court know that he was not informed of his right to remain silent until half an hour after his arrest? Could the mildly incriminating statement he made during the interim be used against him? Did his court-appointed attorney have enough time to prepare an adequate defense? How reliable was the testimony of the government informer? What weight, if any, should be given the defense attorney's failure to cross-examine a key prosecution witness?

Nor can a computer consider that most basic standard for making a judgment—whether the activity that generated the litigation was "reasonable."[51] Scientists, engineers, and the artificial intelligentsia have composed lengthy litanies on the capabilities of computers; "reasonableness," however, is not included in their lists. What would a computer do when confronted by the very commonplace situation (especially in appellate courts) where equally relevant precedents support the contentions of both parties to the dispute? What about the case that raises an issue never litigated before? In a dynamic society, novelty in the courtroom is as common as in the world of fashion. These situations require the exercise of judgment—preferably an informed one. The training and experience that a judge brings with him to the bench make it likely that his judgment will be more informed than that of a programmer or computer scientist.

The Standard of Equality of Treatment

One of the most frequently heard criticisms of today's courts is that judges all too often fail to dispense justice in an evenhanded fashion: that they mete out punishment and reward on the basis of who one is, rather than what one has done. Assuming that there is some merit in such criticism, is it not possible that computerized justice might prove to be a palatable remedy? In addition to the speed with which they work, computers are thoroughly unbiased (assuming, of course, that no "tilt" has been built into the program, which may not be a safe assumption to make). But do we want a literally evenhanded administration of justice?

Too much emphasis on equality of treatment can be counterproductive, even unjust. Consider the separate but equal doctrine, which was the Law of the Land from its enunciation in 1896 until its demise in 1954.[52] According to the Supreme Court, no constitutional violation occurred if public facilities were segregated by race so long as the facilities were themselves equal. Each race—effectively blacks and whites—would receive equal treatment under the law in schools, public transportation, and recreational facilities, but the races would be forbidden to mingle. As Justice Henry Brown said, speaking for seven of the eight participating Justices: "Laws permitting, and even requiring their separation [blacks and whites] in places where they are liable to be brought into contact do not necessarily imply the inferiority of either race to the other." The underlying fallacy, the Court continued, is that the enforced separation of blacks and whites "stamps the colored race with a badge of inferiority." If this be so, "it is not by reason of anything found" in the state's law, but "solely because the colored race chooses to put that construction upon it." If the tables were turned, and blacks enacted the selfsame law relegating "the white race to an inferior position," we are confident that "the white race . . . would not acquiesce in this assumption."[53] The argument is, of course, fatuous. It completely disregards reality. But as stated, it does require equality of treatment: blacks in one railroad car, whites in another—after all, it is still the same train.

Anatole France's ironic statement aptly describes the injustice of a system that limits its focus to equal treatment: "The law, in its majestic equality, forbids the rich as well as the poor to sleep under bridges, to beg in the streets, and to steal bread." But justice was equally administered. Everyone, without exception, was bound thereby. A government would also treat everybody equally if it were to abolish all public welfare and relief programs. No aid to the blind or disabled, no Social Security, no Aid to Dependent Children, no veterans' pensions, no unemployment compensation. Except for veterans' pensions, public assistance is of rather recent vintage. During much of American history, such programs were considered anathema, and not only by businessmen. Consider the words of the Reverend Russell Conwell, one of the most popular lecturers of the last half of the nineteenth century and past president of Temple University:

> ... the number of poor who are to be sympathized with is very small. To sympathize with a man whom God has punished for his sins, thus to help him when God would still continue a just punishment, is to do wrong, no doubt about it, and we do that more than we help those who are deserving.... Let us remember there is not a poor person in the United States who was not made poor by his own shortcomings, or by the shortcomings of some one else. It is all wrong to be poor, anyhow....[54]

Nor need the focus be limited to programs of public assistance. Why should the poor employer be required to comply with minimun wage and maximum hour laws? Is it equitable to outlaw child labor merely because an adolescent is less than sixteen years of age? What about the subsidies government provides to some businessmen, farmers, and manufacturers but not to others? And of course one should not overlook the marvelous provisions of the Internal Revenue Code. Why should childless couples be penalized because deductions are given to families with minor children? Given society's concern over population growth, would it not be more equitable to tax directly those who breed successfully? What about the myriad tax loopholes and shelters? If there must be an income tax, would it not be fairer to tax anything and everything that goes into one's pocket? And even do so at the same rate?

Obviously, everybody is not equal. Ironically, to treat everyone equally produces injustice. Lack of bias is a virtue only up to a point. Beyond that point, it becomes a menace. Human problems cannot be solved by resorting to a single principle of action, even though that principle may be among the noblest ideals that man is capable of striving for. Distinctions must be made; people must necessarily be classified and categorized on the basis of policy considerations. This, indeed, is what politics is all about: the determination of standards of eligibility for public relief; the specification of tax brackets; the establishment of penalties for violation of criminal laws; the determination of liability; the definition of poverty, of a small business, of a defense-related industry, of pollution, of all that constitutes that most undefinable of terms—the "public interest." To expect a computer to make these types of distinctions is no more realistic than to expect an alchemist to turn base metal into gold.

Adaptation to Changing Circumstances and Conditions

Computerized dispensation of justice would have yet another deficiency: it could not be adapted to changing circumstances and conditions. Assume, for instance, that technological progress had advanced to its current level in 1925. Assume further that in that year America's then-existing "noble experiment"—prohibition—was supplemented with a second one: the replacement of judges with computers that were programmed with previous court decisions and were capable of providing an answer to any legal question. The system might have worked tolerably well for five years or so. Thereafter, it would not have worked so well. For beginning in 1929 the United States found itself in the throes of a worldwide depression. Old solutions to traditional problems no longer worked. Furthermore, new problems surfaced for which novel, and somewhat radical, solutions had to be found. The computers, however, were locked in to a fixed point in time. As far as they were concerned, the world had stopped in 1925. Short of a change in the fundamental law, no adaptation to changing circumstances and conditions could occur. Economic relationships were governed by the principles of laissez-faire economics. Freedom of contract was the rule; restraint was the exception. Government was consequently forbidden to regulate prices or fix wages. It was a criminal offense for labor to bargain collectively. Unemployment compensation and Social Security exceeded the taxing powers of Congress. Mining, manufacturing, and agriculture were immunized from regulation at both the federal and state levels of government. In short, though the malaise was an economic one, government was to let nature run its course.

The American public would not likely have tolerated judicial torpedoing of New Deal reforms much beyond 1937, the year in which the Court made its peace with the Roosevelt Administration. The means the Court chose would exceed the capacity of computerized justice. The precedents that precluded effective governmental regulation of the economic system were tossed out on a wholesale basis, and Congress and the states were given carte blanche to do as they wished in matters economic. Nor is it any more likely that the American public would have remained content with other aspects of life as they were in 1925. White male supremacy might have continued for a few more years. Farmers and rural communities might have resisted to the death the apportionment of state legislatures and the House of Representatives on a one-person, one-vote basis. Polluted water and air, and a despoiled environment, might be more serious problems than they are at present. Literary standards would be those of the late Victorian era. Sexual activity would be confined to the bedroom and the back seat of Henry Ford's contribution to the American way of life. Criminal procedure would be limited to the third degree. Poverty law would merely prohibit panhandling. Consumer protection and debtors' rights would be nonexistent: *caveat emptor.*

Computerized justice would thus restrict society to living by the values of a fixed point in history. Only the most stagnant, insulated, and self-segregating society could long tolerate such a situation. If the United

States were to replace its judges with computers, society would soon blow its fuse. Because judges are the most authoritative of America's policy makers, and because they resolve many of the fundamental issues confronting the nation, the responsibility for ensuring adaptation to changing circumstances and conditions rests with them. A stalemate between the President and Congress, between a governor and a state legislature, even when prolonged for a number of years, is often a ho-hum matter, because it is the normal state of affairs. The public at large frequently couldn't care less except for the entertainment value such stalemate enables editorial writers and political cartoonists to provide. Judges, however, in their capacity as American society's professional decision makers, cannot afford such luxury.

Because we live in a dynamic environment, we cannot be the prisoners of our past. Some measure of variability, of adaptation, is essential to survival. Perfectly consistent and predictable behavior is the sign of an endangered species. If justice were computerized, that would be our fate. Of course, perfectly predictable behavior can occur without mechanizing a decision-making process. It does not occur within the Marble Palace. Approximately 12 percent of the Justices' decisions and 15 percent of their votes have been predicted inaccurately. These inaccurate predictions may be due to measurement error, or simply to bad judgment on my part. But just as likely an explanation is that the Justices altered their attitudes and values somewhat because of changing circumstances and conditions. Mention was made earlier in this chapter of instances when the Justices deviated from past performance. There was no way, short of hunch or intuition, in which the Court's decision voiding the states' antiabortion statutes, nor its 1972 decision outlawing the death penalty under procedures then in effect, nor a rather silly 1975 decision concerning the right to counsel could have been predicted.[55]

The facts in the 1975 case were these. A three-time loser in the courts, accused of car theft, was provided a court-appointed attorney because he was unable to afford his own. He politely refused, stating that he was competent to defend himself. But you cannot do that, said the State of California—the government knows best what is good for you, and we have a law that says you must be represented by counsel. There was no question that an individual has the right to an attorney's assistance even if he cannot afford to pay for one. The Warren Court firmly established this principle, and the Burger Court has extended it still further.[56] The Warren Court also stated that if a person wishes to waive a right to which he or she is constitutionally entitled, he or she must do so voluntarily. This issue, however, was not disputed in the 1975 case. But the Court also required that the waiver of the constitutional right be done intelligently. A state, for instance, may protect persons who are mentally incompetent. But the defendant in this case was neither insane nor underage. He simply argued that he could do a better job defending himself than any court-appointed attorney. California, however, disagreed because the trial judge had given the defendant a quiz on the law and he flunked.

But did this suffice as proof of the accused's ineptitude? Ignorance is not the monopoly of laypersons. During oral argument before the Supreme Court, a couple of the Justices observed that many lawyers, including some who practice before the Court itself, are not exactly legal luminaries. To condition legal rights on intelligence would be fine if everyone were an Albert Einstein. American jurisprudence, however, has always assumed that even a fool has freedom of speech. Moreover, self-reliance has always been high in the panoply of America's ideals. Perhaps we live in an iconoclastic age, in which yesterday's truth is today's falsehood. Nevertheless, the Justices' track records in 1975 (especially those of the four Conservative members of the Court—Burger, Blackmun, Powell, and Rehnquist) clearly indicated that none of them was particularly receptive to the notion that Big Brother, paternalistic government, knows best. If anyone was likely to uphold California's law, it would be one or more of the Liberals—Douglas, Brennan, and Marshall. More than the Conservatives, they viewed government as a proper vehicle for succoring the poor and downtrodden. Even so, it was unlikely that any of the Justices would support the government's insistence on protecting people even when they did not want its help. To do so would logically lead to the conclusion that people are irresponsible by nature. Ergo, Big Brother must protect them.

It was consequently predicted that the law would be declared unconstitutional. Though Orwell's *1984* might be California's vision of the ideal society, most assuredly, it was not the Court's. The prediction was correct, but the vote was markedly less than unanimous—6 to 3. The three dissenters were the Minnesota farm boy by way of St. Paul, Warren Burger; the other half of the Minnesota twins, Harry Blackmun; and that son of the wild and woolly West, the Goldwater Republican from Phoenix and hard-nosed assistant attorney general, William Rehnquist. Their rationale was that declaring the act constitutional would add to the burdens of the criminal justice system, and, according to Justice Blackmun, it would write into the Constitution the old legal maxim, "one who is his own lawyer has a fool for a client."

Such unpredictability, though aggravating and sometimes mind-boggling, is inherently healthy. Though researchers and analysts strive to exclude variability from their models of animal and human behavior, such efforts are misleading in the sense that they destroy the validity of the scientific method. Learning theorists, for example, commonly assume that random responses in their subjects will eventually be eliminated when habit or reinforcement become sufficiently strong. The organism's behavior is thus assumed to become less variable as learning progresses because the initial trial-and-error process leads to a highly consistent, never-err state. The criterion of whether the organism has learned whatever is being taught is the number of correct responses. Variation in behavior is deemed incorrect, for it indicates that the learning process has not yet been completed.

Although elimination of unpredictable behavior, of variable responses, may be desirable in some contexts, the fact remains that the world is not static. Organisms and populations must adapt, and thus must be able to maintain a high degree of variability. Organisms that do behave in a completely predictable fashion have lost the ability to respond to novel stimuli and begin to exhibit pathological behavior. As psychologist M. J. Klingsporn has observed, "Rather than cursing the rat who breaks a sequence of seven correct runs through the maze with some exploratory behavior on the eighth trial, we should expect and appreciate that it is just such response variety that represents that organism's learning fitness."[57]

Hence, perfectly accurate predictions, though they would be immensely gratifying, would signify a threat to the continued viability of the Supreme Court. This is especially so because predictions are based upon the Justices' *past* voting behavior. The dynamic forces at work in and on American society make variability essential to survival. Judges, least of all, can ill afford to assume the ostrich posture. In Chief Justice Marshall's classic phrase, "we must never forget that it is a constitution we are expounding"—one "intended to endure for ages to come, and, consequently, to be adapted to the various crises of human affairs."[58]

It is precisely this need for adaptation that precludes substituting computers for judges. Those who work in the field of artificial intelligence may deny this and argue that computers can and do respond to their environments—that they can engage in "creative" decision making.[59] But who or what determines whether the decision shall faithfully follow established precedents or deviate from precedent? Obviously, it would have to be more than a table of random numbers. Contingencies would have to be built into the program and suitably activated when a certain threshold was reached. For instance, the computer could be instructed to deviate from what had previously been decided in cases dealing with unemployment compensation or Social Security benefits when unemployment rose above a certain level or when inflation reached a certain high. The computer would be told that when such a condition, or set of conditions, existed, decisions would be based on some definition of need or hardship. Similarly, a whole range of political, economic, social, and cultural factors could be fed into the computer, some or all of which could trigger a decision if certain environmental conditions were met. Fine and dandy, but the question remains, who is going to define these extrajudicial considerations? Who determines what level of inflation or unemployment is too much, and what social and cultural factors will be the correct input for policy making on which judicial issues? The answer, obviously, can only be the person or persons behind the machine. And if the basic decisions require human discretion, why bother with a machine at all? Moreover, human dispensation of justice works—not always perfectly, of course. No more should be asked of any governmental process. History, after all, does record that most efforts to reform or tinker with viable institutions and processes have proven to be but so many monuments to deficient wisdom.

NOTES

1. Washington, D.C.: Bureau of National Affairs.
2. Philadelphia: Association of American Law Schools and the American Law Institute-American Bar Association Committee on Continuing Professional Education.
3. *Maxwell* v. *Bishop*, 393 U.S. 997.
4. *Maxwell* v. *Bishop*, 398 U.S. 262, at 267.
5. *McGautha* v. *California*, 402 U.S. 183 (1971).
6. *Swann* v. *Charlotte-Mecklenburg Board of Education*, 402 U.S. 1; *Davis* v. *Mobile County Board of School Commissioners*, 402 U.S. 33; *McDaniel* v. *Barresi*, 402 U.S. 39; and *North Carolina State Board of Education* v. *Swann*, 402 U.S. 43.
7. *Branzburg* v. *Hayes*, 408 U.S. 665 (1972), number 41 in Harold J. Spaeth, *Classic and Current Decisions of the United States Supreme Court* (San Francisco: W. H. Freeman and Company, 1977.
8. *Clay* v. *United States*, 403 U.S. 698 (1971).
9. *New York Times* v. *United States*, 403 U.S. 713 (1971), at 714, number 36 in *Classic and Current Decisions*.
10. 403 U.S. 713, at 753.
11. "Burger Calls Court in Fact Unanimous in The Times Case," *New York Times*, July 6, 1971.
12. *San Antonio School District* v. *Rodriguez*, 411 U.S. 1 (1973), number 43 in *Classic and Current Decisions*.
13. *Miller* v. *California*, 413 U.S. 15, number 45 in *Classic and Current Decisions*.
14. *Butler* v. *Michigan*, 352 U.S. 380 (1957), at 383.
15. "State statutes designed to regulate obscene materials must be carefully limited. As a result, we now confine the permissible scope of such regulation to works which depict or describe sexual conduct. That conduct must be specifically defined by the applicable state law, as written or authoritatively construed. A state offense must also be limited to works which, taken as a

whole, appeal to the prurient interest in sex, which portray sexual conduct in a patently offensive way, and which, taken as a whole, do not have serious literary, artistic, political, or scientific value." 413 U.S. 15, at 23–24 (footnote and reference omitted).

16. *Jenkins* v. *Georgia,* 418 U.S. 153 (1974).

17. *Lemon* v. *Kurtzman,* 403 U.S. 602, number 35 in *Classic and Current Decisions.*

18. *Meek* v. *Pittenger,* 421 U.S. 349.

19. See the discussion in Chapter 4 under the heading, "Previous judicial experience."

20. See *Goldberg* v. *Kelly,* 397 U.S. 254 (1970), number 33 in *Classic and Current Decisions.*

21. *California Department of Human Resources* v. *Java,* 402 U.S. 121; and *Graham* v. *Richardson,* 403 U.S. 365.

22. *Goldberg* v. *Kelly, op. cit.,* note 20 *supra.*

23. *James* v. *Valtierra,* 402 U.S. 137 (1971).

24. *Hunter* v. *Erickson,* 393 U.S. 385 (1969).

25. *James* v. *Valtierra,* 402 U.S. 137 (1971), at 141 (reference omitted).

26. *Furman* v. *Georgia,* 408 U.S. 238 (1972).

27. *Roe* v. *Wade,* 410 U.S. 113; and *Doe* v. *Bolton,* 410 U.S. 179 (1973)—number 42 in *Classic and Current Decisions.*

28. *Flood* v. *Kuhn,* 407 U.S. 258.

29. *Federal Baseball Club* v. *National League,* 259 U.S. 200 (1922).

30. *Toolson* v. *New York Yankees,* 346 U.S. 356.

31. *United States* v. *International Boxing Club,* 348 U.S. 236 (1955); *Radovich* v. *National Football League,* 352 U.S. 445 (1957); *Haywood* v. *National Basketball Assn.,* 401 U.S. 1204 (1971).

32. 407 U.S. 258, at 282.

33. *Id.* 284.

34. *Id.*

35. *Id.* at 283–284.

36. *Milliken* v. *Bradley,* 418 U.S. 717; and *United States* v. *Nixon,* 418 U.S. 683— numbers 48 and 47 in *Classic and Current Decisions.*

37. For example, indigents, juveniles, plea bargaining, poverty law, illegitimates, and sex discrimination.

38. *Singleton* v. *Jackson School District* and *Carter* v. *West Feliciana School Board,* 396 U.S. 290 (1970); and *Sweet Briar Institute* v. *Button,* 387 U.S. 423 (1967).

39. *Wright* v. *Emporia,* 407 U.S. 451 (1972), at 474.

40. *Richmond School Board* v. *Virginia Board of Education,* 412 U.S. 92.

41. *United States* v. *Burr,* 4 Cranch 470 (1807); discussed in Robert Scigliano, *The Supreme Court and the Presidency* (New York: Free Press, 1974), pp. 29–32.

42. *Branzburg* v. *Hayes,* 408 U.S. 665, at 688, number 41 in *Classic and Current Decisions.*

43. *Scheuer* v. *Rhodes,* 406 U.S. 233.

44. 1 Cranch 137 (1803), number 2 in *Classic and Current Decisions.*

45. *New York Times,* October 22, 1971.

46. David W, Rohde and Harold J. Spaeth, *Supreme Court Decision Making* (San Francisco: W. H. Freeman and Company, 1976), pp. 109-111.

47. *Youngstown Sheet & Tube Co.* v. *Sawyer,* 343 U.S. 579, number 19 in *Classic and Current Decisions.*

48. Rohde and Spaeth, *op. cit.,* note 46 *supra,* pp. 195–203.

49. For a brilliant and incisive statement of the limitations of computer technology and artificial intelligence, see Joseph Weizenbaum, *Computer Power and Human Reason* (San Francisco: W. H. Freeman and Company, 1976), especially chaps. 8, 10.

50. Quoted in Walter F. Murphy and C. Herman Pritchett, *Courts, Judges, and Politics,* 2d ed. (New York: Random House, 1974), p. 14.

51. See the section in Chapter 3 headed "The test of reasonableness."

52. From *Plessy* v. *Ferguson,* 163 U.S. 537, to *Brown* v. *Board of Education,* 347 U.S. 484—numbers 12 and 20 in *Classic and Current Decisions.*

53. 163 U.S. 537 (1896), at 544, 551.

54. Quoted in Alpheus T. Mason, *Free Government in the Making,* 2d ed. (New York: Oxford University Press, 1956), p. 565.

55. *Faretta* v. *California,* 422 U.S. 806.

56. In *Gideon* v. *Wainwright,* 372 U.S. 335 (1963); and *Argersinger* v. *Hamlin,* 407 U.S. 25 (1972)—numbers 22 and 37 in *Classic and Current Decisions.*

57. "The Significance of Variability," *Behavioral Science* 18 (November 1973): 443.

58. *M'Culloch* v. *Maryland,* 4 Wheaton 316 (1819), at 407, 415, number 5 in *Classic and Current Decisions.*

59. Cf. Weizenbaum, *op. cit.,* note 49 *supra;* Israel Shenker, "Man and Machine Match Minds at M.I.T.," *New York Times,* August 27, 1977.

Is Justice Blind?

The idea that justice should be administered in an evenhanded manner has come under increasing attack in recent years. Are such attacks justified? In this chapter, the two major criticisms of the ideal of judicial blindness are considered. The charge that judges should take into account the personal characteristics of litigants and tilt the scales of justice in favor of those whom society has disadvantaged is considered in the context of affirmative action and quota systems. Allegations that judges do not, in fact, adhere to the ideal of judicial blindness are evaluated by analyzing the Court's decisions in selected areas of its policy making.

THE NORMATIVE IDEAL OF JUSTICE

American justice is symbolized by a blindfolded woman holding the scales of justice evenly balanced in her hand. This representation would lead us to believe that judges approach their responsibilities with a certain myopia, or lack of discernment that prevents the personal attributes of the litigants from influencing the judges' decisions; and that justice is situationally determined. This ideal of American jurisprudence is at least as deeply rooted as the belief that judicial decisions are objective and nondiscretionary—indeed, perhaps more so. Public opinion surveys conducted since the mid-1960's have indicated a greater public awareness that judges are not mere umpires concerned only with how the game is played, but rather that they also have decided preferences as to who should win and who should lose.[1] Does this then mean that the ideal of judicial blindness is as mythical as the perception of judges as operantly conditioned mouthpieces of the law and the Constitution?

Not necessarily. The fact that judges, like the rest of us, have personal policy preferences on which they base their decisions does not prevent them from deciding cases on the basis of the situations in which litigants find themselves rather than on the basis of the litigants' personal characteristics. A judge, in his discretion, can take a dim or a nonchalant view of thievery regardless of whether the accused person wears a white or a blue collar, is amateurish or professional, white or black, male or female. Similarly, a judge, again depending upon his attitudes and values, may hold persons strictly accountable for their actions in personal injury cases, whether such actions be the result of reckless driving, defrauding the public through false and misleading advertising, or failing to make payment on a charge account. He would in no way violate the norm of judicial blindness. Nor for that matter would a judge who took into account the extenuating or aggravating circumstances surrounding an action that resulted in legal proceedings, such as the degree of premeditation or the seriousness of the injury suffered.

Only if the judge based his decision on the personal characteristics of either or both of the litigants would the norm be violated (for example, black-white, rich-poor, educated-ignorant, male-female, young-old). Even so, literal adherence, always and everywhere, to the ideal of judicial blindness is not expected. Some of the major reforms in American law have been based on the desire to lift the blindfold. The system of juvenile courts, for example, was devised to shield minors from the harshness of criminal justice. Although many may protest that this benignly conceived system has produced little monsters that none but Frankenstein would applaud, the fact remains that these minors, solely because of their age—a personal characteristic—are treated differently from miscreants a few years their senior. Similarly, in divorce courts gender still tends to determine who gets child custody, alimony, and child support payments. (Whether the monies are paid regularly after the divorce becomes final is, of course, another matter.)

CRITICISMS OF THE IDEAL OF JUDICIAL BLINDNESS

The Normative Critique

But these and other institutionalized deviations from the norm simply reflect a recognition that justice sometimes needs to be tempered with mercy. Altogether different are recent criticisms—one normative, the other substantive—of the ideal of judicial blindness. At the normative level are the arguments of some radical elements who maintain that to achieve "real" justice, decisions should, at times, be partially or wholly predicated on personal characteristics. Society, they assert, has placed certain groups in a disadvantaged position—so much so and so systematically so that they are unable to pull themselves up by their own bootstraps from the mire in which they are stuck. Some maintain that the color of a defendant's skin should be relevant to decision. If a person is black, for example, the treatment accorded ought to be more lenient than if the person is white. At the time of the highly publicized trials of

Bobby Seale, Huey Newton, Angela Davis, and Joan Little, some militants demanded that all charges be dismissed without trial, regardless of the severity of the alleged crime, on the basis that "white" justice should not be applicable to black defendants. The assertion was not that they were above the law, but rather that the racism of American society had infected all its institutions, including the courts, and thus a truly fair trial was impossible.

In other words, to the extent that judicial blindness is an operative part of American jurisprudence, to that extent is America's notion of fairness inherently unfair. Because the political and economic system has placed certain segments of the population in a permanent position of inferiority, it ought to be the judges' responsibility to "correct" this imbalance by according the disadvantaged preferential treatment. Hence, an individual's race, social position, degree of poverty, and perhaps sex are considered relevant to any decision.

The DeFunis case.　　The argument that some discrimination is necessary to achieve equality reflects the rationale behind various affirmative action programs, quota systems, and preferential placements, such as that of the University of Washington Law School, at issue in the *DeFunis* case, which permitted the admission of minority racial applicants even though their grades and test scores were lower than those of white males who were denied admission. This sort of discrimination is alleged to be of a "benign" nature, supposedly distinguishable from the malignancy of traditional sorts of discrimination. Supporters of this type of discrimination point to legislation dating from the Reconstruction Era that is specifically designed to further the welfare and education of blacks. Given that this legislation has been judicially blessed with a seal of legitimacy, at least some degree of color consciousness is constitutionally permissible.* They further argue that only those classifications that *deprive*

---

*Judges, of course, do have the authority to order the imposition of quotas as a *remedy* for illegal acts of discrimination. Accordingly, if a court finds that a school district has illegally segregated students on the basis of race, it may order each of the schools within the district to enroll the same proportion of blacks and whites as exists within the district's boundaries. See *Swann* v. *Charlotte-Mecklenburg Board of Education*, 402 U.S. 1 (1971), at 22–25; and *Milliken* v. *Bradley*, 418 U.S. 717 (1974)—number 48 in Harold J. Spaeth, *Classic and Current Decisions of the United States Supreme Court* (San Francisco: W. H. Freeman and Company, 1977). The Supreme Court has also excused indigents from the payment of fees that precluded them from appealing their cases to higher courts. For example, *Griffin* v. *Illinois*, 351 U.S. 12 (1956); *Burns* v. *Ohio*, 360 U. S. 252 (1959); and *Hardy* v. *United States*, 375 U. S. 277 (1964). Decisions such as these do not violate the norm of judicial blindness. Where persons have been illegally discriminated against, judges, in their discretion, may take account of such persons' race or sex in order to remedy the effects of the illegal activity. Nor is the norm of judicial blindness violated by the refusal of the High Bench to make access to the courts conditional on ability to pay. As Justice Black said in *Griffin* v. *Illinois*, "all people charged with crime must, so far as the law is concerned, 'stand on an *equality* before the bar of justice in every American court.' " 351 U.S. 12, at 17. (Italics supplied.)

minorities and women of rights are constitutionally forbidden, and that judges are not qualified to evaluate programs designed to increase minority enrollment in colleges and universities and in private institutions that are the recipients of governmental subsidies and to increase the hiring of minorities among the ranks of government employees. Furthermore, educators alone, not judges, are qualified to evaluate applicants to professional schools. These were the arguments presented to the Supreme Court in the first case testing the constitutionality of reverse discrimination.[2]

The opposing arguments were based on the norm of judicial blindness: (1) All applicants must be judged on an equal basis. White applicants should not be rejected when their test scores and grades fall below a certain level if these scores and grades are above those of minority persons who are admitted. (2) If blacks and other minorities may not be excluded from public facilities on racial grounds, then neither may whites. Any other posture elevates "whose ox is being gored" to the level of constitutional principle (that is, goring is constitutional if the ox is yours, but not if it is mine). Blacks would thereby become more equal than whites. (3) Sociologically, quotas not only hurt whites and men; they also stamp minorities and women with a badge of inferiority. Without a leg up on the rest of the population, they cannot compete successfully.

The thrust of the arguments of the proponents of judicial blindness is clear: the government ought to treat everybody alike. The fact that everybody is not alike is irrelevant. Therefore, insistence on equality of treatment results in discrimination. Those who would allow some slippage of the judicial blindfold stand directly opposed: because everybody is not alike, we must discriminate. Discrimination against whites provides opportunities for the disadvantaged to achieve equality. In *DeFunis,* the Court was asked to choose: either strip off the blinders and formally recognize conditions of inequality by legalizing quota systems and affirmative action programs, or tighten the blindfold more securely and thereby ignore the tilt in the scales of justice.

The Court did neither. It adroitly sidestepped the issue altogether, notwithstanding that some sixty organizations (besides the State of Washington and the student denied admission) had filed more than two dozen written briefs hoping to influence the Court's decision. The trial court had ordered the plaintiff admitted and the university complied. Although the State Supreme Court had reversed the trial court's judgment, the plaintiff remained in school pending the outcome of the United States Supreme Court's decision. All this, of course, was known to the Justices. By the time they heard the case in February 1974, the student had only the last term of his senior year to complete. The majority, noting that the law school had said it would allow the plaintiff to complete his final term regardless of the Court's decision, declared the case moot. Four of the Justices dissented, saying that "few constitutional questions in recent history have stirred as much debate." This issue will not disappear, but "must inevitably return to federal courts and ultimately again to this Court."[3]

Of the four dissenters, only Justice Douglas addressed the merits of the controversy. The equal protection clause, he said, required neither an admissions formula based solely on grades and test scores, nor one that precluded consideration of an applicant's prior achievements "in light of the barriers that he had to overcome." What the Constitution does require is "the consideration of each application *in a racially neutral way*."[4] There is, he continued,

> no constitutional right for any race to be preferred. The years of slavery did more than retard the progress of blacks. Even a greater wrong was done the whites by creating arrogance instead of humility and by encouraging the growth of the fiction of a superior race. There is no superior person by constitutional standards. A . . . white is entitled to no advantage by reason of that fact; nor is he subject to any disability, no matter what his race or color.[5]

However, there is "no bar to considering an individual's prior achievements in light of the racial discrimination that barred his way, as a factor in attempting to assess his true potential for a successful legal career."[6] Furthermore, the equal protection clause

> commands the elimination of racial barriers, not their creation in order to satisfy our theory as to how society ought to be organized. The purpose of the University of Washington cannot be to produce black lawyers for blacks, Polish lawyers for Poles, Jewish lawyers for Jews, Irish lawyers for the Irish. It should be to produce good lawyers for Americans. . . .[7]

Douglas also spoke to the desire to give minorities a leg up on the population. This assumption, he said, that "blacks or browns cannot make it" on their individual merit "must be clearly disapproved." That is "a stamp of inferiority that a State is not permitted to place on any lawyer."[8]

In conclusion, Douglas spoke to the need for judicial deference to those responsible for determining admission and eligibility. Educators must be given leeway. "Courts are not educators; their expertise is limited; and our task ends with the inquiry whether . . . there has been 'invidious' discrimination." The educational decision, assuming that the proper guidelines were used, reflects "an expertise that courts should honor."[9]

The Bakke case. Although former Justice Douglas articulated well the norm of judicial blindness in his opinion in *DeFunis,* his views were not shared by his colleagues in their opinions in the *Bakke* case.[10] Six of the nine Justices wrote opinions, with no single opinion garnering majority support. Four of the Justices—Burger, Stewart, Rehnquist, and Stevens—considered the quota system of the medical school at the University of California at Davis, which reserved 16 seats in each entering class for members of a "minority group" (blacks, Chicanos, Asians, and American Indians[11]), a violation of Title VI of the Civil Rights Act of 1964. In pertinent part, the act provides that "No person in the United States shall, on the ground of race, color, or national origin, be excluded from participation in, be denied the benefits of, or be subjected to discrimination under any program or activity receiving Federal financial assistance."[12] In an opinion by Justice Stevens, these four Justices cited the rule that the resolution of a constitutional issue should be avoided if a case can be fairly decided on a statutory basis. Accordingly, they avoided the question of whether the Davis program violated the equal protection clause of the Fourteenth Amendment and focused instead on the language of Title VI, which they considered to be color-blind: The "ban on exclusion is crystal clear: Race cannot be the basis of excluding anyone from participation in a federally funded program."[13]

At the other extreme were Justices Brennan, Marshall, White, and Blackmun, who decided that the Davis quota system violated neither the Constitution nor Title VI. According to their view, preferential treatment is a permissible means "of remedying past societal discrimination,"[14] and Title VI was enacted "to induce voluntary compliance with the requirement of nondiscriminatory treatment." This being so, "It is inconceivable that Congress intended to encourage voluntary efforts to eliminate the evil of racial discrimination while at the same time forbidding the voluntary use of race-conscious remedies."[15]

The opinion of Justice Powell refused to go so far as to prohibit admissions officers "from any consideration of the race of any applicant."[16] But because rights are personal, and because "Racial and ethnic distinctions of any sort are inherently suspect and thus call for the most exacting judicial scrutiny,"[17] and because the medical school had not been found guilty of discrimination, its quota system was unconstitutional:

> . . . the Davis special admission program involves the use of an explicit racial classification. . . . It tells applicants who are not Negro, Asian, or "Chicano" that they are totally excluded from a specific percentage of the seats in an entering class. No matter how strong their qualifications . . . they are never afforded the chance to compete with applicants from the preferred groups for the special admission seats. At the same time, the preferred applicants have the opportunity to compete for every seat in the class.
>
> The fatal flaw in petitioner's preferential program is its disregard of individual rights as guaranteed by the Fourteenth Amendment. . . . Such rights are not absolute. But when a State's distribution of benefits or impo-

sition of burdens hinges on the color of a person's skin or ancestry, that
individual is entitled to a demonstration that the challenged classification is
necessary to promote a substantial state interest. Petitioner has failed to
carry this burden.[18]

The other three opinions that accompanied the *Bakke* decision were
written by the three Justices who concurred in Brennan's opinion. Justice White argued that Title VI provided no private cause of action—
that only governmental bodies, not private persons, could sue because of
alleged discriminatory treatment. Justice Marshall summarized the legal
disabilities that historically had affected blacks in America and concluded that "it is more than a little ironic that, after several hundred
years of class-based discrimination against Negroes, the Court is unwilling to hold that a class-based remedy for that discrimination is permissible."[19] (Two "wrongs" thereby making a right?) Marshall's focus on black
discrimination is itself ironic since the Davis program, between 1970 and
1974, admitted more Asians (53) and Chicanos (39) than blacks (27).[20]
Marshall's statement that discrimination against blacks "has been different in kind, not just in degree"[21] from discrimination against other
ethnic groups is debatable insofar as American Indians are concerned.
No member of the latter group appears to have been admitted to the
Davis medical school during the 1970–1974 period,[22] although perhaps
none applied.

Most surprising is Blackmun's agreement with Brennan's opinion.
Blackmun had not been particularly supportive of racial minorities in
previous litigation. Perhaps his vote is explainable by his close association
with the medical profession during his years as a practicing attorney.
Apart from his statements that "Fourteenth Amendment rights are personal" and that racial classifications "are inherently suspect and call for
exacting judicial scrutiny"[23] (which seem to place him closer to the position of Powell and Stevens than to that of Brennan), his opinion is
largely wishful thinking. For example,

> One theoretical solution to the need for more minority members in
> higher education would be to enlarge our graduate schools. Then all who
> desired and were qualified could enter, and talk of discrimination would
> vanish. Unfortunately, this is neither feasible nor realistic. The vast re-
> sources that apparently would be required simply are not available. And
> the need for more professional graduates, in the strict numerical sense,
> perhaps has not been demonstrated at all.[24]

Not demonstrated? Only if the need for more physicians is conditioned
on an income approaching six figures for the average practitioner.
Of the three main opinions, that of Justice Brennan deviates most
from the norm of judicial blindness. Although he pays lip service to the

necessity that a compelling governmental interest be demonstrated before a racial classification may legitimately be employed, he finds that
such an interest "does not require . . . that recipients of preferential
advancement have been individually discriminated against; it is enough
that each recipient is within a general class of persons likely to have been
the victims of discrimination."[25] Nor does he require judicial determination that the governmental agency engaged in illegal discrimination. His
rationale is that such a requirement "would severely undermine efforts
to achieve voluntary compliance with the requirements of law."[26]
Moreover, the discrimination need not result from the actions of the
defendant. "If there is reason to believe that the . . . past discrimination
[is] . . . that of society at large,"[27] race-conscious programs may legally be
established. In other words, whites, solely because of their race, may be
discriminated against because of American society's discrimination
against blacks. Clearly, no judicial blindness here.

Several difficulties emerge from this focus on the litigants' personal
characteristics. First, constitutional guarantees pertain to "persons," not
groups. If they are possessed by groups, a problem of definition arises.
How is a member of a racial or ethnic group to be defined? Do we return
to the former law of some of the Southern states—"one drop of Negro
blood"? Federal regulations imposed in 1977 define a person as a
"minority group" member if said person had at least one grandparent
who was among the listed groups. What if an individual had two great-
grandparents who were, say, American Indians? Does not one-fourth
equal two-eighths? Not if one does business with federal bureaucrats. If
rights should become based on ancestry, genealogical charts would seem
at least as important as a birth certificate or a Social Security number, and
the Supreme Court would deal with such momentous questions as
whether a person qualified as a black if his only black relative was a
grandmother whose marriage license listed her as "mulatto."

Second, if preference is legitimated for a few groups, where should
the line be drawn? Why not include other groups that have been objects
of discrimination or disadvantaged in some respect: Jews, Catholics,
homosexuals, Poles, Italians, single-parent families, welfare recipients,
abused children, handicapped persons, unskilled workers, women in
general?

Finally, are all blacks, Chicanos, or Asians, by definition, more disadvantaged than any single white? Is a successful black professional or
businessperson, or his or her offspring, less advantaged than an unemployed Appalachian white who dropped out of school in the fourth
grade? Justice Marshall says so: "the racism of our society has been so
pervasive that none, regardless of wealth or position, has managed to
escape its impact."[28] If Marshall is correct, then white supremacy would
seem to be a fact of life, and the only way blacks or members of other

racial and ethnic minorities can compete is by having a leg up on the rest of the population. A more indelibly stamped badge of inferiority is hard to imagine; but it seems to exist. Davis's special admissions program "evaluates applications from economically and/or educationally disadvantaged backgrounds."[29] Yet the record revealed that, to use Justice Powell's words, "although disadvantaged whites applied to the special program in large numbers . . . none received an offer of admission."[30]

Superficially, the doctrine espoused in Brennan's opinion may be justified by his assertion that "no decision of this Court has ever adopted the proposition that the Constitution must be colorblind."[31] Although his statement is correct, so also is that of Powell: "We have never approved a classification that aids persons perceived as members of relatively victimized groups at the expense of other innocent individuals in the absence of judicial, legislative, or administrative findings of constitutional or statutory violations."[32] Significantly, however, Brennan makes no reference to a case decided a short two years before *Bakke—McDonald* v. *Santa Fe Trail Transportation Co.*[33]—in which the Court addressed the succeeding title (VII) of the Civil Rights Act of 1964, which prohibits all employers from refusing to hire, discharging, or discriminating against any person because of race, color, religion, sex, or national origin. In *McDonald,* an employer dismissed two white men who allegedly misappropriated company property, but not the third person involved, who was black. Justice Marshall wrote for a unanimous Court: Title VII "prohibits . . . discriminatory preference for any (racial) group, *minority or majority.*" It proscribes "racial discrimination in . . . employment against whites on the same terms as racial discrimination against nonwhites." It is intended to "cover all white men and white women and all Americans. . . . We therefore hold today that Title VII prohibits racial discrimination against the white petitioners in this case upon the same standards as would be applicable were they Negroes."[34]

Why the distinction between employment and admission to a medical school? Justices Powell and Stevens found *McDonald* relevant to their opinions. Certainly employment discrimination is as pervasive as discrimination in admission to institutions of higher education—arguably more so. A possible explanation may lie in Brennan's statement that "no fundamental right is involved"[35] in admission to a professional school and that consequently governmental activity affecting equal protection need only be "reasonably based." But Brennan's statement that no fundamental right of Bakke was violated is based on the Court's decision in *San Antonio School District* v. *Rodriguez,*[36] which held that education is not a right guaranteed by the Constitution. However, in *San Antonio,* Brennan, Marshall, and White each dissented. And it is most improbable that if *San Antonio* were redecided today, they would concur with the majority that education is not a constitutionally guaranteed right.

The position taken by Stevens, Burger, Stewart, and Rehnquist literally applies the language of Title VI: discrimination against whites is no less reprehensible than that against blacks or other ethnic minorities. If their view had prevailed, would it have meant the end of voluntarily established affirmative action and preferential treatment programs? According to Brennan's and Blackmun's opinions it would. Brennan flatly asserts: "there are no practical means by which . . . [Davis] could achieve its ends in the forseeable future without the use of race-conscious measures. With respect to any factor (such as poverty or family educational background) that may be used as a substitute for race as an indicator of past discrimination, whites greatly outnumber racial minorities simply because whites make up a far larger percentage of the total population and therefore far outnumber minorities in absolute terms at every socio-economic level."[37] Blackmun suspects "that it would be impossible to arrange an affirmative action program in a racially neutral way and have it successful."[38] There is some truth to these statements. Nonetheless, there is more than one way to skin a cat. On numerous occasions, the Court has stated that "in the area of economics and social welfare," governmental activity affecting equal protection need only be "reasonably based."[39] Unlike race, classifications based on such criteria are not "suspect" categories. Accordingly, institutions, businesses, and governmental agencies that wish to recruit disadvantaged persons may readily do so by utilizing such criteria as economic hardship, cultural deprivation, deficient schooling, low social status, or environmental obstacles. Thus, the medical school at Davis could reasonably conclude that the quality of health care among California's migrant workers is abysmally low and that a sensible solution might be the establishment of a quota for the offspring of such persons on the logical assumption that they are more likely than other physicians to practice where migrant workers are concentrated. The fact that those admitted may be predominantly—indeed, perhaps exclusively—Chicano is irrelevant. The basis of the quota is economic, not racial. Similarly, nothing prevents a school from showing a preference for applicants from inner cities (most of whom are black), again on the assumption that such persons are more likely than others to use their training and skills to improve the lot of residents of inner cities.

A final observation needs to be made. The California Supreme Court, in upholding Bakke's argument that the medical school's admission policy violated his right to the equal protection of the law, stated what should be obvious to all: No rule of law requires that determinative weight be given to grades and test scores. They do not reflect a person's abilities or promise as a professional. The Law School Admission Test, for example, merely predicts how successful an applicant will be during the first year of law school—nothing more. But even this assertion is suspect. Many law schools that admit only those scoring high on the LSAT have a very low attrition rate. Students fail to complete their programs only because they drop out or fail to take their final examinations. In such circumstances, scores on the admissions test become a self-fulfilling prophecy. Because only high-scoring applicants are admitted and because of a school's no-fail policy, the test becomes perfectly predictive of success. The words of Justice Douglas in the *DeFunis* case place the matter in proper perspective:

> The Equal Protection Clause did not enact a requirement that Law Schools employ as the sole criterion for admissions a formula based upon the LSAT and undergraduate grades, nor does it proscribe law schools from evaluating an applicant's prior achievements in light of the barriers that he had to overcome. A black applicant who pulled himself out of the ghetto into a junior college may thereby demonstrate a level of motivation, perseverance and ability that would lead a fairminded admissions committee to conclude that he shows more promise for law study than the son of a rich alumnus who achieved better grades at Harvard. That applicant would not be offered admission because he is black, but because as an individual he has shown he has the potential, while the Harvard man may have taken less advantage of the vastly superior opportunities offered him. Because of the weight of the prior handicaps, that black applicant may not realize his full potential in the first year of law school, or even in the full three years, but in the long pull of a legal career his achievements may far outstrip those of his classmates whose earlier records appeared superior by conventional criteria. There is currently no test available to the admissions committee that can predict such possibilities with assurance, but the committee may nevertheless seek to gauge it as best it can, and weigh this factor in its decisions. Such a policy would not be limited to blacks, or Chicanos or Filipinos or American Indians, although undoubtedly groups such as these may in practice be the principal beneficiaries of it. But a poor Appalachian white, or a second generation Chinese in San Francisco, or some other American whose lineage is so diverse as to defy ethnic labels, may demonstrate similar potential and thus be accorded favorable consideration. . . .[40]

On the basis of *Bakke,* where then does the matter of judicial blindness stand? Insofar as quota systems are concerned, those that adversely affect people's rights appear to be illegal or unconstitutional or both. This comports with the ideal of blindness, as do those affirmative action and preferential treatment programs that are based on a compelling governmental interest. Such a basis simply reflects the fact that justice sometimes needs to be tempered with mercy, and that legislative bodies may properly take "suspect" personal characteristics into account if a legitimate governmental objective cannot otherwise be realized. Nonetheless, in the words used in Justice Powell's prevailing opinion, "Racial and ethnic distinctions of any sort are inherently suspect and thus call for the most exacting judicial examination."[41] And though this be his position—and presumably the position of Burger, Rehnquist, Stewart, and Stevens as well—the other four Justices have accepted slippage of the judicial blindfold insofar as preferential admission of racial and ethnic minorities to institutions of higher education is concerned.

The Substantive Critique

The normative criticism of judicial blindness is heard from a few strident voices baying at the fringes of the body politic. Much more significant is the oft-heard allegation that judges do not, in fact, live up to the standard of judicial blindness. This indictment, then, is a substantive critique. Judges are faulted not because judicial blindness is not a commendable ideal, but rather because they are not guided by it—to too great an extent, they base their decisions on litigants' personal characteristics. Such substantive criticism was voiced throughout the colonial era and has continued to be heard ever since American independence.[42] One class, group, or interest is held to be favored over the others: creditors over debtors, merchants over landowners, railroad men over shipowners, men over women, capital over labor, rich over poor, young over old, East over West, North over South—or vice versa. Such chronic complaining is an example of the "poor me" syndrome—a means of blowing off steam, to be sure. Nonetheless, occasionally it reaches a certain collective intensity that produces an undercurrent of discontent that surfaces in the form of political action of one sort or another. In the second half of the twentieth century, group discontent has produced the McCarthy hearings, a manifestation of soft-on-Communism hysteria; racist resistance, first in the South, subsequently in Northern cities, to court-ordered desegregation; the "Impeach Earl Warren" billboards protesting a coddling of criminals; and, most recently, reverse discrimination and its threat to the status and job security of white middle- and working-class males. Given the pervasiveness of such criticism, it is worthwhile to ascertain whether it is true or false.

Is the substantive critique accurate?   In Chapter 5, the methods of determining why the Justices vote as they do were explained. The key construct was "attitude," which has two primary functions. First, it provides a conceptual framework with which to structure and arrange, in a manageable fashion, the wide variety of stimuli that impinge upon individual consciousness. Second, attitudes cause individuals to respond, to act, in one manner rather than another. The need to distinguish between "attitudes toward objects" and "attitudes toward situations" was also noted. To explain a decision maker's actions, it is not sufficient merely to know that person's attitudes toward such "objects" as blacks, women, students, indigents, criminal defendants, business, and labor unions. It is also necessary to know the decision maker's attitudes toward what that "object" is doing—toward the situation in which the decision maker encounters the "object."

To categorize the Court's decisions, several dozen cumulative scales were constructed, each on the basis of an attitude object and an attitude situation. A number of these scales had the same attitude object but different attitude situations. It was therefore possible, using these sets of scales, to determine whether the Justices' votes were a result of their attitudes toward the objects (the litigants) or their attitudes toward the situations within which the litigants were encountered. If justice is truly blind, the Court, for example, ought to treat business or blacks differently from one situation to another. If, on the other hand, justice is not blind, then business or blacks should be accorded the same treatment regardless of the situation in which they are encountered.

Several sets of cases drawn from the last eleven terms of the Warren Court (1958–1968) are suitable for testing whether the norm of judicial blindness guides the Court's policy making.[43] Because of the longer time span of the Warren Court, its decisions are more numerous than those of the Burger Court to date and hence more amenable to analysis.

Two sets of cases pertain to business and labor, respectively. Although criticisms that the Court is pro- or antibusiness or labor have not been especially widespread during the past quarter century, denizens of executive suites have undoubtedly grumbled about the prolabor proclivities of the Warren Court, just as porkchoppers in the back rooms of union headquarters have probably muttered about the probusiness orientation of the Nixon-constituted Burger Court. The business cases tested for this purpose constitute four separate cumulative scales, in each of which the attitude object is business. The four situations to which these scales pertain are: (1) alleged violations of the antitrust laws; (2) state taxation of business; (3) federal versus state regulation of business; and (4) federal regulation by means other than regulatory commissions. The determination of whether the Justices' policy making is situationally determined is straightforward. If the cases in these four scales may be combined to form one acceptable scale according to the statistical criteria described in Chapter 5, then a strong *prima facie* case exists that justice is not blind—that the Justices' attitudes toward business, rather than their attitudes toward the situations in which businesses found themselves, controlled their votes. Supplementary tests can also be employed to determine whether justice is situationally determined, but they need not detain us. However, it is possible to determine, albeit roughly, the relative importance of attitude toward situation and attitude toward object by comparing the rank order of the Justices on one scale with their rank orders on each of the others. If these correlations, which range from

+1.00 to −1.00, are high and positive, then the impact of the litigants is much more important than that of the situations that produced the controversy. In other words, if the correlations are uniformly high across the situations in which a class of litigants is encountered, then it is safe to conclude that the Justices' voting resulted from their attitudes toward the litigants rather than their attitudes toward the encountered situations.‡

The results of the analysis show that the business cases cannot be combined to form an acceptable scale and that the rank-order correlations among these four scales average only +.30.§ Attitudes toward situation thus clearly dominate those toward business, and in this set of cases, at least, justice was administered blindly. That is not to say that the attitude object, "business," had no effect whatsoever on the Justices' decisions. As was pointed out in Chapter 5, behavior is a function of the interaction between attitude toward object and attitude toward situation. The fact that the average rank-order correlation among the four business scales is positive, albeit low, indicates that the Justices' attitudes toward business had some impact on their decisions in these cases. But by the same token, situational considerations appear to have been at least twice as important as the fact that the litigants were businesses.

Similar results can be obtained from a set of four cumulative scales in which the attitude object is labor unions. The "situations" to which these scales pertain are: (1) the sanctions that labor unions use against business (such as strikes, picketing, collective bargaining, representational elections); (2) the sanctions that businesses use against organized labor (such as discharging and locking out employees and discouraging union membership); (3) the applicability of federal antitrust legislation to anticompetitive labor union activity (such as secondary boycotts and uniform industry-wide working conditions); (4) the legality of making union membership a condition of employment—that is, of allowing closed, union, and agency shops. These sets of cases could not be combined into one cumulative scale, and the average rank-order correlation among the scales was only six points higher than it was for the business cases: +.36.

Is the blindness with regard to the business and labor cases typical of other issue areas in which there is a common class of litigants? The answer, perhaps unfortunately, perhaps not, is "no." During the 1958–

---

‡ If, for example, the rank orders (with regard to their support of business) of the eleven Justices who sat on the Court during the 1958–1968 terms (Harlan, Stewart, White, Goldberg, Fortas, Clark, Marshall, Warren, Black, Brennan, and Douglas) were substantially the *same* in *each* of these scales, then their attitudes toward the object (business) rather than their attitudes toward the diverse situations in which businesses were encountered controlled their decision making.
§ Clearly, then, no constant ordering of the Justices occurred. Rather, the order of the Justices varied greatly from one business scale to another.

1968 terms, the Court decided 103 cases in which one person sued another for damages suffered due to negligence. Although such cases pose mundane, commonplace issues, the Court deems some of them of sufficient importance to warrant its attention. These cases constitute three separate scales, in which the situations are: (1) sufficiency of the evidence—whether the injured person has presented enough evidence to permit the jury to determine whether compensation should be provided; (2) election of remedies—what laws, state or federal, specify the remedies that an injured person is entitled to; (3) liability—what responsibility, if any, the person being sued has for the injury suffered.

In this set of decisions, unlike the cases in the business and labor scales, there are two distinguishable attitude objects: physically injured employees and nonphysically injured persons. The former, which are worker's compensation cases, pertain primarily to railroad workers, longshoremen, and merchant seamen. The latter cases involve damage to privately owned property. This set of decisions, then, allows us to test the effects of a common situation across different attitude objects. This was not possible in the business and labor cases because each of those sets had only a single attitude object—business and labor, respectively. When the cases involving physically injured employees and nonphysically injured persons are separately scaled across the situations in which these litigants found themselves, very acceptable results are obtained. Indeed, the nonphysically injured persons scale is perfect: it does not contain so much as a single inconsistent vote by any participating Justice. Furthermore, the two attitude objects may even be combined to produce a scale that is far above minimal acceptability. The rank-order correlation among the different situations that the two attitude objects encountered is also extremely high: +.855. In short, no matter how these cases are compared, the conclusion is inescapable: the attitude objects are overwhelmingly dominant; the situations are all but irrelevant. In this set of cases, then, justice is not only *not* blind; it possesses 20-20 vision.

Another set of scales also exists in which it is possible to test the effects of a common situation on a pair of discrete attitude objects. These scales concern various issues pertaining to civil and political rights. In some of these cases, the litigants were black; in the remainder, they may be designated as "nonblacks." The "situations" are as follows: (1) First Amendment freedoms—conventional First Amendment freedom cases, excluding those which pertain to freedom of religion, establishment of religion, and obscenity. (The religion and obscenity cases constitute separate scales in which the race of the litigants is almost exclusively white.) (2) Voting—cases concerning the right to vote, plus cases concerning electoral and ballot qualifications. (3) Comity—cases concerning the principle of nonintervention by the federal judiciary in ongoing state court proceedings. (The issue here is whether cases being heard in state courts, which are also within the jurisdiction of the federal courts, may be resolved by the federal courts before the remedies available under state law have been exhausted.) (4) Protest demonstrations— cases that dispute the use of demonstrations to communicate ideas and beliefs, frequently by nonverbal means. (Defendants in these cases justify their activity on the basis of freedom of speech, press, assembly, and/or association.) (5) Sit-in demonstrations—cases that dispute the use of sit-in demonstrations to achieve desegregation of public facilities and accommodations. (Unlike the defendants in protest demonstration cases, the defendants in these cases justify their actions on the basis of the equal protection clause of the Fourteenth Amendment.) In this scale, unlike the others in this set, all of the litigants were black.

Analysis of the Justices' votes in these five scales shows that the Court did not decide these cases on the basis of whether the litigants were black or nonblack. Although the cases in which the litigants are black do form a marginally acceptable scale (those involving nonblacks, by contrast, do not), marked improvement results when the cases in which blacks are a party are limited to a single situation. Moreover, when the rank orders of the Justices are compared, controlling for both situation and object, situation dominates. In other words, scales with a common situation (voting, comity) produce much higher correlations (even though the object in one is black and object in the other is nonblack) than do scales in which the object is held constant across situations. For example, the correlation between the black First Amendment freedoms and protest demonstration scales is 40 points less than the correlation between the black and nonblack First Amendment freedoms scales, and 32 points less than the correlation between the black and nonblack protest demonstration scales. ‖ Therefore, in litigation involving political and civil rights to which both blacks and nonblacks were party, the Warren Court behaved in a way that indicated a selective myopia—not to the extent that it did in cases concerning business and labor, to be sure, but sufficiently so to warrant a judgment that its blindfold was reasonably well in place.

A final issue is internal security. (The Court was much criticized by Senator Joe McCarthy and his ilk because of its decisions in this area.) Three cumulative scales relate to this issue, in each of which the attitude object may be designated as a "security risk"—a person whose beliefs and/or behavior was deemed "un-American" or "subversive." Three distinguishable types of litigation concerned them: (1) Legislative investigation: the legality of the statesmanlike activities of the House Un-

---

‖ In other words, the First Amendment freedom cases and protest demonstration cases fit less well together (even though only the cases involving black litigants were combined) than was true when black and nonblack litigants were combined into a single First Amendment freedom scale and a separate protest demonstration scale.

American Activities Committee and related state investigative bodies. (2) Public employment or benefits: the dismissal of public employees, admission to the bar, and the constitutionality of loyalty oaths. (3) Federal legislative sanctions: the interpretation and application of federal legislation (the Subversive Activities Control Act, the Internal Security Act, and the Smith Act) designed to control the spread of subversive ideas.

When the cases in these three scales are combined, a scale even better than that attained in the set of personal injury cases results. Furthermore, the mean rank-order correlations among the three security risk scales reaches a high of +.75. The attitude object, beyond question, dominated the Justices' votes in this set of cases. The Court, therefore, was at least as perspicacious as the gimlet-eyed guardians of political orthodoxy themselves.

Explanations for deviation from the norm of judicial blindness. The Court appears to have adhered to the norm of judicial blindness in three of these five sets of data. Superficially, this is not a very impressive record. One may ask, however, if extenuating circumstances may not explain the Court's deviation from the norm in the areas of personal injury and internal security. I think they do.

The security risk cases, for the most part, date from the McCarthy era, a period in which the fear of subversion and the threat of Soviet aggression loomed large in the public mind. No more damning an indictment could be leveled against an individual than that he was a "security risk" or "subversive." The question that one must consequently ask is whether it is reasonable to expect courts to dispense justice blindly when a climate of fear of vigilantism pervades society. Throughout history, judges themselves have succumbed more often than not to the force of mass hysteria. On balance, the United States Supreme Court during this period did not. Rather, it adhered to another, equally important, norm: that judges should be especially protective of those who are the victims of lawlessness; that they should not legitimate the activity of frenzied zealots, of heedless horsemen, who would punish those who do not share their vision of the ideal society. Of the Court's 71 security risk decisions during this period, 45 (63 percent) favored the accused.

A completely different extenuating circumstance may explain the Court's failure to adhere to the norm of judicial blindness in the personal injury cases. Congress has never seen fit to enact a workers' compensation law. As a remedy for the impotence of Congress in this regard, the Court has assumed the role of a federal workers' compensation commission for those fortunate few who manage to secure access to itself.[44] It would seem that the Court has been deliberately performing this function, at least since 1939.[45] From the standpoint of those who have suffered injuries, the Court has done a reasonably good job. The thrust of its decisions, during the 1958–1968 terms at least, has been highly supportive of injured persons, especially injured employees, 76 percent of whom emerged victorious.

The types of litigants who seek redress before the court of last resort are by no means confined to these issue areas. Other groups and classes, such as indigents, women, debtors, public employees, and persons accused of crime, likely also have their controversies resolved with the blindfold reasonably well in place. Some of the Justices may have been prone to make decisions based on the litigants' personal characteristics rather than on the situations that gave rise to the controversies. But the Court's decisions are a group product, and as a group the Court appears to adhere to the normative ideal, or to other ideals it deems equally important.

NOTES

1. See John H. Kessel, "Public Perceptions of the Supreme Court," *American Journal of Political Science* 10 (May 1966): 167–191; Walter F. Murphy and Joseph Tanenhaus, "Public Opinion and the United States Supreme Court," *Law and Society Review* 2 (May 1968): 357–384; Greg A. Caldeira, "Judges Judge the Supreme Court," *Judicature* 61 (November 1977): 208–219.

2. *DeFunis v. Odegaard,* 416 U.S. 312 (1974).

3. *Id.* at 350.

4. *Id.* at 331, 334.

5. *Id.* at 336–337.

6. *Id.* at 340–341.

7. *Id.* at 342.

8. *Id.* at 343.

9. *Id.* at 344.

10. *Regents v. Bakke,* 46 LW 4896 (1978).

11. *Id.* at 4898.

12. 42 U.S.C. §2000d.

13. *Regents v. Bakke,* 46 LW 4896, at 4935.

14. *Id.* at 4912.

15. *Id.* at 4914.

16. *Id.* at 4910.

17. *Id.* at 4902.

18. *Id.* at 4909–4910.

19. *Id.* at 4931.

20. *Id.* at 4898, note 6.

21. *Id.* at 4931.

22. *Id.* at 4898.

23. *Id.* at 4932.

24. *Id.*

25. *Id.* at 4921.

26. *Id.*

27. *Id.* at 4923.

28. *Id.* at 4931.

29. *Id.* at 4897, note 1.

30. *Id.* at 4898.

31. *Id.* at 4914.

32. *Id.* at 4906.

33. 427 U.S. 273, 49 L Ed 2d 493 (1976).

34. 49 L Ed 2d 493, at 500–501.

35. *Regents* v. *Bakke,* at 4919.

36. 411 U.S. 1 (1973), number 43 in *Classic and Current Decisions.*

37. *Regents* v. *Bakke,* at 4924–4925.

38. *Id.* at 4933.

39. For example, *Dandridge* v. *Williams,* 397 U.S. 471 (1970).

40. *DeFunis* v. *Odegaard,* 416 U.S. 312, at 331–332.

41. *Regents* v. *Bakke,* at 4902.

42. See Lawrence M. Friedman's excellent work, *A History of American Law* (New York: Simon and Schuster, 1973), especially Part II, chaps. 4-7, and Part III, chaps. 7-10. Also Robert J. Steamer, "The Court and the Criminal,"*William and Mary Law Review* 8 (1967): 319-342.

43. The following analysis is based upon Harold J. Spaeth, *et al.,* "Is Justice Blind: An Empirical Investigation of a Normative Ideal," *Law and Society Review* 7 (Fall 1972): 119–137.

44. James C. Connor, "Supreme Court Certiorari Policy and the Federal Employer's Liability Act," *Cornell Law Quarterly* 43 (Spring 1958): 451–468; Glendon Schubert, "Policy Without Law: An Extension of the Certiorari Game," *Stanford Law Review* 14 (March 1962): 284–327.

45. For example, *Bailey* v. *Central Vermont R. Co.,* 319 U.S. 350 (1943), at 354–359; *Stone* v. *N.Y.C. & St.L. R. Co.,* 344 U.S. 407 (1953), at 410–413; *McAlister* v. *United States,* 348 U.S. 19 (1954), at 23–25; *Rogers* v. *Mo. Pacific R. Co.,* 352 U.S. 500 (1957), at 559–564.

After the Lawsuit Is Over: Compliance with the Court's Policies

Given the creative and innovative policy making of the Warren Court and, to a lesser extent, the Burger Court, to what extent are the Court's decisions complied with? The conventional assumption is that compliance occurs naturally, like thunder after lightning. But compliance with the Court's rulings on such issues as school prayers and school desegregation has been difficult to enforce. Nor is noncompliance a recent problem. In response to the Court's ruling in *Worcester* v. *Georgia*,[1] Andrew Jackson is alleged to have commented, "John Marshall has made his decision, now let him enforce it."[2]

Compliance means to behave in conformity with the law.[3] Although numerous studies, in whole or in part, suggest that at least certain decisions either have not been complied with or have had little impact[4] (for example, the desegregation of Southern schools,[5] school prayer,[6] obscenity,[7] and criminal law—specifically, *Mapp* v. *Ohio* and *Miranda* v. *Arizona*[8]), the position taken in this chapter is that compliance is the rule, disobedience the exception. But compliance tells not the whole story. It is certainly possible that though those subject to the Court's ruling may comply, the decision may nonetheless have little impact—for all practical purposes, business continues as usual. For example, although employment discrimination is illegal, the procedure that women and minorities must follow to seek redress (request state or federal administrative agency action, then resort to the courts if the agency's decision is unfavorable or is appealed to the courts by the employer) appears not to have effectively eliminated such discrimination.[9] Similarly, though the Court in *Miranda* v. *Arizona*[10] wrote a manual of police procedure that requires suspects to be informed of their rights to refuse to answer

questions and to have the assistance of an attorney, one study found that
during a three-month period in one community, "there [was] no evidence indicating that the warnings given . . . caused many suspects to
refuse to talk or ask for counsel."[11] But this conclusion ought not cloud
another aspect of a decision's impact: though business may continue
substantially as usual, at least the objectionable practices and conditions
may not have worsened. For example, the ruling in *New York Times* v.
Sullivan,[12] that public officials could not secure damages for libel unless
they could show actual malice, may not have made discussion of public
issues more robust; in this sense the decision had little impact. But it
most assuredly did prevent public officials from muzzling adverse criticism by the media, and in this sense the Court's ruling had a most
pronounced impact. From which perspective should the impact of this
case be judged? To assume compliance is probably at least as realistic as
to assume noncompliance by those who consider the Court's decisions
merely so much sound and fury.

REASONS FOR NONCOMPLIANCE

Several arguments superficially support judgments that compliance with
the Court's mandates may be less than complete.

Justices Lack Coercive Capability

The Justices possess neither the power of the purse nor that of the
sword. Hence, they must depend on the executive branch to give force
and effect to their decisions when resistance occurs.[13] The sole weapon
the Court has at its disposal is its moral authority, and though moral
authority may appear to be a fragile weapon when compared with dollars, nightsticks, nuclear weapons, and other elements of *Realpolitik,* the
Court's policy-making capacity—based on the respect and reverence accorded Justices, the perceived legitimacy of the Court's decisions even
when they are disapproved of by substantial segments of society, and the
factors described in Chapter 1[14]—compares favorably with these tangible forms of persuasion, whether they are gently or roughly applied.

Decisions Bind Only the Parties to the Litigation

The decision of a court, at all levels of the judicial system, technically
binds only the parties to the litigation. Other persons, though similarly
situated, are under no legal duty to comply. Even so, the Supreme Court
virtually never finds it necessary to spend time applying a decision to
other persons simply because they were not formally parties to the litiga-

tion.[15] School desegregation and obscenity do constitute important exceptions, however. Other exceptions are cases that are already on their way to the Court at the time the Court announces its decision. These merely receive summary treatment; that is, the Court simply cites its controlling decision as authority for the action to be taken. Thus, four days after its July 1976 death penalty decisions, in which the Justices declared that a mandatory sentence of death upon conviction for premeditated murder constituted cruel and unusual punishment,[16] the Court took summary action in the cases of 63 other persons who were under sentence of death: 38 from North Carolina, 9 from Georgia, 7 from Oklahoma, 6 from Florida, and 3 from Louisiana. In each instance, the summary action was based on the formal decisions that had been announced four days earlier.[17]

The Court's 1976 decisions were not its first encounter with the death penalty. Four years earlier, in *Furman* v. *Georgia,* the Justices, with one fell swoop, had voided the capital punishment laws of 39 states plus the District of Columbia. In the words of Justice Stewart, "These death sentences are cruel and unusual in the same way that being struck by lightning is cruel and unusual. For, of all the people convicted of rapes and murders ... many just as reprehensible as these, the petitioners are among a capriciously selected random handful upon whom the sentence of death has in fact been imposed." The Constitution "simply ... cannot tolerate the infliction of a sentence of death under legal systems that permit this unique penalty to be so wantonly and so freakishly imposed."[18] Thereupon, 35 states and Congress enacted new legislation to comply with what they perceived to be the Court's mandate, even though the laws *of only two states*—Georgia and Texas—were at issue in *Furman.* But over half of these states found that their new laws still failed to pass muster when the Court handed down its 1976 decisions, which held that a death sentence is constitutionally permissible, at least for murder,[19] only if the judge and jury have been given adequate information and guidance to enable them to take account of the aggravating and mitigating circumstances of the crime and the character of the defendant before passing sentence.[20]

As evidence of compliance, the states' response to the Court's decisions regarding capital punishment is instructive. From the time the Court first grappled with the constitutionality of the death penalty in a 1968 decision,[21] until Utah's execution of Gary Gilmore in January 1977, not a single one of the several hundred occupants of death row was executed—notwithstanding American society's overwhelming endorsement of capital punishment (noted in the prevailing opinion in *Gregg* v. *Georgia*[22]) and the rapidity with which all but fifteen of the fifty states successfully managed to crank up their creaky legislative machinery in order to comply with the Court's 1972 decision that declared existing capital punishment statutes constitutionally defective.

The Court Does Not Always Make the Final Decision

As was noted in Chapter 5,[23] four constitutional amendments have been adopted that overturned previous Court decisions. And, of course, if the Court has ruled on the meaning of a provision of an act of Congress rather than a provision of the Constitution,[24] Congress is free to overrule the Court simply by changing the wording of the act's provision. For example, in September 1977 the Senate passed and sent to the House of Representatives a bill that would amend Title VII of the Civil Rights Act of 1964 to require employers to include pregnancy benefits in any disability plan that they provided their employees. If approved by the House and signed by the President, the legislation would overturn a controversial Court ruling that the exclusion of pregnancy-related disabilities did not constitute sex discrimination in violation of Title VII.[25]

Furthermore, the Justices, as a matter of policy, typically refrain from overruling decisions in cases originating in the states' courts with which they do not agree, preferring to remand the case to the state supreme court "for further proceedings not inconsistent" with their opinion. This the Court does for two reasons. First, as was pointed out in Chapter 1, ours is a federal system of government in which the states, as well as the federal government, are entitled to a substantial measure of autonomy. Diplomacy accordingly decrees that the Court treat the states as so many semisovereign entities. The Justices also theorize that more will be gained if the Court is mindful of the states' sometimes tender sensibilities. Second, as was explained in Chapter 2, the Supreme Court's jurisdiction, insofar as it affects the states, extends only to "federal questions"—those that pertain to provisions of the Constitution, acts of Congress, and treaties of the United States. Such questions invariably come interwoven with issues of state law and procedure. As a result, the party who emerges victorious from the Marble Palace occasionally ends up the loser after the case has been remanded to the state court. Georgia's electrocution of Aubrey Williams, described in Chapter 2, is a striking case in point.[26]

The Court's Opinions Lack Clarity

It was observed in Chapter 2 that a majority of the Justices must agree on an opinion for it to become the opinion of the Court.[27] When the Court is closely divided, bargaining, negotiation, and compromise among the majority coalition are especially costly and difficult to come by. Sometimes the majority Justices cannot accommodate their differences, and in such cases all that results is a "judgment of the Court." These judgments provide little guidance to the lower courts or to those affected by the Court's decision.[28] Even those who desire to comply with the Court's mandate find determination of the Court's position as difficult as navigating with a cockeyed compass. Nonetheless, compliance typically occurs. Consider again the Court's 1972 death penalty decision.[29] Although the opinion of the Court was announced *per curiam* rather than as a judgment of the Court, it approximated the latter more than the former. In pertinent part it read as follows:

> The Court holds that the imposition and carrying out of the death penalty in these cases constitute cruel and unusual punishment in violation of the Eighth and Fourteenth Amendments. The judgment in each case is therefore reversed insofar as it leaves undisturbed the death sentence imposed, and the cases are remanded for further proceedings.[30]

Each of the five Justices who constituted the majority wrote his own separate opinion. Nonetheless, as has been mentioned, fully 70 percent of the states and the Congress promptly rewrote their capital punishment laws, hoping that they had accurately fathomed the Court's inscrutable position on the subject of the death penalty. More than half of these states found that they had guessed wrong when the Court handed down its five 1976 death penalty decisions,[31] every one of which was announced via a judgment of the Court to which only Justices Stewart, Powell, and Stevens subscribed.

But even when every single Justice joins the opinion of the Court, its position may still be no more clear than mud. The decisions in *Brown* v. *Board of Education* are an apt illustration.[32] The Court first said that "separate educational facilities are inherently unequal" and that the segregation the plaintiffs complained of deprived them of the equal protection of the laws guaranteed by the Fourteenth Amendment.[33] This was a perfectly clear and comprehensible statement. The Court then addressed the matter of implementation, and one year later ruled that public schools must desegregate "with all deliberate speed" and that the task of eradicating this racist legacy belonged to the federal district courts "because of their proximity to local conditions."[34] Needless to say, the formula "with all deliberate speed" hardly lent itself to consensual application. No wonder that a decade elapsed before any appreciable changes occurred in the Deep South—especially since the Court itself chose to say virtually nothing more on the subject until 1965, when it tersely asserted that "delays in desegregation of school systems are no longer tolerable."[35] Not until the Burger Court was the matter of implementation clarified. And then clarity resulted only because the Court tossed the "all deliberate speed" formula aside:

> . . . continued operation of segregated schools under a standard of allowing "all deliberate speed" for desegregation is no longer constitutionally permissible. . . . the obligation of every school district is to terminate dual school systems at once and to operate now and hereafter only unitary schools.[36]

Thus did desegregation finally come to the South, the border states, and parts of the North, aided and abetted by provisions in the Civil Rights Act of 1964 that permitted a cut-off of federal funds from school districts that failed to desegregate. If the fifteen-year interval between 1954 and 1969 constitutes noncompliance with the Court's mandate in *Brown* v. *Board of Education,* the blame should be placed on the occupants of the Marble Palace—especially those who, in 1896, formulated the separate but equal doctrine that constitutionally blessed racially separate schools—rather than Southern school officials, state legislators, and assorted governors.[37]

A lack of clarity may also result when the Court focuses on fundamental principles rather than on the specific controversy before it—that is, in deciding certain cases the Court focuses on the larger question or issue, of which the case before it represents only a part. The opinion of the Court is, after all, the core of the Justices' policy-making power. The opinion lays down the broad constitutional and legal principles that bind the lower courts, other governmental instrumentalities, and affected private persons; establishes precedents for the Court's future decisions; and, least importantly, resolves the litigation at hand.

Thus, in *M'Culloch* v. *Maryland,*[38] Chief Justice Marshall upheld the power of Congress to establish a national bank and, concomitantly, prohibited the states from either taxing or regulating it. If the outcome of the controversy were analyzed twenty years after the decision was announced, the conclusion would be inescapable: the "case was more interesting as a monument to judicial impotence than as an example of judicial power."[39] In 1832, President Jackson vetoed a bill to extend the charter of the Bank of the United States. One year later, he withdrew federal funds from the Bank's vaults, and in 1837 its charter expired. The Bank, a shell of its former self, lingered for a few more years until bankruptcy put it out of business in 1841.

But the significance of *M'Culloch* v. *Maryland* is not that it affected the eventual fate of the Bank, but rather that in that decision, Marshall formulated the doctrine of implied powers. His assertion of this principle was the basis for the expansion of federal power and the rise of the welfare state that began during the depression of the 1930's. Though these developments did not occur until more than a century after *M'Culloch* v. *Maryland,* the decision in that case doomed the strict constructionists of federal power to defeat; thereafter, assertions that that government is best which governs least would have an unmistakably hollow ring.

Similarly, before 1852 the Court had wrestled with the basic issue of the extent to which the states might enact legislation that would affect interstate commerce, but it had not formulated a policy that would serve as a permanent guide for the future. The Constitution vests Congress with the power to regulate interstate commerce, but the states, on the basis of their power to legislate for the health, welfare, morals, safety, and convenience of their residents and on the basis of their power of taxation, had continually enacted regulations that affected licensing, inspection, transportation, and navigation—and thus interstate commerce. The question was whether the states could so legislate; and if so, where did their authority end? Only after it had rejected a number of principles did the Court accept one—"selective exclusiveness"—on the basis of which future controversies concerning this aspect of the relationship between the federal government and the states would be resolved.[40]

Short-Term Noncompliance versus Long-Term Compliance

There is a tendency to view noncompliance from a short-term perspective. A pair of cases dealing with released-time programs of religious instruction for public school pupils is a good illustration. In 1948, in *McCollum* v. *Board of Education,* the Court held that even though the religious teachers were not paid by the schools and parental consent had been secured, such programs were not compatible with the establishment of religion clause of the First Amendment if they were held during school hours and on school grounds.[41] Given the assumption that all such programs were unconstitutional, the decision created a furor in religious circles and was widely ignored. But not all released-time programs were banned, as the Court made clear when it next addressed the question four years later, in *Zorach* v. *Clauson.*[42] If the program took place either off school grounds or not during school hours, no constitutional violation occurred. In other words, if the program took place off school grounds, it could be given during school hours; alternatively, if it were offered in the school building, it had to be at a time other than during the regular school day. Although many school districts did not adjust their programs so that they met the criteria of *Zorach* v. *Clauson,* others did. These programs, of course, were in compliance, even though, immediately after *McCollum,* it could have been argued that they were not. Be that as it may, no additional cases reached even the lower federal courts in the decade following *Zorach.*[43] If sectarian programs are still offered during school hours and on school grounds, they most certainly are a well-concealed fact.

The same must be true of prayer in the public schools, the subject of two decisions that were received with rancor when handed down in the early 1960's. In the first, the Court declared unconstitutional a 22-word prayer composed by the governing body of New York State's educational establishment that was to be recited at the start of each school day.[44] The Court's opinion unequivocally stated that "it is no part of the business of government to compose official prayers for any group of the American people to recite as part of a religious program carried on by govern-

ment."[45] One year later, the Court went a step further, ruling that a
school prayer is a school prayer, whether it is composed by a school
board or whether it consists of selected passages from somebody's ver-
sion of the Bible.[46] Both decisions were widely ignored, especially in
rural areas and in the Southern Bible belt.[47] Within a decade, however,
school prayer had ceased to be a burning issue. Some districts continued
to disobey the Court's mandate, and some undoubtedly still do so—they
are small, religiously homogeneous districts where conformist pressures
make parents reluctant to subject themselves and their children to ob-
loquy and ostracism. And though such behavior may appear scornful, if
there is consensus within a community that school prayers are desirable,
and if the school has not been ordered to desist, and if no one complains,
who is hurt?

Notwithstanding the lack of short-run compliance with its released-
time and school prayer decisions, the Court had not become gun-shy, as
some commentators surmised.[48] Beginning in 1971, the Burger Court
began to systematically demolish state-established programs of financial
assistance to nonpublic schools—better known as parochiaid. Adher-
ing to a Warren Court decision that upheld only the *loan* of secular-
subject textbooks to parochial school students,[49] the Court beat back
state efforts to supplement the salaries of teachers of secular subjects in
nonpublic schools and to reimburse private schools for instructional
costs in specified secular subjects;[50] a scheme to reimburse pupil-testing
and record-keeping costs;[51] the partial repayment to parents of tuition
paid for their private-school children;[52] direct money grants for the
maintenance and repair of certain facilities in nonpublic schools, partial
reimbursement of tuition paid by low-income families who sent their
children to private schools, and tax relief for middle- and upper-income
families;[53] and the loan of instructional materials and equipment and
the provision of special educational personnel and services to nonpublic
schools.[54] The Court did, however, allow the provision of diagnostic
speech, hearing, and psychological services to parochial school children,
as well as the provision of therapeutic, guidance, and remedial services
at sites that were physically and educationally separate from nonpublic
schools.[55] By no stretch of the imagination, however, can these services
be deemed anything other than commonplace health and social—rather
than educational—programs. And though the parochiaiders complained bitterly, noncompliance was notable by its absence.

The Nature of the Mandated Compliance

Decisions regarding actions emanating from fervently held beliefs—
such as the recitation of a brief prayer in a public school classroom—are
much more likely to result in noncompliance than decisions regarding
the provision of money or other tangible goods. The absence of public

support for a decision may also encourage noncompliance, as will the absence of effective and zealous organizations supportive of the Court's decision. Offsetting these considerations is the very essence of our adversary system of justice, in which two opposing parties engage in litigation.[56] Assuming that the litigants are proper parties and are in the proper forum,[57] one of them must of necessity win. The victorious party thus has his or her claim legitimated and is entitled to the relief decreed by the court. This does not mean automatic vindication. Effectuation of the court's judgment may well require action by other governmental personnel. For example, a magistrate or friend of the court may have to dun an ex-spouse for court-ordered alimony or child support; the police or a marshal may have to take possession of wrongfully secured property; or bureaucrats may have to alter their standards and procedures so that they comport with the legal rights of an aggrieved person.

COMPLIANCE BY THE OTHER BRANCHES OF GOVERNMENT

The most potentially dramatic impact of Supreme Court policy making occurs when the Court orders a coequal branch of government to do or not to do something. Two recent examples are instructive. One involved Congress and, by extension, the state legislatures; the other involved the President.

Congress

In 1962, the Supreme Court decided the first in a rapid series of cases that, in the words of one observer, "involved the most remarkable and far-reaching exercise of judicial power in our history."[58] The issue was the reapportionment of Congress and the legislatures of each and every one of the fifty states. The Court initially asserted that legislative apportionment was properly a matter for judicial resolution,[59] thereby overruling a previous decision in which Justice Frankfurter had held such controversies to be political questions and therefore not appropriate for courts to decide.[60] In his dissent in *Baker* v. *Carr*, Frankfurter had asserted that the belief that courts "could effectively fashion" a remedy for "the abstract constitutional right" of electoral districting was mere "judicial rhetoric . . . not only a euphoric hope. It implies a sorry confession of judicial impotence in place of a frank acknowledgment that there is not under our Constitution a judicial remedy for every political mischief, for every undesirable exercise of legislative power." Appeal for relief, he said, "does not belong here," but belongs rather "to an informed, civically militant electorate." He then predicted: "there is nothing judicially more unseemly nor more self-defeating than for this Court to make *in terroram* pronouncements, to indulge in merely empty rhetoric, sounding a word of promise to the ear, sure to be disappointing to the hope."[61] The majority paid him no heed and, in the process, proved him to be a false prophet, and his words to be merely another monument to deficient wisdom. In its next decision, the Court stipulated that within a single legislative constituency the operative districting principle must be one person, one vote.[62] This was followed by a ruling that in congressional elections, one person's vote "as nearly as is practicable . . . is to be worth as much as another's."[63] The Court topped off its policy making four months later when it made its one-person, one-vote standard binding on *both* houses of the state legislatures.[64] Lest the Court appear to be riding herd only on Congress and the state legislatures, it should be noted that the Justices subsequently penned all popularly elected local governmental officials in the same barnyard as the legislators.[65] Thus, in the 27-month period from March 1962 to June 1964, the Court utterly abolished the stranglehold that farm and rural interests had had on the nation's legislatures since the time of Thomas Jefferson. This was no mean accomplishment for the governmental branch that possesses nary a smidgen of coercive capability—especially since it concerned a matter that is not exactly of minor moment to legislators. The name of the legislators' game is re-election, and re-election depends on the boundaries and characteristics of their constituencies. Nonetheless, within one year of the decision in *Reynolds* v. *Sims,* 45 of the 50 states took action to comply with the one-person, one-vote principle. It ought also be kept in mind that the Court's reapportionment policy making coincided with the Court's school prayer decisions of 1962 and 1963; that at this same time "delays in desegregation of school systems" were about to be prohibited;[66] police, prosecutors, and law-and-order elements were muttering about the Court's revolutionizing of criminal procedures;[67] and prudes and bluenoses were dismayed and distraught that the Court was about to preside over the demise of Victorian morality.[68]

The President

The other recent example of conflict is the Watergate Tapes controversy, described in detail in Chapter 6.[69] The circumstances that gave rise to the litigation were without precedent—President Nixon dared the Court to force him to turn over his confidential papers. Federal District Court Judge John Sirica had ordered Nixon to hand over 64 specified tapes and documents that related to private conversations between himself and his closest and most trusted advisers so that they could be used as evidence in a pending criminal trial involving seven of those advisers, all of whom had been previously indicted by a federal grand jury for various offenses including conspiracy to defraud the United States and obstruction of justice. On several occasions Nixon and his henchmen had hinted that they might not comply with a decision ordering the surrender of the tapes unless it was considered a "definitive" ruling by the Court. (Nixon himself presumably would determine whether the Court's decision was definitive.) The Justices, however, were not intimidated. They accepted the gauntlet thrown down by Nixon; and with a lapse of only sixteen days between oral argument and the announcement of their decision, the Justices delivered a unanimous opinion (written, ironically, by the man whom Nixon himself had nominated as Chief Justice) that unequivocally subjected the President to the rule of law. That decision stated that the aphorism "the King can do no wrong" has no place in the American constitutional system; and that when a President claims the privilege of confidentiality in his communications, that claim "cannot prevail over the fundamental demands of due process of law in the fair administration of criminal justice. The generalized assertion of privilege must yield to the demonstrated, specific need for evidence in a pending criminal trial."[70]

The same day the Court announced its decision, July 24, 1974, the House Judiciary Committee began final deliberation on the impeachment of the President. On August 8, Nixon resigned. If any doubts still lingered about the authority of the Court's decisions, Watergate should have consigned them to the same fate that befell the thirty-seventh President of the United States.

SOURCES OF COURT SUPPORT

One final observation: the Court never stands alone. Not only does the nature of our adversary process assure that one party or interest must necessarily win in every case that a court decides—with consequent support from those persons and groups who benefit from the court's decision—but the Supreme Court also shares the task of protecting and advancing the cause of human liberty and freedom with other policy-making bodies. In recent years, for example, the state courts, to the astonishment of many observers, have rid themselves of the rampant parochialism that was reflected in so many of their decisions as late as the 1950's and 1960's,[71] and have begun to exercise a measure of constitutional leadership beyond that manifested by the Supreme Court itself. Not even the wildest imagination would have envisioned state courts leading the efforts to eradicate inequities in the financing of public education,[72] or state courts construing the bitterly criticized decision in *Miranda* v. *Arizona*[73] more liberally than the Supreme Court itself[74]—so liberally that the Court felt compelled to caution the states that they "may not impose such greater restrictions as a matter of *federal constitutional law* when this Court specifically refrains from imposing them."[75] Or a Wisconsin court refusing to comply with the United States Supreme Court's decision in *General Electric* v. *Gilbert*[76] that a disability plan providing employee benefits except for pregnancy did not violate the sex discrimination provisions of the Civil Rights Act of 1964. Instead, the Wisconsin court ruled that the exclusion of pregnancy did violate the state's own Fair Employment Law, even though the pertinent language therein "is strikingly similar to the applicable provisions of Title VII" of the federal Act.[77] Or the Supreme Court of South Dakota—after the United States Supreme Court had reversed and remanded one of the South Dakota court's search-and-seizure decisions[78] (search and seizure, incidentally, is an issue about which law-and-order elements feel rather strongly)—insisting that

> We are mindful that the U.S. Supreme Court's decision in South Dakota v. Opperman . . . is binding on this court as a matter of federal constitutional law. However, we are free to provide an individual with *greater protection* under the state constitution than does the U.S. Supreme Court under the federal Constitution.
> . . . We find that logic and sound regard for the purposes of the protection afforded [by South Dakota's constitutional provision against unreasonable searches and seizures] warrant a *higher standard* of protection for the individual in this instance than the United States Supreme Court found necessary under the Fourth Amendment. (Italics added.)[79]

And so, the Supreme Court's decisions affect not only the litigants who are parties to the cases it hears, but the entire society in which it stands as the most authoritative of all decision and policy makers. Since the time of John Marshall, the Court "has shaped as well as reflected our political life, social structure, economic system, cultural heritage, and religious traditions—in short, all that goes to make up 'the American way of life.' "[80] That issues so deeply controversial as the death penalty, school desegregation, school prayers, abortion, criminal procedure, legislative reapportionment, and Watergate are authoritatively resolved by the Court speaks volumes about its policy-making capabilities. It is no exaggeration to say that the Supreme Court, more than any other component of the governmental system, has shaped and directed the course of American society. The fact that it has successfully done so for almost 200 years is the best guarantee that it will continue to do so as long as the constitutional system endures.

NOTES

1. 6 Peters 515 (1832).
2. The controversy concerned white missionaries working among Georgia's Cherokee Indians who had been convicted of violating a state law requiring them to procure a license from Georgia's governor. At issue was the Indians'

fate, not that of the missionaries. Georgia wished to subjugate the Indians and, if possible, to remove them to lands west of the Mississippi. The Court voided the legislation and ordered the missionaries released. Georgia resisted, but the Court did not seek Presidential enforcement of its decision, nor did it institute a contempt action against Georgia's officials. A year later the matter was resolved when the missionaries, upon agreeing to leave the state, were pardoned by the Governor. See Robert Scigliano, *The Supreme Court and the Presidency* (New York: Free Press, 1971), pp. 36–39.

3. Stuart S. Nagel, "Causes and Effects of Constitutional Compliance," in J. Roland Pennock and John W. Chapman, eds., *Political and Legal Obligation* (New York: Lieber-Atherton Press, 1970), p. 221. Also see James P. Levine, "Methodological Concerns in Studying Supreme Court Efficacy," *Law and Society Review* 4 (1970): 583–611; and Malcolm Feeley, "Coercion and Compliance," *ibid.*, pp. 505–519.

4. See, generally, Stephen L. Wasby, *The Impact of the United States Supreme Court* (Homewood, Ill.: Dorsey, 1970); Theodore L. Becker and Malcolm Feeley, eds., *The Impact of Supreme Court Decisions*, 2d ed. (New York: Oxford University Press, 1973); Samuel Krislov, *et al.*, eds., *Compliance and the Law* (Beverly Hills, Ca.: Sage, 1971); and Harrell R. Rodgers, *Community Conflict, Public Opinion, and the Law* (Columbus, Ohio: Merrill, 1969); Harrell R. Rodgers and Charles S. Bullock, *Coercion to Compliance* (Lexington, Mass.: Lexington Books, 1976); and George A. Tarr, *Judicial Impact and State Supreme Courts* (Lexington, Mass.: Lexington Books, 1977).

5. See the books by Albert P. Blaustein and Clarence Clyde Ferguson, Jr., Robert C. Crain, Robbins L. Gates, Hugh Davis Graham, Jack Greenberg, Benjamin Muse, J. W. Peltason, Reed Sarratt, Don Shoemaker, Bob Smith, and Melvin M. Tumin listed in Wasby's bibliography, *op. cit.*, note 4 *supra*, pp. 288–289; and also the articles listed therein by Samuel Krislov, Robert B. McKay, Walter F. Murphy, Melvin M. Tumin and Robert Rotberg, and Micheal W. Giles and Thomas G. Walker, "Judicial Policy Making and Southern School Desegregation," *Journal of Politics* 37 (1975): 917–936.

6. William Beaney and N. Edward Beiser, "Prayer and Politics," *Journal of Public Law* 13 (1964): 475–503; Robert Birkby, "The Supreme Court and the Bible Belt," *American Journal of Political Science* 10 (1966): 304–319; Richard Johnson, *The Dynamics of Compliance* (Evanston, Ill.: Northwestern University Press, 1967); Ellis Katz, "Patterns of Compliance with the Schempp Decision," *Journal of Public Law* 14 (1965): 396–408; William K. Muir, Jr., *Prayer in the Public Schools* (Chicago: University of Chicago Press, 1967); Stuart Nagel and Robert Erickson, "Editorial Reaction to Supreme Court Decisions on Church and State," *Public Opinion Quarterly* 30 (1966–1967): 647–655; Donald Reich, "The Impact of Judicial Decision Making," in David Everson, ed., *The Supreme Court as Policy Maker* (Carbondale: Public Affairs Research Bureau, Southern Illinois University, 1968); and M. Frank Way, Jr., "Survey Research on Judicial Decisions," *Western Political Quarterly* 21 (1969): 189–205. Also see the articles by Frank J. Sorauf and Gordon Patric mentioned in note 43 *infra*.

7. Thomas E. Barth, "Perception and Acceptance of Supreme Court Decisions at the State and Local Level," *Journal of Public Law* 17 (1968): 308–350; Ira Carmen, *Movies, Censorship and the Law* (Ann Arbor: University of Michigan Press, 1966); Richard S. Randall, *Censorship of the Movies* (Madison: University of Wisconsin Press, 1968); Parker Shipley, "Obscene Publication Prohibition," *Nebraska Law Review* 40 (1961): 481–491; Stephen L. Wasby, "Public

Law, Politics, and the Local Courts," *Journal of Public Law* 14 (1965): 105–130; and Wasby, "The Pure and the Prurient," in Everson, ed., *op. cit.*, note 6 *supra.*

8. Bradley C. Canon, "Organizational Contumacy in the Transmission of Judicial Policies," *Villanova Law Review* 20 (1974): 50–79; David Manwaring, "The Impact of *Mapp* v. *Ohio*," in Everson, ed., *op. cit.*, note 6 *supra;* Richard J. Medalie, *et al.*, "Custodial Police Interrogation in Our Nation's Capital," *Michigan Law Review* 66 (1968): 1347–1422; Peter O. Mueller, "Right to Counsel at Police Identification Proceedings," *University of Pittsburgh Law Review* 27 (1965): 65–88; Michael J. Murphy, "The Problem of Compliance by Police Departments," *Texas Law Review* 44 (1966): 939–946; Stuart S. Nagel, "Testing the Effects of Excluding Illegally Seized Evidence," *Wisconsin Law Review* 1965 (1965): 283–310; Herbert J. Reiss, Jr., and Donald J. Black, "Interrogation and the Criminal Process," *Annals* 374 (1967): 47–57; James Ridella, "Miranda: One Year Later—The Effects," *Public Management* 49 (1967): 183–190; Richard H. Seeburger and R. Stanton Wettick, Jr., "*Miranda* in Pittsburgh—A Statistical Study," *University of Pittsburgh Law Review* 29 (1967): 1–26; Arlen Specter,"*Mapp* v. *Ohio:* Pandora's Problems for the Prosecutor," *University of Pennsylvania Law Review* 111 (1962): 4–45; Otis H. Stephens, Jr., "Police Interrogations and the Supreme Court," *Journal of Public Law* 17 (1965): 241–257; and Michael Wald, *et al.*, "Interrogations in New Haven: The Impact of *Miranda*," *Yale Law Journal* 76 (1967): 1519–1648; Neal Milner, *The Court and Local Law Enforcement* (Beverly Hills, Ca.: Sage, 1971).

The Court itself, in Part IV of its opinion in *United States* v. *Janis*, 428 U.S. 433 (1976), discussed the effect of its rule in *Mapp* v. *Ohio* mandating the exclusion of illegally seized evidence. See especially the discussion of Bradley Canon's article, "Is the Exclusionary Rule in Failing Health? Some New Data and a Plea against a Precipitous Conclusion," *Kentucky Law Journal* 62 (1974): 681–700, in note 22 of the Court's opinion.

9. Roger Wilkins, "New Legal Effort to End Job Discrimination," *New York Times,* January 9, 1978.

10. 384 U.S. 436 (1966), number 29 in Harold J. Spaeth, *Classic and Current Decisions of the United States Supreme Court* (San Francisco: W. H. Freeman and Company, 1977).

11. Wald, *et al., op. cit.*, note 8 *supra,* quoted in Walter F. Murphy and C. Herman Pritchett, *Courts, Judges, and Politics,* 2d ed. (New York: Random House, 1974), p. 640.

12. 376 U.S. 254 (1964).

13. A notable example is the action taken (albeit reluctantly) by President Eisenhower in 1958: he ordered in the National Guard to enforce the desegregation order at Central High School in Little Rock, Arkansas. *Cooper* v. *Aaron*, 358 U.S. 1 (1958). Details are included in J. W. Peltason, *Fifty-Eight Lonely Men: Southern Federal Judges and School Desegregation* (New York: Harcourt, Brace & World, 1961), chaps. 5–7.

14. See Walter F. Murphy and Joseph Tanenhaus, *The Study of Public Law* (New York: Random House, 1972), pp. 40–44.

15. As a classic example, consider *Miranda* v. *Arizona*, 384 U.S. 436 (1966), number 29 in *Classic and Current Decisions,* in which a bare majority of the Justices, in an opinion by Chief Justice Warren, undertook to write a manual

of police procedure that required arresting officers to inform suspects of their constitutional rights prior to being questioned. Three other cases were joined with the opinion in *Miranda*—one each from New York and California, and one involving the federal government. Though the Chief Justice was figuratively hanged in effigy in every police station in the land because of this decision, the Court reviewed no subsequent cases in which *Miranda* had been deliberately disregarded. Indeed, in its subsequent decisions, the Court—with the addition of Nixon's appointees—has eased rather than tightened *Miranda*'s strictures: for example, *Harris* v. *New York*, 401 U.S. 222 (1971); *Michigan* v. *Tucker*, 417 U.S. 433 (1974); and *Oregon* v. *Hass*, 420 U.S. 714 (1975). But not invariably: see *United States* v. *Hale*, 422 U.S. 171 (1975); and *Doyle* v. *Ohio*, 426 U.S. 610 (1976). No suggestion is made here that *Miranda* was immediately and everywhere implemented. But it was clear that the nation recognized that the Supreme Court had spoken and that its word, not those of station house commanders or cops on the beat, was the Law of the Land. For better or for worse, suspects now possessed a major weapon against incriminating statements, which defense attorneys were quick to utilize.

16. *Gregg* v. *Georgia*, 428 U.S. 153, and *Woodson* v. *North Carolina*, 428 U.S. 280—number 52 in *Classic and Current Decisions; Proffitt* v. *Florida*, 428 U.S. 242; *Jurek* v. *Texas*, 428 U.S. 262; and *Roberts* v. *Louisiana*, 428 U.S. 325.

17. These summary decisions may be found in 49 L Ed 2d 1205–1215, 1217–1221, 1226.

18. *Furman* v. *Georgia*, 408 U.S. 238 (1972), at 309–310 (footnote omitted).

19. In 1977, the Court ruled out imposition of the death penalty for rape, at least when the victim is an adult woman. *Coker* v. *Georgia*, 433 U.S. 584.

20. See note 16 *supra*.

21. *Witherspoon* v. *Illinois*, 391 U.S. 510.

22. 428 U.S. 153, at note 25.

23. See the section headed "The Court of Last Resort."

24. See the section in Chapter 3 headed "Strict Construction."

25. *General Electric Co.* v. *Gilbert*, 429 U.S. 125 (1976).

26. See the section headed "Review of state court decisions." Cf. Lawrence Baum, "Implementation of Judicial Decisions: An Organizational Analysis," *American Politics Quarterly* 4 (1976): 94–101.

27. See the section headed "The Writing of Opinions."

28. See note 25 in Chapter 2. Also see Stephen L. Wasby, *Small Town Police and the Supreme Court: Hearing the Word* (Lexington, Mass.: Lexington Books, 1976).

29. *Furman* v. *Georgia*, 408 U.S. 238.

30. *Id.* at 239–240.

31. *Op. cit.*, note 16 *supra*.

32. 347 U.S. 484 (1954) and especially 349 U.S. 294 (1955), number 20 in *Classic and Current Decisions*.

33. 347 U.S. 484, at 495.

34. 349 U.S. 294, at 301, 299. The manner in which the federal district courts assumed this responsibility is discussed in Peltason, *op. cit.*, note 13 *supra;*

Robert J. Steamer, "The Role of the Federal District Courts in the Segregation Controversy," *Journal of Politics* 22 (1960): 417–438; and Kenneth N. Vines, "Federal District Judges and Race Relations Cases in the South," *Journal of Politics* 26 (1964): 337–357.

35. *Bradley* v. *Richmond School Board*, 382 U.S. 103, at 105; and *Rogers* v. *Paul*, 382 U.S. 198, at 199.

36. *Alexander* v. *Holmes County Board of Education*, 396 U.S. 19 (1969), at 20.

37. For a comprehensive overview of school desegregation in the South, see Wasby, *op. cit.*, note 4 *supra*, pp. 169–185.

38. 4 Wheaton 316 (1819), number 5 in *Classic and Current Decisions*.

39. Murphy and Tanenhaus, *op. cit.*, note 14 *supra*, p. 56.

40. *Cooley* v. *Board of Wardens*, 12 Howard 299 (1852), number 8 in *Classic and Current Decisions*.

41. 333 U.S. 203.

42. 343 U.S. 306 (1952).

43. Frank J. Sorauf, "The Released Time Case," in C. Herman Pritchett and Alan F. Westin, eds., *The Third Branch of Government* (New York: Harcourt, Brace & World, 1963), p. 146. Also see Gordon Patric, "The Impact of a Court Decision: Aftermath of the McCollum Case," *Journal of Public Law* 6 (Fall 1957): 455–464; and Frank J. Sorauf, "*Zorach* v. *Clauson:* The Impact of a Supreme Court Decision," *American Political Science Review* 53 (September 1959): 777–791.

44. *Engel* v. *Vitale*, 370 U.S. 421 (1962).

45. *Id.* at 425.

46. *Abington School District* v. *Schempp*, 374 U.S. 203 (1963), number 23 in *Classic and Current Decisions*.

47. Wasby, *op. cit.*, note 4 *supra*, pp. 129–135, and the references cited on pp. 285–286.

48. "Decisions of the Court are greatly influenced by the viability and the impact of its earlier decisions in the same area. For example, the widespread evasion of the school prayer decision [*sic*] might be expected to inhibit the Court's extension to other areas of its separation of church and state philosophy since blatant evasion of too many decisions would undermine its influence and prestige. At the same time, if the Court did extend this policy, the widespread evasion of the earlier decisions might be expected to encourage a similar lack of compliance." Thomas E. Barth, "Perception and Acceptance of Supreme Court Decisions at the State and Local Level," *Journal of Public Law* 17 (1968): 308–350, reprinted in Walter F. Murphy and C. Herman Pritchett, *Courts, Judges, and Politics*, 2d ed. (New York: Random House, 1974), p. 636.

49. *Board of Education* v. *Allen*, 392 U.S. 236 (1968).

50. *Lemon* v. *Kurtzman*, 403 U.S. 602 (1971), number 35 in *Classic and Current Decisions*. In its opinion in this case, the Court formulated an imposing test, all three parts of which had to be met before a parochiaid program could be constitutionally sustained.

51. *Levitt* v. *Public Education Committee*, 413 U.S. 472 (1973).

52. *Sloan* v. *Lemon*, 413 U.S. 825 (1973).

53. *Committee for Public Education* v. *Nyquist*, 413 U.S. 756 (1973).

54. *Meek* v. *Pittenger,* 421 U.S. 349 (1975).

55. *Wolman* v. *Walter,* 433 U.S. 229 (1977).

56. See the section in Chapter 2 headed "The adversary process."

57. See the sections headed "Standing to Sue" and "Jurisdiction" in Chapter 2.

58. Richard C. Cortner, *The Apportionment Cases* (New York: Norton, 1970), p. 253. The subsequent pages (pp. 253–256) include a succinct and insightful statement of considerations affecting compliance with the Court's decisions.

59. *Baker* v. *Carr,* 369 U.S. 186 (1962).

60. *Colegrove* v. *Green,* 328 U.S. 549 (1946).

61. 369 U.S. 186, at 269–270.

62. *Gray* v. *Sanders,* 372 U.S. 368 (1963).

63. *Wesberry* v. *Sanders,* 376 U.S. 1 (1964), at 7–8 (footnote omitted).

64. *Reynolds* v. *Sims,* 377 U.S. 533 (1964), number 24 in *Classic and Current Decisions.*

65. *Avery* v. *Midland County,* 390 U.S. 474 (1968); and *Hadley* v. *Junior College District,* 397 U.S. 50 (1970). *Avery* extended the equal population principle to a mere 80,000 local governmental units. See Cortner, *op. cit.,* note 58 *supra,* p. 256. *Hadley* further extended the principle to the nation's 18,000 school districts and 21,000 special-purpose governmental bodies (such as water, sewer, sanitation, and pollution boards), whose members are popularly elected and whose activities do not "disproportionately affect" a subset of the district's population. *Salyer Land Co.* v. *Tulare Water District,* 410 U.S. 719 (1973), at 728, 729.

66. *Op. cit.,* note 35 *supra.*

67. For example, *Escobedo* v. *Illinois,* 378 U.S. 478 (1964).

68. For example, *Manual Enterprises* v. *Day,* 370 U.S. 478 (1962); *Jacobellis* v. *Ohio,* 378 U.S. 184 (1964); and *A Quantity of Books* v. *Kansas,* 378 U.S. 205 (1964).

69. In the section headed "The Watergate Tapes Case."

70. *United States* v. *Nixon,* 418 U.S. 683 (1974), at 713, number 47 in *Classic and Current Decisions.*

71. Bradley C. Canon, "Reactions of State Supreme Courts to a U.S. Supreme Court Civil Liberties Decision," *Law & Society Review* 8 (1973): 109–134; Neil T. Romans, "The Role of State Supreme Courts in Judicial Policy Making," *Western Political Quarterly* 27 (1974): 38–59.

72. Compare *Serrano* v. *Priest,* 96 Cal. Rptr. 601, 487 P. 2d 1241, 5 Cal. 3d 584 (1971), with *San Antonio School District* v. *Rodriguez,* 411 U.S. 1 (1973), number 43 in *Classic and Current Decisions.*

73. *Op. cit.,* note 10 *supra.*

74. For example, *Michigan* v. *Tucker,* 417 U.S. 433 (1974); and *Oregon* v. *Hass,* 420 U.S. 714 (1975).

75. *Oregon* v. *Hass,* 420 U.S. 714, 43 L Ed 2d 570 (1975), at 576 (footnote omitted).

76. 429 U.S. 125 (1976).

77. *Time Insurance Co.* v. *Dept. of Industry, Labor and Human Relations,* 46 LW 2369 (1978). The court further held that neither the National Labor Relations Act nor the Employee Retirement Income Seniority Act of 1974 pre-empted

Wisconsin from enforcing its Fair Employment Law in the decreed manner. *Id.* at 2369–2370.

78. *South Dakota* v. *Opperman,* 428 U.S. 364 (1976).

79. *State* v. *Opperman,* 45 LW 2283 (1976).

80. Harold J. Spaeth, *An Introduction to Supreme Court Decision Making,* rev. ed. (San Francisco: Chandler, 1972), p. 7. Also see Jonathan D. Casper, "The Supreme Court and National Policy Making," *American Political Science Review* 70 (1976): 56–73.

Table of Cases

Index

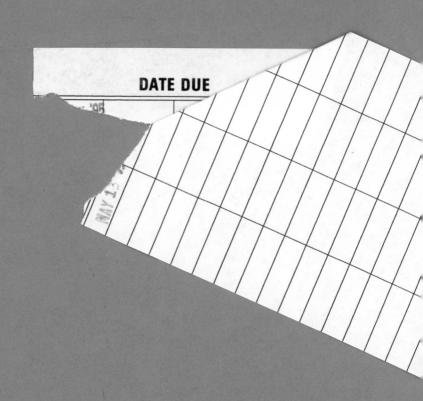

DATE DUE

MAY 13